MONTANA WOMEN HOMESTEADERS

A Field of One's Own

EDITED BY SARAH CARTER

FARCOUNTRY
PRESS

Helena, Montana

ISBN 10: 1-56037-449-7
ISBN 13: 978-1-56037-449-7

© 2009 by Farcountry Press
Text © 2009 by Sarah Carter

For more information on our books, write Farcountry Press, P.O. Box 5630, Helena, MT 59604;
call (800) 821-3874; or visit www.farcountrypress.com.

CIP data is on file at the Library of Congress.

Created, produced, and designed in the United States.
Printed in the United States.

14 13 12 11 10   2 3 4 5 6

To Amy McKinney's great-grandmother
Petrina Peterson Pogreba, a homesteader at
Box Elder, Montana, and to all
Montana's solo women homesteaders.

PHOTO COURTESY OF THE RALPH McKINNEY FAMILY.

COVER PHOTO: *Eva Iddings of Indiana stands in front of her claim shack in Pleasant Valley, northwest of Fort Benton, Montana. Eva and her brothers, Morris and Harold, filed for homesteads in 1910. They were later joined by another brother, Fred Iddings, and two aunts Iva and Sadie, who also filed for homesteads. Eva Iddings proved up on her homestead in 1912 and later married Harold Roudebush.* BARROWS COLLECTION, OVERHOLSER HISTORICAL RESEARCH CENTER, FORT BENTON, MONTANA. 1910-BC11. 244.

Contents

Acknowledgments

THE IDEA FOR THIS BOOK grew out of a conversation between editor Caroline Patterson and Ken Robison, historian at the Overholser Historical Research Center at Fort Benton, Montana. Ken knew that I was compiling material for an academic study comparing land policies on both sides of the forty-ninth parallel and that I had become intrigued by the wealth of material on solo women homesteaders. He put Caroline in touch with me and the book was born. Thanks to Ken and also to Henry L. Armstrong of the Overholser Center.

Special thanks to Amy McKinney for her invaluable assistance with this book at many stages, including research and transcribing, and to researcher Gretchen Albers—doctoral students at the University of Calgary. Thanks to Michel Hogue at Carleton University for his research on Valley County in Washington, D.C. Many Montana archivists and librarians have been very helpful and supportive, particularly the staff at the Montana Historical Society Research Center in Helena. Special thanks to Sharon Emond, curator at the Phillips County Museum in Malta.

The Social Sciences and Humanities Research Council of Canada and the Killam Program (Canada Council for the Arts) provided the support that resulted in this book and the comparative study to follow, with a standard research grant and a Killam Research Fellowship, respectively.

I am particularly grateful to Caroline Patterson; her encouragement, enthusiasm, knowledge, and editorial skills have been critical to the completion of this book.

Sarah Carter
Edmonton, Alberta
June 2009

MY GOVERNMENT CLAIM
Written in 1912

I'll write a few lines, if only I can,
And tell you about my excellent plan.
You will find me out here on a West bench plain,
Working hard on a government claim.
Hurrah, for this country, the land of the free,
Home of the rattlesnake, bugs, and the flea.

O, I tell of its joys, and sing of its fame,
While starving out here on my government claim.
My mansion is built so it doesn't cover much soil,
The walls erected, according to Hoyle.
The roof hasn't much pitch, is quite level and plain,
And I'll sure get wet if it ever rains.

I have a good time, I live at my ease,
On canned goods, old crackers, bacon, and cheese.
Then come to this country, there is a home for you all,
Where the wind never ceases, and the rain never falls,
Where the sun never sets, but sweetly remains,
Till it burns up our crops on our government claims.

O, how happy I feel on my government claim,
There is nothing to make a person hard and profane.
I've nothing to eat, nothing to wear,
The mosquitoes possess both our water and air,
It's here we are settled, and here we must stay,
Our money's all spent and we can't get away.

There's nothing to loose, and there's nothing to gain
While living out here on a government claim.
Hurrah for this country, where storm clouds arise,
Where the sun never sets, and the mustard never dies.
Come, join in the chorus and sing of the fame,
Of the ones who stuck to their government claims.

This was written by a woman who lived about 20 miles from my homestead. This is a pretty true story of the Homestead Days. I spent 9 years out on the prairie, 35 miles from town. —Mrs. Adelia Elizabeth Hawkins Sturm Glover

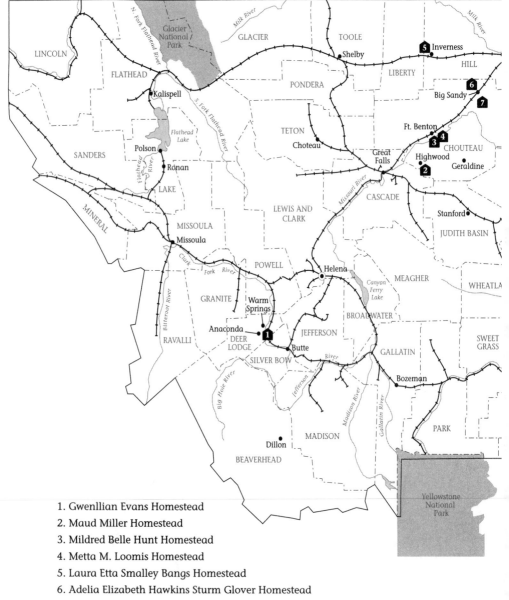

1. Gwenllian Evans Homestead
2. Maud Miller Homestead
3. Mildred Belle Hunt Homestead
4. Metta M. Loomis Homestead
5. Laura Etta Smalley Bangs Homestead
6. Adelia Elizabeth Hawkins Sturm Glover Homestead
7. Nan ("Nannie") Pritchard Francis Homestead
8. Nellie T. Holt Homestead
9. Anna Scherlie Homestead

Montana Solo Women Homesteaders

Homestead locations are approximate.

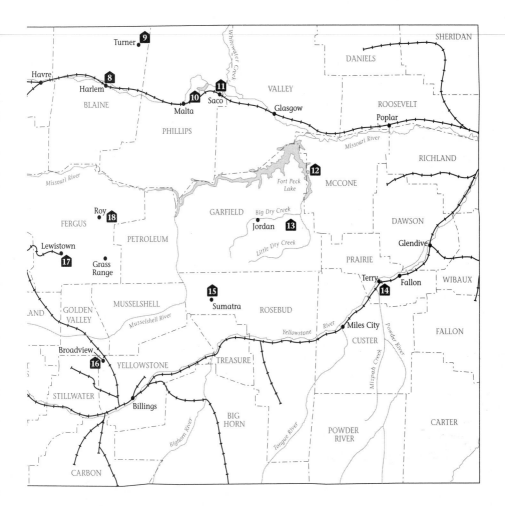

10. Mattie T. Cramer Homestead
11. Nora Nereson Homestead
12. Pearl Danniel Homestead
13. Catharine Calk McCarty Homestead
14. Janet ("Jennie") Williams Homestead
15. The Homesteads of Grace Binks, Ina Dana, and Margaret Majors
16. Ada Maud Melville Shaw Homestead
17. Irene Van Kleek Homestead
18. Mia ("May") Anderson Vontver Homestead

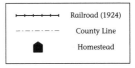

	Railroad (1924)
	County Line
	Homestead

Anna Scherlie's homestead near Turner in Blaine County, just south of the Canadian border. Scherlie laid claim to her land in 1912 at age thirty-two; she proved up in 1916. PHOTO BY NELLIE CEDERBERG. MONTANA HISTORICAL SOCIETY RESEARCH CENTER, MONTANA STATE HISTORIC PRESERVATION OFFICE, 24BL1561.

Introduction

MONTANA'S SOLO
WOMEN HOMESTEADERS

ANNA SCHERLIE'S SHACK REMAINS much as she left it when she sold her land in 1967. It is furnished with a bed, a table, a bench, and a rocking chair. Her two-burner kerosene stove is there, her wood box stands neatly filled, beside the washstand. Scherlie never had electricity, believing she was too old for modern conveniences when rural electrification arrived in "Big Flat" in 1946. She hung on through drought and depression, choosing not to replace her homestead shack with a more substantial dwelling, as did most of her neighbors. She could have afforded a larger house. Finances were not a problem as she had sold half of her land for five thousand dollars in 1928 to the Great Northern Railway for the town site of Turner. When she died in Havre in 1973 at age ninety-three, eighteen nephews and nieces shared an estate of $107,575. There is a stone marker, under a favorite lilac bush in the yard, with Anna Sherlie's name and the dates of her birth and death.

The Anna Scherlie homestead shack was built in 1913 in an area known as the "Big Flat" near what became the town of Turner in Blaine County, Montana.[1] As a single, thirty-two-year-old woman, Scherlie had claimed this land as her homestead a year earlier when she arrived from North Dakota to join her three brothers and two sisters who

Anna Scherlie's well was located on her homestead, which she still owned when she died in 1973 at the age of ninety-three. Her homestead was placed on the National Register of Historic Places on November 5, 1998.
PHOTO BY NELLIE CEDERBERG. MONTANA HISTORICAL SOCIETY, MONTANA STATE HISTORIC PRESERVATION OFFICE, 24BL1561.

were homesteading in the area. In 1916, she "proved up" and earned her patent to this land. Scherlie remained single and lived in her one-room house, although she spent many winters in Saint Paul, Minnesota, where, according to local legend, she worked as a governess for the children and grandchildren of James J. Hill, founder of the Great Northern Railway.[2] In the mid-1990s, Nellie and Leon Cederberg, who farmed Anna Scherlie's land, had the foresight to nominate her homestead to the National Register of Historic Places. It is a rare survivor of the thousands of homestead shacks that once dotted Montana's landscape. Many were owned by single women similar to Scherlie or women who were widowed, divorced, or otherwise out on their own. Many arrived during Montana's homestead "boom" of the 1910s and 1920s, but numerous women homesteaders date from much earlier.

Women homesteaders were everywhere in Montana, although no one has determined how many there were among the nearly 200,000 people that homesteaded in Montana between 1900 and 1921.[3] The

Final Affidavit Required of Homestead Claimants.

Act of May 20, 1862.

I, *Margaret Macumber (Widow)*, having made a Homestead entry of the *E ½ of SE ¼ & E ½ of NE ¼* section No. *24*. in township No. *2 South*, of range No. *5 East* subject to entry at *Bozeman M. T.* under the first section of the Homestead Act of *May 20th 1862*, do now apply to perfect my claim thereto by virtue of the first proviso to the second section of said act; and for that purpose do solemnly *swear* that *She is* a citizen of the United States; that I have made actual settlement upon and have cultivated said land, having resided thereon since the *9th* day of *September*, 187*0*, to the present time; that no part of said land has been alienated, but that I am the sole bona fide owner as an actual settler; and that I will bear true allegiance to the Government of the United States.

Her
Margaret X Macumber
Mark

I, *E. W. Willett Register*, of the Land Office at *Bozeman M. T.*, do hereby certify that the above affidavit was taken and subscribed before me this *14th* day of *Sept*, 1875.

E. W. Willett Register

Margaret Macumber proved up on her homestead in this final affidavit dated September 14, 1875. Note the "X" in lieu of her signature. UNITED STATES NATIONAL ARCHIVES AND RECORDS ADMINISTRATION, MTMTAA056560.

distinction of Montana's first woman homesteader should probably go to Gwenllian Evans, who filed a statement on May 12, 1870, testifying that, on April 20, 1870, she had settled on 160 acres of land on Warm Springs Creek, near Anaconda.[4] A widow from Wales who arrived in Anaconda in the late 1860s, Evans ran one of Montana's early post offices.[5] Her house was a substantial home built in the 1880s, located

5 miles east of Anaconda. Her granddaughter still lived there in 1936 when journalist Walter Ed Taylor wrote a column under the title, "Landmark Stands Near Anaconda: Old House Located on First Plat Ever Filed on By a Woman."[6] Unfortunately Evans' house was torn down.

Although Evans is first by filing date, she may be second in actual settlement to Margaret Macumber, who filed on her homestead in Gallatin County in July 1870 and "proved up" her claim in 1875.[7] A widow and citizen of the United States, Macumber signed her name with an "X." In her July 1870 affidavit, she swore that she was already a resident and had made "valuable improvements to tract of land I now seek to enter as a homestead." Macumber may have settled her homestead in advance of Evans, although official paperwork puts her in second place.

What did it mean to homestead? We may think of it as synonymous with farming or generally establishing a home in a rural area, but in the later nineteenth century and early twentieth century in the United States and Canada, the word "homestead" had a much more specific meaning. A survey that carved up western North America and has been described as "one of the most astonishing man-made constructs on earth" was the first step in creating the homestead system.[8] The "immaculate grid" of perfect squares—a stunning patchwork quilt—is particularly striking from the sky.[9] While the same units of survey were used from the Rio Grande to the Arctic Ocean, the Great Plains provided the most ideal raw material and was the true showpiece of the surveyors' art. The grid survey set the stage for the federal government to become a real estate developer on a grand scale. Land was distributed, bought, and sold in an uncomplicated and timely manner. However, some of it should never have been contemplated for agricultural settlement.

From the late 1860s to 1917, three homestead acts profoundly changed the face of the American West and the lives of thousands of people who packed up everything to head out to file on 160 acres of "free" land. The original Homestead Act of 1862 that embraced the concept of "free" homesteads emerged after decades of stormy Congressional debates. There were those who favored purchasing lands to provide funds for the federal government and those who argued that, as Thomas Jefferson had envisioned, free homesteads would create industrious, agricultural families who would strengthen democracy by creating wealth and building communities.

Free homesteads were also intended to flood public lands with settlers and undermine Indian land rights, a "least-cost strategy to secure ownership."[10] In short, as economic historian Douglas W. Allen wrote, "due to the Indians' simultaneous claim on public lands and the costs imposed by this dispute over property rights...homesteading is a substitute for direct military force and acts to mitigate the costs of violence."

The gender-neutral wording of the Homestead Act of 1862 provided that "any person who is the head of a family, or who has arrived at the age of twenty-one years," was permitted to make entry on 160 acres of land. American citizens and immigrants who had declared their intention to become citizens were eligible to file on homestead land for a small fee. A homesteader could live on the land for six months, then buy it for one dollar and twenty-five cents an acre (this was called the commutation clause); or live on it for five continuous years (later reduced to three), cultivate it, and build a habitable home. Having met these conditions, the homesteader could then apply for title or patent to the land by having two neighbors vouch for the truth of her or his statements that government regulations were satisfied.

The Enlarged Homestead Act of 1909 recognized that successful agriculture required more land in the arid West, so the number of acres an individual could claim as homestead was increased from 160 to 320 in areas classified as dry farming lands not suitable for irrigation. The original 160-acre allotment was based on farming the lush lands of the eastern third of the continent. As Wallace Stegner wrote about farming on the unpredictable Great Plains in *Beyond the Hundredth Meridian,* even if spring was green and promising, "the brassy sky of drouth might open to let across the fields winds like the breath of a blowtorch, or clouds of grasshoppers, or crawling armies of chinch bugs....And if drouth and insect plagues did not appear there was always a chance of cyclones, cloudbursts, hail. It took a man to break and hold a homestead of 160 acres even in the subhumid zone. It took a superman to do it on the arid plains."[11]

In 1912, Congress enacted the Three-Year Homestead Act, which reduced the "proving up" period from five to three years and permitted the homesteader to be absent for five months each year. Promotional material provided specific advice about the legislation but highly misleading advice about the climate. In the Great Northern Railway's 1913 pamphlet "Montana: Homesteads in Three Years," for example, prospective homesteaders were told, "it is questionable if any state in the union has a better climate." The winters were described as "less severe than in areas farther east" and the cold spells were said to be "of short duration." In summer, "hot winds that wither vegetation are but little known."[12] Testimonial letters from homesteaders enticed others with headlines such as "Made a Great Mistake – By Not Coming Sooner," and "Success of a 'Lone' Woman" (which is included in this book).

The 1913 pamphlet advised homesteaders to first locate their land and become acquainted with its characteristics before filing a claim at the local land office.[13] Homesteaders had to follow detailed rules to gain ownership of their land. They were advised to establish a permanent residence within six months from the date of filing, and were permitted five months' continuous absence each year upon application to the nearest land office. Once they applied for a land patent, one-eighth of the homesteader's total entry had to be under cultivation. Settlers who "squatted" on unsurveyed land had to make improvements at once and reside continually upon the land until it was surveyed. At that point, they had ninety days prior right to file for the land at the nearest land office. Three witnesses were required to swear that the "squatter" had lived on the land and made the required improvements. To perfect the title, the amount of time a settler made improvements on the unsurveyed land was deducted from the years necessary to live on a homestead.

The Homestead Act allowed women to apply for land under the same conditions as men, but they had to be over the age of twenty-one and unmarried (single, divorced, widowed, or otherwise the head of a household).[14] Providing for single women landowners was controversial, but their inclusion, as historian Tonia M. Compton wrote, "reflected the belief that civilization required the presence of white women who would bring with them the structures that made society operate—churches, schools, town socials, and an abhorrence of social ills such as alcohol, gambling, and prostitution. Women as wives, mothers and civilizers—and therefore a key component to securing the empire in the West—motivated Congress' adoption of legislation that granted women the right to claim the western lands in their own name."[15]

"If a female desires to possess a home, and is willing to conform to the requirements of the law, there is no reason why she should be an alien to the justice or the charity of her country," declared Congressman William Taylor Sullivan Barry of Mississippi about the 1862 homestead bill. "If she is unfettered by marriage ties she has the same natural right to be provided a home from the public domain than the unmarried man of the same age has."[16]

Married women, however, were not permitted to homestead—although there were exceptions. Under the doctrine of marital unity, married women had no legal existence. A married woman could not apply as "head of the family" because the husband was the "head" during the marriage. As a commissioner of the U.S. General Land Office explained in 1864, a woman's services and labor were "due and belonging to her husband" and that if she, as a twenty-one-year-old, was permitted to claim land, "the legal restrictions growing out of her matrimonial relations would at once be violated."[17]

As often happened, if a single woman married before she proved up, the status of her homestead became complicated. The issue was particularly murky when both the bride and groom had homestead entries, another frequent occurrence, because the Homestead Act stipulated that each settler had to live on and cultivate his or her entry.

Over the years, the Department of the Interior kept changing its position on how to handle homestead claims when homesteaders married. First, it claimed marriage did not bar an entrywoman from completing her claim as long as she complied with the legal requirements of residence and cultivation. Then, in 1886, department policy changed and it was decided that if a single woman filed on a homestead and married before she proved up, she forfeited her right to the land. This generated protest because it appeared to discourage marriage when "the policy of the law is to encourage matrimony."[18] Some couples postponed marriage in order for each to file and prove up on claims.[19] The department changed its approach to allow a homestead couple to prove up one claim and relinquish the other. Homestead couples tried solving the problem by occupying a house built on the line between claims, but this was ruled illegal in 1887.

In 1912, Montana's newly married homesteaders who had claims that were not yet proved up were advised that they could not do this—that they could not "maintain separate residences on homestead entries held by each of them," and that they had to decide which homestead "they will retain, and relinquish the other."[20] They could convert the claim to a cash payment and receive title to the land.

Finally, the Act of 1914 stated that a married couple who had both filed on land both had the right to a patent as long as they had both complied with the residency laws for at least one year. One was the "residence claim" where the couple would live, and the other was the "residence waiver" and only the cultivation requirement was enforced. The husband was designated as the person to decide which of the entries would become their home.

The homestead legislation opened the doors for diverse groups of women to acquire land. As clearly itemized in the legislation and the published guides for prospective homesteaders, marital status was the critical criteria. Widows such as Gwenllian Evans and Margaret Macumber were eligible as long as their husbands had not exercised their homestead privileges. (A widow was still considered one person with her

4—1003-R.

The United States of America,

To all to whom these presents shall come, Greeting:

WHEREAS, a Certificate of the Register of the Land Office at **Helena, Montana,**

has been deposited in the General Land Office, whereby it appears that, pursuant to the Act of Congress of May 20, 1862,

"To Secure Homesteads to Actual Settlers on the Public Domain," and the acts supplemental thereto, the claim of

Mary E. Smith

has been established and duly consummated, in conformity to law, for the **west half of the west half of Section twelve in Township five north of Range two west of the Montana Meridian, Montana, containing one hundred sixty acres,**

according to the Official Plat of the Survey of the said Land, returned to the GENERAL LAND OFFICE by the Surveyor-General:

NOW KNOW YE, That there is, therefore, granted by the UNITED STATES unto the said claimant   the tract of Land above described; TO HAVE AND TO HOLD the said tract of Land, with the appurtenances thereof, unto the said claimant   and to the heirs and assigns of the said claimant   forever; subject to any vested and accrued water rights for mining, agricultural, manufacturing, or other purposes, and rights to ditches and reservoirs used in connection with such water rights, as may be recognized and acknowledged by the local customs, laws, and decisions of courts; and there is reserved from the lands hereby granted a right of way thereon for ditches or canals constructed by the authority of the United States.

IN TESTIMONY WHEREOF, I,   **Woodrow Wilson,**

President of the United States of America, have caused these letters to be made

Patent, and the seal of the General Land Office to be hereunto affixed.

GIVEN under my hand, in the District of Columbia, the   SECOND

(SEAL.)   day of   AUGUST   in the year of our Lord one thousand

nine hundred and   TWENTY   and of the Independence of the

United States the one hundred and   FORTY-FIFTH.

By the President:

By

Secretary.

Recorder of the General Land Office

RECORD OF PATENTS: Patent Number   **765832**

Each homesteader who successfully proved up received this document granting him or her a patent to the land, signed by the president of the United States. Mary E. Smith obtained title to her 160 acres on August 2, 1920.

COURTESY OF JUANITA LARSON, HELENA, MONTANA.

husband in the eyes of the law even though her husband was deceased.) Single women, unwed mothers, and divorced women were permitted to make entry, even if they were not yet twenty-one years of age, because they were considered heads of the family.[21] Under certain circumstances, married women were permitted to homestead; a wife, "whose husband is a confirmed drunkard," was considered the head of a family.[22] So was a married woman who had been "actually deserted" by her husband or a woman whose husband was in the penitentiary or "incapacitated by disease or otherwise from earning a support for his family."[23] Mormon women who were plural wives were permitted to enter for homesteads because their marriages were not recognized as legal.[24]

Thousands of solo women claimed and proved up on homesteads in the West.[25] Before 1900, women homesteaders constituted less than 10 percent of all entries, but their numbers grew dramatically thereafter.[26] Numbers varied from state to state; one study of forty-three townships in North Dakota reveals that the number of women homesteaders varied from 1 to 22 percent with an average of 10 percent.[27] In two Colorado counties, women entrants were at 11 percent before 1900 and nearly 18 percent after that date. During the peak homestead rush from 1900 to 1918 in Cochise County, Arizona, 14 to 21 percent of the homesteaders were women.[28]

Women homesteaders were everywhere in Montana. In her study of the Yellowstone River Valley, Sunday Anne Walker-Kuntz found that between 1909 and 1934, the federal government issued 4,066 land patents in Yellowstone County; of these 18 percent, or 746, were issued to women who together claimed more than 150,000 acres.[29] My research in eastern Montana's Valley County shows a similar percentage—17 percent, or more than 900 women—proved up on Valley County homesteads.

Women homesteaders were as successful at "proving up" as their male counterparts.[30] Felice Cohn, whose work as a federal assistant superintendent of public sales of Indian lands took her to the land offices of Montana, wrote in 1917 that, "The woman homesteader always lives up to the land regulations of the government. The homestead inspectors seldom have occasion to make an adverse report on a woman who is proving up on her land. Every regulation is always faithfully complied with."[31]

The majority of women homesteaders were single; in North Dakota 83 percent were single, 15 percent were widows, and 1 percent were divorced.[32] Like their male counterparts, women often homesteaded in clusters—sisters, cousins, and friends filed together and near each other. Three Chmelik sisters from Minnesota—Anna, Mary, and Emily—took up adjoining homesteads in Chouteau County in 1910. Anna was a teacher and Mary a seamstress. Their brother helped them build their cabins and break sod for their first crops.[33] In 1912 Lena J. Michels and her cousins, Mary and Frances Lambert, left South Dakota and filed on adjoining homesteads near Stanford, Montana, by the Genou post office.[34] One settlement in the Hawarden district near Fort Benton was called "Ladyville" because of the preponderance of women homesteaders.[35] Daughters arrived with mothers, and all took out homesteads. Homesteaders built "twin shacks" close together, but on their own claims, divided by the survey line. Sophia Jefferson and Mildred Hunt filed on adjoining homesteads on the North Bench near Fort Benton in 1910; their cabins were known in the area as "twin shacks." (Hunt's diary is featured in Chapter Nine.) Adelia Elizabeth Hawkins Sturm Glover and her mother homesteaded near Big Sandy in Chouteau County, where they had twin shacks on their homesteads as well (Glover's account is featured in Chapter Two.)

Families plotted to increase their holdings when they filed for land. Daughters helped expand the family land base by taking out homesteads—filing alongside brothers, sisters, fathers, uncles, aunts, or other relatives. Ann Yoctorowic Obie filed on land near the homesteads of her father, sister, and three brothers near Joplin in Liberty County.[36] Women arrived in Montana with their "sweethearts" and delayed marriage while both homesteaded.

The great majority of the women homesteaders in Valley County—81 percent—were from the United States. Most were from Minnesota, with Iowa, Wisconsin, North Dakota, and Illinois following. If they were of "foreign" birth, most were from Norway, then Canada, followed by Germany and Sweden, then England. Most were women in their twenties, twenty-five to twenty-nine, when they filed on their land, although some were much older—the oldest was eighty. Forty-six percent of the women were single while 28 percent were married and must have been in the deserted category, or else their husbands were incapacitated. Seven percent were widows, while the marital status of the remaining women is not clear from the documents. Things shifted somewhat by the time single women homesteaders applied for their patents—a good many had married in the interval. Fifty-one percent were married, and 23 percent remained single.[37]

Typical experiences of women homesteaders in Valley County include Mabel Peterson's. Born in South Dakota in 1894, Peterson was working as a teacher there in 1915 when her cousin reported that there was plenty of good land available[38] (she was on land that later became part of the Fort Peck Reservation). Her father, an aunt, and a neighboring young man together filed on homesteads of 320 acres at the Glasgow land office in 1916. Peterson taught school while proving up, and in 1919 she married and the couple moved to her homestead, where they lived until the 1930s.

Two sisters from Norway, Karen and Oline Johansen, were working in New York in 1908 when they heard that homestead lands were "up for grabs" in Montana.[39] They filed on homesteads near their two brothers north of Glasgow, where they raised cows, horses, sheep, chickens, and turkeys and sold eggs. They required help only when their windmill and pump needed repairs. They never married, and they remained on their land until Oline's death in 1943 and Karen's in 1954.

Addie May Michael, from North Carolina, arrived in Glasgow in the spring of 1913 with her father and mother. She filed on 160 acres next to her parents' land, and later acquired an adjoining homestead of 160 acres.[40] When another daughter and her husband also took out a 320-acre homestead, the whole family held a block of 960 acres. Addie

May worked in a ladies clothing store in Glasgow, driving her horse and buggy back and forth to town 7½ miles each day.

There was some ethnic diversity among Montana women homesteaders. Homesteader Louise C. LaFournaise was Metis, the daughter of Joseph Napoleon and Marie Therese McGillis LaFournaise.[41] Born in Canada, LeFournaise came to Glasgow in 1898 with her parents and filed on a homestead in 1915 near Opheim, close to the Canadian border. She successfully proved up in 1918. A nurse and graduate of the Saint Ignatius Training School for Nurses in Colflax, Washington, LaFournaise was issued a Montana State Nurses' Certificate in 1917. After enlisting with the U.S. Army Expeditionary Forces in 1918 and working at various evacuation hospitals on the front lines in France, she was decorated with two Great War chevrons, the victory medal service ribbon, and one Bronze Star, for her service in the evacuation hospital of the St. Mihiel offensive. These decorations are currently on display at Glasgow's Valley County Museum.[42]

An African-American woman from Missouri, homesteader Bertie (Birdie) Brown of the Gilt Edge district of eastern Fergus County filed on her homestead in 1907 at the Lewistown land office. She stated that she was "a deserted woman, have not seen my husband for ten years and have supported myself and am head of a family."[43] When she applied for her patent in 1912, she stated she was a widow. At that time, she had a log house, stable, chicken house, garden, and 25 acres of wheat, oats, and barley. In addition, her land was fenced. These improvements were estimated at a value of one thousand dollars. In the local history of that area, Bertie Brown was described as a very kind-hearted woman who loved children. Her homestead cabin was "lovely," with two main rooms, an addition for a kitchen, and a wraparound porch.[44] She raised Leghorn chickens but was best known for her homemade brew, reputed to be the "best in the country." When her still blew up in 1933, Bertie was severely burned. She died the next day and was buried in the Lewistown City Cemetery.

Solo women homesteaders all had other forms of income. Bertie

In Bertie Brown's October 28, 1907, homestead affidavit, she describes herself as "a deserted woman, have not seen my husband for ten years and have supported myself and am head of a family." When she applied for her land patent in 1912, Brown had a log house, stable, chicken house, garden, and twenty-five acres of wheat, oats, and barley. She was also known for her homemade brew. UNITED STATES NATIONAL ARCHIVES AND RECORDS ADMINISTRATION, MTLTN 0004062.

Brown may have been the only bootlegger, but other women worked a variety of jobs to meet expenses. Some were restaurant owners or bank clerks; others worked for wages as waitresses or office help.

Many, such as Ruth Giles Fischer, worked as teachers. As she explained in her memoir about homesteading in Chouteau County in 1917, her mother helped pay for her train ticket from Martinsville, Virginia, to Havre—nearly two hundred dollars—but when she arrived, she had to build a house, fence her land, and put in crops.[45] She hired labor: Breaking sod cost from five dollars to six dollars and fifty cents per acre, backsetting four dollars per acre, and discing and seeding was one dollar and twenty-five cents per acre. Seed wheat was two dollars and fifty cents to three dollars and fifty cents per bushel. Building materials had to be hauled from over 30 miles away. "Luckily," she wrote, "I was teaching and could meet expenses." She started out earning sixty-five dollars per month, but after upgrading her Virginia Professional Teacher's Certificate and attending regional summer school, she earned one hundred dollars and later one hundred and thirty-five dollars per month. She proved up in 1921.

Still other women worked as nurses, midwives, cooks, postmistresses, and newspaper editors. Josephine Krug, a widow with five children when she arrived in Great Falls in 1908, filed on a homestead north of Fort Shaw in 1910 and moved her family there. A registered nurse, she rode on horseback to her patients, often maternity cases.[46] Krug was the only medical specialist in the district until the arrival of Dr. Rose Russell, another homesteader who was located south of Fort Shaw. After she arrived in Carter in 1914 with her two siblings and her mother who also homesteaded, Agnes Burdick and her family ran Villa Café in Carter.[47] The family made good money as they sometimes served as many as thirty-five people for meals and catered sandwiches at night for saloon patrons. A number of women also worked as postmistresses. Marian Chausse, who had a claim south of Ismay in Carter County, circulated a petition for a post office in her cabin. It was established in 1915.[48] Her stepfather and two sisters also homesteaded in Carter County. With the financial help of her sisters, Chausse built an addition to her cabin the next year and opened a store. The Chmelik sisters, mentioned above, found work in private homes, hotels, and a hospital.

Several women edited newspapers—Mattie T. Cramer and Nellie Holt in this book are examples. A central job of these small papers was to publish the notices of intention homesteaders were required to make when applying for final proof to establish their claims (see the Sumatra women homesteaders notice of intention).

Marriage was a desired outcome for many women homesteaders, as well as a sound financial decision. As postmistress Marian Chausse wrote, she had some of her land broken by neighbor Paul Petter, and "we finally decided he needed a cook and I needed a farmer."[49] Ollie E. Silvernale's account of her homestead years near Verona seems to sum up the dual purpose of her homesteading adventure: "I Won a Homestead and a Husband."[50]

Solo women homesteaders were, and continue to be, criticized. They did not conform to the late nineteenth- and early twentieth-century definition of farmers: they had other occupations, they had to purchase labor, and some women sold up shortly after they proved up. Several women homesteaders in this book experienced this criticism directly. Ada Melville Shaw found disapproving neighbors, and Nellie T. Holt's homestead shack may have been removed by unfriendly townspeople.

In a 1905 federal government *Report of the Public Lands Commission,* solo women homesteaders were singled out for criticism.[51] In the section on the commutation clause permitting homesteaders to pay for their land after fourteen months, it was declared that "a large portion of the commuters are women, who never establish a permanent residence and who are employed temporarily in the towns as school-teachers or in domestic service, or who are living with their parents. The great majority of these commuters sell immediately upon receiving title."[52] (The Sumatra women, in this book, were such "commuters.") This was not in keeping with the object of the homestead law, the report continued, which was "to give to each citizen, the head of a family, an amount of land up to 160 acres, agricultural in character so that homes would be created in the wilderness." Instead, the "homestead shanties of the commuters may be seen in various degrees of dilapidation, but they show no evidence of genuine occupation. They have never been in any sense homes."

In her study of homesteaders in western South Dakota, historian Paula M. Nelson described solo women (and many men as well) as "absentee" homesteaders who had no intention of remaining permanently, who sought only to prove up and leave.[53] Their commitment to the region was weak, they "visited" rather than lived on their claims, and their experiences resembled an "extended vacation." They were not "real" farmers; their "real" work was outside the home. She concluded that, "Most women homesteaders were not farmers, however, and they did not contribute to the agricultural development of the west river country, although they did much to aid social development, albeit temporarily. It could be argued that their long-term impact was negative because their commitment was limited. They helped form organizations that later had to be abandoned or greatly reduced due to a lack of membership, to the great resentment of people who stayed in the region. Agriculturally, their small plowed patches attracted weeds, especially Russian thistles, to the detriment of bona fide farmers."[54]

Sociologist H. Elaine Lindgren, author of *Land in Her Own Name: Women as Homesteaders in North Dakota*, the most sustained study of women homesteaders, wrote that sceptics often asked her, "Did women 'really' homestead?"[55] Lindgren found that 94 percent of the women in her study oversaw the operation of their land. They did domestic work but also contributed a great deal to "outdoor" work on their homesteads. They purchased labor but so did male homesteaders, as there were "hired men" and harvest hands throughout the West. Like male homesteaders, some proved up and sold their land, while others stayed all their lives. Lindgren also noted that the domestic work women did must be seen as valuable and important. "Domestic work...always has been devalued, and those doing it have been considered dependent and less important," Lindgren wrote. "The question, 'Did they 'really' homestead?' reflects this evaluation. The question has no meaning unless 'women's work' is defined as requiring little initiative and skill and as being less important than 'men's work.'"

What did independence mean for these solo women homesteaders? Were these women deliberately striking out on their own, challenging the gender norms and conventions of their age? In the earliest scholarly studies, solo women homesteaders were celebrated as "exemplars of female independence, proof that the frontier liberalized women's roles."[56] In the last decade, however, scholarship has downplayed this characterization, stressing that many filed on land to assist their families. Historian Sherry L. Smith pointed out that even the best known woman homesteader, Elinore Pruitt Stewart of Wyoming, author of *Letters of a Woman Homesteader*, was married one week after she filed on her homestead.[57] This, Smith suggested, indicated that Stewart and her new husband were seeking to increase the newly formed family's land holdings. Nor did she ever prove up on her homestead; Stewart feared she would not legally meet her residency requirement so she relinquished her claim to her mother-in-law, Ruth C. Stewart, a seventy-three-year-old widow who claimed the land so it could remain in the family's control.

Historian Dee Garceau stressed that property ownership and independence held a variety of meanings for women, and that we must take care when romanticizing solo women homesteaders as "intrepid pioneers" and "as models of female liberation."[58] While the published success stories about women homesteaders in mass-circulation magazines in the early twentieth century "celebrated female independence" and "presented homesteading as a vehicle for transforming gender identity," Garceau said the land records present a more complex story. A woman often filed next to the claim of her fiancé, parent, or brother, combining forces with them to accumulate property. Group cooperation and family service were critical factors in the decisions of many women to file on land as, Garceau wrote, "homesteading was difficult to do alone, both physically and financially."

For some solo women, however, Garcaeu said economic gain and independence were the goals. There were single women "investment"

In 1912, the Great Northern Railway promoted homesteading for single women with a photograph of Miss Nickey's homestead, located 36 miles north of Harlem, Montana. MONTANA HISTORICAL SOCIETY RESEARCH CENTER, FROM MONTANA FREE HOMESTEAD LAND, *GREAT NORTHERN RAILWAY CO., 1912.*

homesteaders who sold after they proved up, and who financed their claims as teachers, stenographers, bank clerks, and horse trainers. In this way, Garceau wrote, "homesteading did contribute to the liberalization of women's roles, in that it provided an opportunity for capital accumulation unequalled in other occupations available to women on rural frontiers. Neither lone ranchers nor cooperative members of a family ranch, the entrepreneurial homesteaders were, quite simply, real estate speculators. For these women, property became an individualistic asset, a means of advancing their personal fortunes."

Women homesteaded in Montana for the enhancement of family land holdings, for individual or family economic security and profit (if any), for adventure and escape, and for a healthier environment. Ephretta J. Risley, for example, came west because of a family obligation. As she wrote in *The Golden Triangle: An Account of Homesteading in Montana by One Who Lived It,* "It was a very blustery day in March in the year 1910 that I received a telephone call from my father telling me that he had returned from Montana, where he had filed on a homestead and had reserved 320 acres adjacent to his claim, in my name, and that it would be necessary for me to go to Montana as soon as possible to file on this land."[59] She had just turned twenty-one, had recently completed a business course at Grand Forks, North Dakota, and was a secretary for a hardware firm.

For Nena S. Anderson, homesteading was a personal goal. In 1914, she visited friends near Winifred, Montana, who homesteaded and taught, and "those two weeks in Winifred were so eventful they really sold me on Montana. I wasn't, at the time, old enough to homestead, but I was determined to wait until I could. It was three years before I finally found what I wanted. Those three years were spent as a bookkeeper at the Fad Shoe and Clothing Co. During this time I made many friends; among them was the Shanklin family who homesteaded east of Roy, Montana, near the Missouri River. Mr. Shanklin told me he had found a place for me six miles from them...I soon had a homestead."[60]

More examples of varying motivations appear in the accounts of the woman homesteaders that follow. In the Yellowstone River Valley, Sunday Anne Walker-Kuntz sensibly concluded women homesteaded for the same reasons as men. Tracing the individuals who were issued land patents between 1909 and 1934, she found that, "data suggests women followed the same trends as men, indicating [that] whatever compelled men to homestead, appears to hold true for women as well."[61] Lindgren's conclusions were similar—that men, too, homesteaded near family in order to increase family holdings. Some sold soon after proving up but others persisted, and that while "reasons for homesteading were many and sometimes complicated...the possibility to achieve some measure of independence as a result of land ownership was a strong incentive."[62]

Nearly 200,000 people homesteaded in Montana between 1900 and 1921.[63] They flocked to Montana, enticed by the inspiring and optimistic rhetoric of James J. Hill, chairman of the Great Northern Railway, about Montana's fertile soil and how the state could become the nation's breadbasket. Homesteaders were also assured that new, scientifically approved dry farming methods would make arid regions arable.[64]

While it was "common knowledge" that eastern Montana could be dry, dry farming advocates claimed that by following recommended cultivation techniques, the soil would not only produce high yields, but would retain enough moisture to pull a farm through a period of drought. Between 1909 and 1920, virtually all organizations supplying information to homesteaders advocated dry farming techniques. The Montana Agricultural Experiment Station published numerous pamphlets about how to adapt to dry land conditions.

Dry farming practices, however, may have actually hastened homestead failure. Advice about dry farming and a lack of accurate weather information led to the dense settlement of the Great Plains on farms that proved to be unsustainable.

Then the droughts came. As economic historian Gary D. Libecap wrote, "Dryfarming doctrine and homesteading bloomed together and they jointly wilted between 1917 and 1921."[65] There were droughts in 1904 and 1910, but in 1917 a severe five-year drought began. Dry farming advocates were confident that the drought could be withstood. The first year of the drought followed the wettest year of the twentieth century to date (1916). Unfortunately, Montana homesteaders made 15,000 new entries in 1917, and this drought was a catastrophe for many of them. On many homesteads, there was no crop at all. From 1900 to 1916, 25 bushels was the average yield per acre; in 1919 the yield was 2.5 bushels. What was produced was worth little, as wheat prices plummeted after World War I.

Of all the upper Great Plains, eastern Montana was the most affected—it had the nation's highest rate of farm abandonment and loan foreclosure. An estimated 11,000 farms, or one out of five, failed. According to Montana writer Joseph Kinsey Howard: "The dreams of great men often live a long time, as dreams. That of Jim Hill, which he sought to bring to life in fact, became a witless nightmare. His trains rattled empty through dying towns. His neat little green fields were transformed as if an evil spirit had sped overhead, laying a curse upon them: suddenly they were fenced deserts in which the trapped tumbleweed spun and raced nowhere all day. The little houses stood slack-jawed and mute, obscenely violated by coyotes, rats and bats, and finally faded into the lifeless fields."[66]

The homesteaders in this book experienced the optimistic and heady years of homesteading, as well as the devastation of the drought years. Some persisted, making important and long-term commitments and contributions to their communities and their state, while others sooner or later sold up or gave up and deserted. Those featured here documented their experiences in writing or photographs. These records are varied—some were written during the homestead years and for publication, others are unpublished accounts composed for family years later, others are diaries that capture the moment-to-moment experience, and still others are memoirs that present slightly grittier accounts. The accounts are as close to the original as possible, including mispellings, grammatical errors, and sentence fragments.

As a historian of western Canada, I was astonished by the extent, variety, and richness of the records left by Montana's solo women homesteaders. Single women were deliberately excluded from the privilege of homesteading under Canada's legislation. The result is that there is only one account (that I know of) of a solo woman farmer in western Canada—Englishwoman Georgina Binnie-Clark's *Wheat and Woman* (1914). Binnie-Clark had to purchase her land, as she could not homestead as a single woman. Her book documents the injustices of Canada's land laws.

The rural landscape was remarkably different just south of the border, where each county had hundreds of women homesteaders. These women clearly had a keen idea that they were playing a vital role in the history of their state and region, that they were stepping beyond the bounds of what was regarded as typical feminine behavior; they were understandably motivated to leave a record of their lives and work. As I found this wealth of material in the course of my research comparing land policies on both sides of the forty-ninth parallel, I couldn't help but be captivated and engaged. The traces left by these women homesteaders help us today to nourish a new western history that challenges and complicates older approaches.

The homestead accounts included here are not terribly diverse, although there are some differences of class, age, and ethnicity. While these various accounts display courage, tenacity, and adventurousness, we need to also realize that these women were part of the "army of occupation" that dispossessed Native Americans of their land.

Dee Garceau wrote that literary women homesteaders published their accounts in popular magazines in the early twentieth century at a time when women's roles were in transition, and "homesteading became a compelling metaphor for female transformation."[67] They "presented their experience as a vehicle for developing emotional self-reliance, economic autonomy, and political clout." Metta Loomis, whose account was originally published in the January 1916 *Overland Monthly,* was an example of this genre. She was a single woman proving herself in an unorthodox way by testing traditional assumptions about her gender, and she touted the advantages of homesteading for single women.

Unpublished accounts that were composed for family and not public consumption—often long after homesteading days had ended—are complex, as anthropologist Seena B. Kohl wrote. In retrospective accounts, she argued, "time, intent, and audience affect subject matter, permitting narrators to transform and give new meanings to experience."[68] There tends to be little anger, pain, frustration, and exhaustion, for example, in the often massive community histories that compiled settlers' stories. These histories, Kohl wrote, "characteristically regret the decrease in the sense of community, altruism and independence." The reader cannot escape the inference that the past, "although hard, was better." In retrospective "life reviews," negative or discordant elements may appear, but there is a tendency toward a positive and instructive view of the past. Some of the homesteader accounts included here present the past with this "roseate glow."[69]

The memoirs in this compilation, including May Vontver's and Pearl Danniel's, challenge and disrupt cherished myths of a happier, cooperative time, and some of them question the wisdom of homestead settlement. Vontver tells stories of children stealing mittens from each other and trying to sell them back to their owners; Pearl Danniel writes of eating wild horses to survive. Others, such as Nora Nereson, who died when her shack was picked up and blown away by a cyclone, never had the opportunity to leave much record of their presence at all.

Chapter One

A LONE WOMAN HOMESTEADER: MATTIE T. CRAMER

IN A 1913 GREAT NORTHERN RAILWAY *Bulletin,* a testimonial letter from Malta, Montana, homesteader Mattie T. Cramer was published under the headline "Success of a 'Lone' Woman." Her letter, written at the request of an immigration agent of the Great Northern Railway, described Montana as "the land of unlimited opportunities." Cramer claimed she had filed on her homestead in 1908 with less than one hundred dollars to her name, but by 1913 she had a two-story house worth one thousand dollars, a barn and other outbuildings, and 21 acres under cultivation. She also had two lots in the town of Malta; on one of these, she had a five-room cottage that she rented. Over the next two years, Cramer received hundreds of letters from would-be homesteaders throughout the United States and Canada, primarily requesting information about homesteading in Montana, although three marriage proposals were also included. The Great Northern Railway printed a two-page circular letter for her to send in reply.

There are few details about Cramer's life before she homesteaded. Mattie T. Cramer, born in Nora Springs, Iowa, was the daughter of William and Eliza (Slec) Mathers.[1] Her father, born and raised in Quebec, was a sailor, policeman, interpreter of Spanish and Portuguese, farmer, and harness maker. Her mother was from England, but immigrated to Canada at age eighteen. William and Eliza were married in Chicago in 1850 and had twelve children.

In the 1890s, Cramer was a newspaper reporter and editor for the *Iowa City Herald*, then worked as a traveling salesperson for a clock and jewelry manufacturer. She married B. Frank Cramer; they were living in Utica, New York, where son Harold was born in 1896. What happened to her husband is unknown—he is not mentioned at all in any of her personal papers.[2] And just what Cramer did in the twelve years between the birth of her son and her move to Montana is a mystery. According to census data, Martha (Mattie) Cramer was living with her mother in Rock Grove, Iowa, in 1900. She was listed as married but with no husband in the household; her son Harold Cramer, now three years old, was with her.

In her own brief letter to Ellery Sedgwick, editor of *Atlantic Monthly*, (included here), Cramer wrote that "I had been in school and newspaper work for years and was in a newspaper office in the Middle West in 1908, when I decided to go to northern Montana and take up a homestead." While she may have been widowed, in her homestead documents she described herself as "unmarried" and "single."

Cramer and son Harold lived continuously on her homestead in the Strater community near Malta from May 1908 until 1912, except, according to Cramer's brief biographical account included here, for the winter months beginning in late November 1910, when they moved to Malta so that Harold could attend school.[3] She proved up on this land in 1912, and in 1916 entered on another nearby quarter section under the Enlarged Homestead Act, proving up on this in 1921. She was also editor and manager of the Malta *Enterprise*. Cramer began work with the paper in 1908, and was there only a few months when it was announced that the paper had been taken over by the Malta Enterprise Publishing Company under the management of Mattie T. Cramer.[4]

Some members of Cramer's family followed her out West. Cramer's mother Eliza Mathers had moved to Malta and proved up on 120 acres

Before she moved to Montana in 1908, Mattie T. Mathers, who later married B. Frank Cramer, worked as a newspaper reporter and editor for the Iowa City Herald. She may have used this 1893 editorial train pass on the Burlington Cedar Rapids and Northern Railway in the course of her reporting. MONTANA HISTORICAL SOCIETY RESEARCH CENTER, MATTIE T. CRAMER PAPERS, MC255, BOX 1, FOLDER 11.

in 1916.[5] Mathers died in 1919. Perhaps as a result of visiting her aunt and grandmother, one of Cramer's nieces, Florence Ethel Mathers, married Malta's attorney, John A. Tressler.

Cramer established the first library in Malta by collecting donated books and magazines and loaning them to the community from a corner of her cluttered office at the *Enterprise*. When her mother became ill in 1914, Cramer resigned from the *Enterprise* to care for her. After three years of crop failure (1917, 1918, 1919), and with the invalidism of her mother, Cramer's debts accumulated, and she had to find work. She moved to Puget Sound where she worked for the *Oracle* in Orting, Washington, returning to her homestead in 1926. She continued to publish articles in Montana newspapers, including the *Great Falls Tribune* and

Phillips County News. In 1954, when she was ninety-six, she entered a short story in a contest that was held to "discover and encourage talent in this State." It was sponsored by the Bozeman's Writers' Group of Montana Institute of the Arts. In the 1950s she moved to Great Falls. She died there on July 2, 1959 and is buried in the Malta cemetery, beside her son Harold, who died in 1946.

Mattie T. Cramer's papers at the Montana Historical Society Research Center include some of these stories and fragments of stories. For example, she wrote a celebratory history of James J. Hill, in which she championed his dream of "growing frontier towns and the country roundabout settled by happy, thrifty, successful homesteaders; all the arable land under cultivation, bountiful crops flourishing, prime livestock on the ranges."[6] She had helped to promote this dream through her testimonial letter and replies to prospective homesteaders.

But the fragment of another story she wrote suggests that she was keenly aware of the tragic results for many homesteaders. A woman farmer "realized as she never realized before how the poverty and hardships had in a certain sense taken out of her life much of the richness, the beauty and the sweetness which should have been there....Hope had died that season when scarcely any rain fell, and the grain in the fields turned yellow, then brown, when it was scarcely four inches tall. The pastures were sear and brown the first of July. Even the leaves on the trees began to wither and turn yellow when they should have been gloriously green and flourishing. The creeks were dry and the beds of them cracked and caked."

In 1927, back on her homestead, Cramer offered to tell the story of her homestead days in a series of articles she proposed to Ellery Sedgwick, editor of the *Atlantic Monthly*. She had just read a serialized account by Hilda Rose, "The Stump Farm: A Chronicle of Pioneering," and offered to share many "thrilling experiences." Sedgwick had published accounts of solo women homesteaders before, including the letters of Elinor Pruitt Stewart, later published as a best seller, *Letters of a Woman Homesteader*. Sedgwick's reply, if any, has not survived, and if

Cramer did write her life story it has yet to be found.

The following excerpts are from the Mattie T. Cramer papers at the Montana Historical Society Research Center. What is interesting about her testimonial letter—with their renderings of a woman facing not only the challenges of the prairie but also the condemnation of the society she was leaving—was the enthusiasm it sparked among readers, many of whom were women. Her readers asked her many practical questions: How do I find free land? Are there plots next to yours? Did you have trouble getting people to help you work on your land? But, mixed among those, were more fearful questions: What do I say to people who think I am crazy? How do I get the courage to homestead? Cramer had clearly struck a chord, even to the tune of wedding bells, in the case of a few lonely bachelors. Misspellings and grammatical mistakes in the letters have not been corrected.

SUCCESS OF A "LONE" WOMAN TESTIMONIAL LETTER: "MONTANA: HOMESTEADS IN THREE YEARS," GREAT NORTHERN BULLETIN, 1913[7]

Montana Historical Society Research Center

Malta, Montana, October 1, 1913.

E. C. Leedy,

St. Paul, Minn.

Dear Sir:—

Some of my relatives back in Iowa City, Iowa, thought I was mentally deranged when I announced to them in 1908 that I was going to take my little boy and move to Montana. They could not understand how a "lone woman" could ever expect to get along out in that wild country as they termed it; however, I filed on a homestead near Malta May 4, 1908, having less than $100.00 at the time, built a house on the claim that cost me $100.00, and accepted a position with the Malta Enterprize. As my homestead was only four miles from town, I lived on it and have been working with the newspaper here now for four years. In that time I have built a two story frame house on my claim, costing $1,000, a barn, chicken house, dug a well, fenced all the land, and 21 acres is under cultivation. Besides, I bought two lots in town and built a five room cottage which I rent. I consider this the land of unlimited opportunities. A poor man can secure homestead land north of here or he can buy at a very reasonable price, and as there is plenty of work to be found, he can absent himself from his farm and earn a little extra to keep him going. I have raised all kinds of vegetables, berries, small fruits, grains, etc., and the soil is as productive here as in any section I have ever been.

Mattie T. Cramer

SELECTED LETTERS TO MATTIE T. CRAMER FROM PROSPECTIVE HOMESTEADERS[8]

Tibbetts Callaway Co. RH2,

Tibbetts, Mo.

Oct. 14, 1914

Dear Madam:—

I have noticed your name in a circular I have hear about Homesteads. I would like for you to give me some information about the free land. I am kind a interested in it. I have often thought that I would like to take up a claim if I could. If the climate is not too severe. I suppose the soil is very fertile and the climate not too cold. I don't mind some cold weather: I live here in Missouri and it is noted for extremes of weather either so hot or so dry or so wet you can't hardly live. I have any home now. My mother is dead and my father is in the hospitle. I have one sister and two Bros. I am the youngest of the four. My oldest Bro. could take up a claim I expect. He is 18 will be 19 yrs in Nov. If you would give me some pointers I would sure be obliged to you. Tell me how you got to where you are living. I close happy to hear from you soon.

Your's Respt.
Miss Jewell Brown.

1336 So. State Street

Syracuse, N.Y.

Jan. 24, 1913.

Mrs. Mattie T. Cramer

Malta, Montana.

Dear Madam:

I saw your letter in a book from Montana and would like to hear from you. I intend to make my home in Montana and my four daughters are coming with me.

Is there any free homestead land out near you that I could take up and how far would I be from the town and depot? Would I have any trouble getting someone to help me work my land or are the neighbors willing to help you work your land? Is there a high school in the town of Malta? If there is any free homestead land near you, how large are the tracts? I would be glad to hear from you.

Sincerely yours,

Mrs. Mary Campbell

Frederick, Illinois March 13, 1914
Mattie T. Cramer.
Malta, Montana:

My Dear Mrs. Cramer:—

Being much interested in a homestead in Montana and upon reading your testimony I write you in regard to the country.

First I shall speak of myself. I am a single lady 22 years old. For 5 years I have been a successful school teacher and hold a first grade certificate. I am a graduate of a Normal (State) School. I wondered if I could homestead and also teach school, thus earning a little for expenses. Just what part of the state would you advise me to locate in? I am not coming alone, but with a party. They had thot of locating in the Yellowstone River valley near Forsythe. What capital would one need to build a home and get things ready for winter, for one person. Any thing which you can write me will be greatly received and obliged I am,

> Yours very truly
> Emma St Cashman

Nov. 28th 1913
Mattie T. Cramer
Malta, Mont.

Dear Madam:

Noticed your testimonial in the Great Northern Bulletin. Being very anxious to take up a homestead am writing directly to you for information.

Being a woman I feel a bit timid about taking up land in a strange state and a letter from you would be very encouraging—thus proving that women can make good in Mont.

Please write me of the soil, climate, oppertunities and anything else you feel would help an inexperienced "would-be-homesteader."

I thank you in advance,
Bessie Christopher

P. S. Enclosed find stamped self addressed envelope for reply.
[2109 Washington, Parson's, Kansas]

Paris, Ill
Sep 27, 1913
Mrs. Mattie T. Cramer,

Kind Friend:—

I read of your success in Montana and as I am thinking of taking up a claim I will write you for infermation.

I want to know about the soil near you is it very productive? How far north would one have to go to take a claim? Are the winters severe? Are the snow storms bad?

I am a school teacher. I have taught almost twelve years.

I want to know if I could still continue teaching.

Are the schools in the country paying very good salaries?

What salaries are paid in town?

Would you send me the county superintendents name, so I could write him about schools?

How long a school term do they have in the city also country?

I am a girl that has to make my own way so I am greatly in sympathy with all working women.

You surly have had success and when I read your testimony I thought I too could share in the claims of Montana.

So trusting you will answer my letter and give me any further information you think I should know I will close.

Very Resp.
Nellie Maple.

Add.
Miss Nellie Maple
811 Shaw Ave,
Paris Ill.
4957 Washington Av

St. Louis, Mo
Jany 24, 1914
Mrs. Mattie T. Cramer
Malta, Montana

My Dear Madam:

Your letter of October 1st addressed to Mr. E. C. Leedy, St. Paul Minn, and published in The Great Northern Bulletin has been read by me with great interest and I am taking this privilege of writing to you asking for some more information regarding your part of Montana.

Is there any good land in your region available for homesteading now?

Could a lady with her son of 22 succeed in homesteading there on a capital of say $1,000?

Though neither of us are farmers, we are fully acquainted with ranch life, and desire to undertake it.

Would March 1st be a good time to locate there?

Do you know of any good homesteading land outside of your region?

Will you favor me with an early reply? It will be appreciated.

Very truly yours,
Edith M. Callaway

[Editor's note: Edith M. Callaway proved up on a homestead in Valley County in 1918.]

701 South 13th St

Feb 5, 1914

Mrs. Mattie T. Cramer,

Malta, Mont.

My dear Mrs. Cramer,

I trust you will not throw this letter into the waste basket without first replying because it is of vital interest that I learn something about the country in which you live.

You're lucky to have made a success of homesteading and consequently I write you for particulars.

Did you find it difficult to get laborers to build your first little home and make the necessary improvements during the three years that the law requires? Are there laborers available and about what is the average daily wage?

What do the new settlers do for water and fuel until they get a footing there? Is there employment for women who are willing to work at serving or keeping house boarders during the time not required to be on the homestead?

A friend and I want to homestead. We are two lone women fifty years of age and there is a party going from here in Apr. to Mont. and we are considering the matter very seriously.

Any information will be gladly rec'd. I have about $500.00 to start in with. Will that tide us over do you think?

Please let me hear from you at your earliest convenience because we must begin to plan if we go so soon.

Trusting I am not intruding and claiming more of your time than you can give,

I am Yours sincerely,
Helen M. Hull

February 10, 1914
847 Lincoln Ave
St. Paul, Minn

Dear Mrs. Cramer;

Have seen your testimonial in the Montana circular and as I am a "lone" woman also am writing to you. I have been unexpectedly thrown on my own resources and thought a claim would be a good thing as so many write so very favorably of it. I would be able to do all that was necessary in the line of improvements until I proved up and got money from the crops, but of course have no idea of the prices of things and how much money would be needed at the start. I would like to take 320 acres and have a friend who will take the same amount so we would want a section.

You having lived there six year and having been so successful know a great many of the important facts in the case as well as the less important things, which a person would be entirely ignorant of who have never been there. When you take up "squatters claims" do you have to remain there continuously until surveyed? When a locator takes you out to see the land do you have to stay there, or can it be fixed in some way so you can go back to town for a few days to get things out there without danger of anyone taking your land in the meantime?

These questions probably sound very foolish to one acquainted with the "ins and outs", but you can't have any idea of conditions until you have seen for yourself or found out from one familiar with the land. Would be very grateful for any information you could give and enclose stamp for a reply. I hate to bother you this way but as you are alone like myself felt you could help me more than any one else.

Most sincerely,
Helen L. Meier

[Editor's note: Helen L. Meier proved up on a homestead in Phillips County in 1918.]

Angola, Ind
March 21st, 1914
Mattie T. Cramer
Montana

Dear Mrs. Cramer,

I read in the Montana bulletin of your success in Montana. I have read it over many times for I do admire your pluck and energy. I too am a lone woman have been a widow for nearly 32 years. I too have made some success in life and now have what they call here Montana fever. I fear I will not get over it till I take the cure which I suppose can only be had by going there. I am anxious to go and I just felt that you might wisely and truely advise me. I am 60 years old, I have a Grandson 13 years old that would go with me but I must educate him he is now in the 1st year of high school and a bright boy.

I have a friend here that filed on a half section of land 12 miles north of Coburg they will go to settle on it in June. It is what they call dry farming. Now I wish you would tell me what you know of the success of dry farming. This bulletin tells of large crops but some think here that those people that report such crops have means of irregation and that they could not do so in the dry territory. Please tell me do you have irrigation or is it dry farming? I see you are near Milk river. Can one readily hire plowing and other work done? Of course I would have to hire my work done, as I am 60 years old. I am active yet and more active than most younger women so please think of me as one physically able to endure. I have the courage and determination and I am sure if any other lone woman can make it—I can too. I could not do the work you are doing but I can do many another thing I will enclose stamp for a reply and I wish you to tell me as near as you can about what they can do with this dry farming, tell me about what the average per acre of wheat is also potatoes and do they put out shade trees and will they grow or is it too dry. I am asking a great deal of you to

give to a stranger but I am sure I would delight to help someone myself
and feel sure you are the same.

I shall look for a speedy answer.
Please address Harriet Miller
208 So Darling St
Angola, Ind
I wish the average crops per ACRE in dry farming.

[Editor's note: Harriet Miller proved up on a homestead in Hill County in 1924.]

Mrs. Mattie T. Cramer.
Malta, Montana.

Dear Madam:—

I have read your letter in a "Northwestern" Bulletin on Montana. I want to take up a homestead claim in Montana next spring but my family cannot be convinced that a lone lorn damsel can establish her lone lore self on a claim way in Montana and accomplish anything. I am 29 years old, without a chick or child or cent to my name. I believe I can borrow the money for a start and pay out by the end of three years.

I am attracted to the territory around Big Sandy for no special reason except that I know the two people in Hill Co (at Havre) and thought it would help me to fight homesickness to be within a few hours of somebody who knows me. Now I would like to impose on your good nature enough to ask you to write me some facts to help me convince my parents and older sisters and brothers that I don't need a man to manage in order to work up to making final proof on those blessed acres.

I'm convinced myself but need a little outside help to convince them and believe a letter from you would help.

Thanking you for a reply, I am Very truly,
(Miss) Grace W. Stebbins

Hinton, Okla
2/20 x 1915
Dear Madam

Kind Lady Mrs. Mattie Cramer,

I am just affal, anxious to marri Some sweet loving Lady. For me, a Good Sweet Loving and fine and Jolly Sweet wife you seem, to be, a Good woman. I am honest but I am poor man. I am a Good hand to work. I take cair of Stock. I wood like to bee your husband and help you take care of everything. I can give you good references if need Bee. I am staying down here now with my Good old mother. My age is 39, But I can doo loots of yard work yet I am healthy and Stout. I am a Good hand with horses. Taking caire of them also with [cattle] and hogs. Will you please write me and tell me if you wood like to marrie You probely, have been married before and you now what married Life is. I never was but wood wood like to be, soon. How, old is your Little Girl you sayed in your Letter Sompthing about her when you rote to me Last March 15 x 1914, about that country I am affal anxious to here from you. Please find a stamp in this letter so please send me your photo and I will send you one of mine.

I, am your True Friend and future husband if you want to marrie me Sow Goodby.

Rite me soon to Hinton, Okla, Box #4.

With much Love,
Fred M. Dixon

FRAGMENT OF MATTIE T. CRAMER'S CIRCULAR LETTER

[Editor's note: This is a fragment of the letter Mattie T. Cramer sent in reply to the hundreds of people who contacted her for advice. It was printed by the Great Northern Railway.]

[page 1 missing]

Building material is cheaper now than when I built and I know people who have lived in and made final proof in a "shack" costing less than $100.

Breaking costs from $4.00 to $4.50 per acre but since so many gas engines or tractors have been brought into the country, one can get the breaking done for $2.00 per acre on a share-of-the-crop basis.

I have lived in York State, Illinois and Iowa and to me Montana is THE state of states for people with little or no money, and with its 146,000 square miles of area there's plenty of room for you. The climate is unrivalled, it so invigorates that you want "to do things."

You can raise fruit and vegetables of all kinds just as successfully as you can elsewhere, and everything produced has a much better flavor.

From fifty strawberry plants set out in May, 1912, I picked this last summer, 1913, thirty quarts, (I measured them) of large, luscious berries, some measuring three and one-half inches in diameter, and I'm inexperienced and did not know "the how" as perhaps you do. I have been delighted with good yields of flax, wheat, oats, corn and potatoes, having seventy acres under cultivation last year. This raw prairie land even in my inexperienced hands has yielded just as much as my father's farm did years ago in Iowa and that same land my father owned changed hands recently and the purchaser paid $135.00 per acre for it.

I trust you may secure a good homestead near here and that after filing you may be successful and satisfied, for, after all it is in the individual to succeed or fail and not entirely in the environment, though favorable conditions help a great deal.

Work of all kinds can be easily secured and the salaries and wages are much higher here than in the eastern and middle western states.

Yours very respectfully, [Mattie T. Cramer]

LETTER, MATTIE T. CRAMER TO ELLERY SEDGWICK,
THE ATLANTIC MONTHLY

Malta, Montana,
October 7, 1927
Mr. Ellery Sedgwick,
Boston, Mass.

Dear Sir:

Since reading the experiences of Mrs. Rose on a stump farm in Idaho, in your valuable magazine, it has occurred to me to ask if you would like a narrative of my homesteading life on a United States government claim of 160 acres of land in northern Montana. Unlike Mrs. Rose, I was exceedingly fortunate or successful and had more enjoyment and many thrilling experiences than out of any other period of my existence thus far.

I had been in schoolwork and newspaper work for years and was in a newspaper office in the Middle West in 1908, when I decided to go to northern Montana and take up a homestead. I was a widow with a son twelve years of age, and when I informed my relatives of my intentions, they decided I must be going "crazy," and did not hesitate to point out imaginary dangers and difficulties that I would be sure to encounter. Then, too, my near relatives in Chicago, those who had been born and reared there and had never lived elsewhere, were most apprehensive of our safety, pointing out in letters to me that cruel savages, mountain lions, tigers, bears and wolves infested the region for which we were bound, and if we were scalped alive, or eaten by these ferocious beasts, I would not be blameless.

Despite the awful picture that had been drawn for our consideration May, 1908, found us settled in a one-room shack on a 160-acre homestead four miles northeast of Malta, a typical western town containing a large number of saloons. I had only been in Malta forty-eight hours when I again entered a newspaper office, that of *The Enterprise*, the only newspaper, a weekly, published in the town. In September, 1908, I became the editor and manager of it and continued in that capacity for about four and a half years.

After filing on my claim, for a period of six weeks, or until I had earned funds with which to purchase a horse and buggy, my son, Harold, and I walked into Malta each morning, (He was in school) and walked back to the homestead at night, much to the amazement of the "natives" who walked but little. At the claim, or "our farm" as we began to call it, we were very busy and exceedingly happy, in fact at times wild with joy anticipating what the future seemed to offer and in the enjoyment our new life in this new world afforded us. That first summer was brimming over with interesting incidents of a unique and charming character. Here we saw sunrises and sunsets and most wonderful, the aurora borealis, for the first times in our lives. The thought of proprietorship was sweet. I had never owned a home before and to be the owner of 160 broad acres of land caused a feeling of freedom and buoyancy never before experienced.

In July my mother came out from the east and joined us and with but two short intervals visiting her old home, she spent the remainder of her life here, crossing the Great Divide in 1919. For five years prior to her demise, she was blind and an invalid and I resigned my position and nursed and cared for her.

By request of Mr. E. C. Leedy, then immigration [agent] of the Great Northern Railway, I wrote a letter for one of their booklets, which must have had a wide distribution for I received between two and three hundred inquiries from doctors, lawyers, teachers, farmers, in fact people of almost every walk in life and from nearly all the states in the union. These inquiries came so thick and fast that the Great Northern company had a two-page circular printed for me to send to these inquiring, or prospective homeseekers. I am enclosing my letter to Mr. Leedy and also one of the two-page form letters that Mr. [L. H.] Hill had printed for me.

In 1919, I leased the homestead and went to the Puget Sound country, (Harold had employment at Great Falls, Montana) and engaged in newspaper work. In May, 1926, I returned to the dear old homestead, almost a wreck, physically. In February, 1926, I had endured intestinal flu (For I am always well), and this was followed by small-pox which nearly extinguished life. And so I came back to the dear old home, and for weeks and months put up a great fight. But now, (With God everything is possible, and in him we live, and move, and have our being) I am well and strong again and to me there is an indescribable glory in the sun and air and amid these charming and beautiful environs, little wonder that a miracle has been wrought.

I have featured numerous articles for Sunday issues of our leading state dailies; contributed articles to farm journals, wrote a juvenile short-story for Little Folks, Salem, Mass., which has since ceased publication, have had acceptances from *Grit and Ginger* and when out in Washington contributed feature articles to The (Sunday) Tacoma Ledger and the daily Tribune and have contributed several articles to newspaper associations that supply small weeklies with what is called "ready prints."

You may not read this far, Mr. Sedgwick, but if you do, I would like to apologize for saying so much about myself. If you care for my story, I'll write a whole lot about the country—this wonderful state of Montana which is most appropriately called The Treasure State. My son is living in San Francisco and would like me to come and live with him but since my illness, I am tired of cities. Mrs. Mary Pfotenhauer, to whom you recently wrote for letters written by Mrs. Rose, is a dear friend of mine and she and I have kept up a correspondence for over a quarter of a century.

I am aware you do not use pictures to accompany stories but am enclosing a few snapshots so that you may see a few features of the homestead, etc. On the reverse side of each you will find a description.

Enclosed you will find a stamped addressed envelope for the return of the pictures and the circular or form-letter and clipping of letter sent

Mr. Leedy. And should you not care for my narrative, I will still be grateful to you for considering it.

Yours truly,
[Mattie T. Cramer]

Addendum: I still have all those letters written to me by prospective homeseekers. I have been urged to write a book about my life but have not done so, and so far I have refused being interviewed for publication. There were three proposals of marriage in those letters.

Through the columns of *The Enterprise* while I was its editor, people were asked to contribute books and magazines with which to start a town library. There were generous responses. I kept the books in The Enterprise office and gave them out from there, and from time to time published the names of contributors. Thus the town library was established and carried on until today we have a fine County Carnegie library with thousands of volumes of good books. I featured the foundation of the library for a Sunday daily. The times of my librarianship was full of amusing and interesting incidents.

I am wondering if I have made it clear that this letter is simply an inquiry, containing a few facts? That "copy" would need to be prepared entirely differently. I will be perfectly willing to submit a story of whatever length you desire for your approval or refusal.

M.T.C.

The homestead of Adelia Elizabeth Hawkins Sturm Glover, who came west in 1912 and proved up in 1917. OVERHOLSER HISTORICAL RESEARCH CENTER, FORT BENTON, MONTANA, *2006-AHG-002.*

Chapter Two

A SHACK NEAR BIG SANDY:
ADELIA ELIZABETH HAWKINS STURM GLOVER

"THIS IS TO MY CHILDREN, so that they may know something of the Life on a Homestead,"[1] wrote Adelia Glover, in 1971, at the age of eighty, when she sat down to write her homesteading memoir. Adelia Hawkins was twenty-one in 1912 when she filed on her 320-acre homestead near Big Sandy, Montana, in Chouteau County, between Great Falls and Havre, not far from the Canadian border. She came west with her two brothers, Will and Clair, and mother Celia (a nurse and midwife)—all homesteaders as well. Born and raised in New York, Adelia moved with her family in 1909 to Des Moines, Iowa, and then to Minneapolis. She was working for a real estate company there, when her brothers decided to homestead in Montana. During her first winter in Montana, she worked for a family in Great Falls.

In 1914, Adelia married Martin Sturm from Iowa, who was helping his cousin build a homestead shack. They shared an interest in music; he played the violin and she the piano. They lived on her homestead but worked elsewhere to make ends meet. Shortly after they were married, they worked on a ranch in the Bears Paw Mountains. Adelia was a cook for a fencing crew that included her husband and brother. Their first child, Marjorie, was born in 1915 on the homestead; Adelia's

Adelia Hawkins Sturm Glover's homestead shack is to the left, and her mother Celia's is to the right. Glover came west in 1912 with her mother (a nurse and midwife) and two brothers—Will and Clair. Glover, Clair, and her mother proved up five years later. OVERHOLSER HISTORICAL RESEARCH CENTER, FORT BENTON, MONTANA, 2006-AHG-001.

mother assisted with the delivery. Son Robert was born in 1918. Brother Will gave up and headed back East, but Glover, her mother, and Clair persisted. She received the patent to her homestead in 1917 as Adelia Sturm.[2] At that time she had a house estimated to be worth three hundred dollars, a barn worth one hundred dollars, 55 acres broken, a well, and a hen house.

In 1921, however, they all decided to "get out or starve," as 87-year-old Glover told a journalist in *The Post-Journal* of Jamestown, New York, in 1978.[3] "The drought had killed our last chance of surviving...When we left we just pulled out, notified the bank and gave up all we had worked nine years for. We never heard from the bank, so I guess it was all right. Our house was still standing in 1960 when a man bought it and made it into a garage." The family moved to Jamestown, where Martin died in 1957. Ten years later Adelia married Lafayette Glover.

At age twenty-one, Adelia Hawkins Sturm Glover stands at a fencepost on her homestead in the spring of 1912, the year she filed on her 320-acre plot near Big Sandy, between Great Falls and Havre. OVERHOLSER HISTORICAL RESEARCH CENTER, FORT BENTON, MONTANA, 2006-AHG-005.

Her concluding words to the journalist were, "Those were tough, turbulent times. But I feel we were a part of the settling of the West and I do not regret a minute of it."

Adelia Sturm Glover took all of the photographs that appear here. One of her prize possessions was a small box camera called a "Brownie," but she later graduated to a better camera and, as she describes in her memoir, she and her husband learned to develop the prints. Approximately half the memoir is about proving up on her homestead with her husband. This is representative of experiences of many solo women homesteaders, who started out as single women but soon married.

ADELIA HAWKINS STURM GLOVER MEMOIR
Overholser Historical Research Archives

St. Valentines Eve
Feb. 14, 1971

This is to my children, so they may know something of the Life on a Homestead:

In the fall of the year of 1909, my mother, my two brothers, and I left N.Y. State for the West. Clair and Will had some idea about going into the manufacturing of silos, but somehow it did not materialize. We spent a year in Des Moines, that was where they thought they would do this. I got me a job there working for S&H Green Stamp Co, but the first thing I knew the boys said we were moving to Minneapolis, They had both got a job as salesmen for Nebraska Silo Co, and sold all through Minn. We all liked Minneapolis, joined the church there, I got a job working in a Real Estate office in the Plymouth Bldg. Mother got a job in the hospital there, everything was going along fine, I thought. I had met some nice young people in the church. I also met a young man from Middletown, and we got to go together real steady, then suddenly, the men had decided we were going to Montana and take up a homestead.

Well, this just about floored me and I said, "I'm not going" but mother said she would not go unless I went, so every nite when I came home from the office, she had packed some of my clothes, and so off we went. The Great Northen R.R. was putting out great ads and making special rates for people who were going to take a carload of goods or stock and that is what we did. Half the car lord was household goods, the other was stock the men bought in Minn.

I think it was in February that we landed in Big Sandy. We rented a small house, the men found some place to put the horses. It was still winter, so we stayed there until the roads got so they could go out on the prairie, 35 miles, and have our homesteads staked out, we had two sections of land all joining.

In case you don't know what a homestead consists of—320 acres, you are required to live there so many months of the year, plow so much each year, get it into grain, fence so much, live there three years, then if you have not starved to death in that time, they give this land to you.

It was almost April before the boys got out there. They set up a tent, took a load of lumber out with four horses, some grubb, an old stove to cook on. They would use that lumber up and come back to town for more. It was pretty cold sleeping out in a tent, but as soon as they got some kind of a shelter up and an outhouse, they moved us out there. If you ever saw a desolate place, that was it. We hauled our water from a nearby "coolie", it was really melted snow in a little valley like, that was all the water there was. The men rigged up a stone boat affair, put two barrels on it and that's the way the water went. We learned to be economical with water, as well as everything else. So we all lived in one shack until they could get the others built. It took time and money and the boys had to get some plowing in that spring. Will and Clair were both workers, hard workers, they had to get some kind of a shed and a corral up for horses, and they had a cow so we could have milk....

I hadn't been there only two weeks, when one Sunday, two young men, cowboys, drove up to the door on horses and they had an extra horse with them, all saddled to ride. They said they heard there was a young girl out here and they just thought she might like to go for a ride. Well, I had never been on a horse in my life, but I was game, and away we went. So after that I never had to haveva horse of my own. I was about the only single girl within a radius of 25 miles, so I had a lot of cowboys coming to see me and taking me for a ride. There was no place to go but to the other ranches and have dinner with another bunch of cowboys, they were lonely and so was I. Some times we would ride to a sheepherder's camp and get our own dinner, he always had bacon, ham and a lot of canned goods. Sometimes it was pretty hot, we would just eat a can of peaches and some crackers.

One day one of the cowboys and I rode into town to a dance, it took most of the day. We danced until early morning, slept a couple of hours, got on the horses and back to the prairie, that was a 35 mile ride one way. I carried the dress I was going to wear in a bag on the back of the horse. It rained so we had to don slickers. It did rain a little the first two years, not much but a little. I was having too much fun then to worry about it being dry, my brother was taking care of my land then. I used to go up to the White House Ranch, that was the owners summer home. I used to help the cook during Round Up and branding time. The cook and I were the only females around then. I was going quite steady then with a young cowboy. We decided to go back to my home at nite, we got lost, but we finally found the ranch fence and followed it to a gate. I did not get home that nite but stayed at the Ranch. It was pretty easy to get lost, as the lights from the shacks looked so far away and then you would drop into a little coolie and when you got out of that, you lost the light.

One of the first things the boys had to do was get a well dug for water. My brother Will had a well driller come out. He got water but had to go down about 500 feet and it was just alkali, terrible water to drink but the stock drank it. We used to go down to the Creek about two miles away and get water to drink. Will put up a windmill. I guess we missed water to drink as much as anything. It was very hot in summer. No shade trees. We did discover a sprong, about two miles away. We used to go over there with a canvas bag and carry water back to drink. Boy, did that ever taste good on a hot day.

We had no Post Office, so the neighbors and my folks decided we better see what we could do about it, so we started going over to meet the stage 7 miles across the big field. I did my share of this. We rode horseback, tied the mail on the horse, and had a lot of Montgomery Ward catalogues. We did this for seven months to prove to the government that we needed a P.O. My mother was appointed to be Post Mistress so the boys built a shed on her house, and she named it Eagleton,

Glover inscribed the following caption on this 1912 photograph of herself perched on a horse: "This snap shot was taken up in the Bearpaw Mountains at the White House Ranch, the summer home of McNamara and Marlow. I was helping the cook during roundup time." OVERHOLSER HISTORICAL RESEARCH CENTER, FORT BENTON, MONTANA, 2006-AHG-004.

the name of the creek that passed through that country was called Eagle Creek, that's how she arrived at that name. Burleson was the Post Master General at that time. This certificate is now at the county seat, Fort Benton, Montana. The place is no more so I sent it to the Historical Society. I think it was discontinued about the year of 1924.

This was 1912 when we first landed on the prairie, it is now 1913. My mother's shack is built and my shack 8 x 10 was built, a root cellar in between the two shacks. Mother and I ate most of our meals together. I had a little two lid iron stove to cook on, no oven. Mother had a four lid stove with an oven so we got along pretty good. This was all new stuff for us, we had always lived in town. The shacks were all built with no foundation, plain boards for siding, then black tar paper to cover – held in place by nailing lath to it. The wind blew every day. These shacks had no ceiling, therefore they got pretty cold in winter. Winter got to be 40 and 50 degrees below zero many days, the shack would sway a little in the wind but they never blew over. It hadn't rained much so far but everyone thought it would, maybe next year. My brother Will did most of the plowing with unbroken horses. He got the use of them if he could break them to harness and work. He had quite a time with four horses hitched to a plow, and they just wanted to lay down and act up.

I used to get pretty lonesome days, I would go up on a little knoll, sit on a sheep herder's pile of rocks, and strain my eyes, just to see if I could not see someone on horseback coming my way. No, they most always went another direction. You could sleep nites, the coyotees would howl off in the distance, a pretty weird sound. More people were coming in this section all the time, and one morning, my mother was sweeping off a little porch she had on her shack and I was playing my piano, a very nice looking young man came to get the mail, he heard me playing and he said, "Who is that playing?" My mother said, "It's my daughter," and he said he hadn't heard any music since he came out about a mouth ago, so my mother invited him in and he played the violin that he had brought with him. He was from Iowa. My mother invited him over for supprer Sunday nite and he brought his violin. This young man turned out to be Martin V. Sturm, whom I married within three months. He just came out to help his cousin build his homestead shack. He was not going to stay in that "God forsaken' country," but I managed to convince him to stay. At times I thought he was not going to stay. I met Martin in April and we borrowed two horses and a buckboard wagon from neighbors, drove to Big Sandy, left the horses there at the livery, took a train to Fort Benton (the county seat) and got there at almost closing time so we just barely got the license in time. We were married at 7:30 in the M. E. Parsonage. This was July 3, 1914, the next day was the 4th, it was a blistering hot 103. on the street, and they had big "doings" there but we just went over to the river and soaked our feet in the Missouri. There were a few trees there and that seemed good too. Then 4th of July nite we went back to Big Sandy, where a dance was in full swing, so we danced most of the nite away, had to sit up in the hotel lobby, there was no room at the inn. We were not long there, all the chairs were full of people. Sunday we drove back to the homestead. Monday my brother had a job fencing a big field for those two men that owned everything, [including the bank in Big Sandy and eight ranches] and he said he would give Martin a job and I could go u[p] near the Bear Paw Mts. And cook for five men for about a month, so this is where we spent our honeymoon. The log cabin was about 9 x 10, with a two lid stove and bunks. Martin put up a tent and we slept in that...

I forgot to mention, the winter of 1913, I went to Great Falls, I am single then, I did housework, mostly cooking for a nice family. My friend from Minneapolis had been out on the prairie to visit me and so he went to Great Falls and got work. That was when I found out more about him. When I got back on the prairie I met Martin and then I knew for sure, this fellow from Minneapolis wasn't for me, and immediately wrote and told him so. I got a mean letter from him, but I did not see or hear from him again. I think he wrote he was going to join the Army, I think this was the Spanish War.

Now, Martin and I were married, we had to enlarge my shack. We decided it was too close to my relatives, and we should be in another part of our land, so we moved the shack, about three quarters of a mile away. Martin was a good carpenter and said we were going to have a better house. We started out well, built a house with one bedroom, a combination living room and kitchen and a little room aside, like a pantry. We shingled this, and stained the shingles brown and the roof green. I helped put the shingles on and also held up the rafters for him, and it was real windy that day. We had a fairly decent looking house, then later we decided to put in a screened in porch, the mosquitoes were bad. Well, we didn't seem to have much time to sit out there in summer so we decided to board it up and make a kitchen of it, but it was cold out there in winter, the water pail froze solid, and we could not throw the water away. I used to bake pancakes, with my feet on the stove hearth, and hand the pancakes in to the family through the window. Our house never got any inside ceiling, things did not seem to be improving, as far as rain was concerned but we still had HOPE. Money was scarce.

In the fall of 1914, we decided to go to Iowa to visit Martin's folks, he had a lot of relatives in Lenox, Iowa and they all wanted to see me as well as Martin. He was a big help to them too, he got right out and helped in corn husking time, etc. I helped all I could about the house, we stayed until April. I discovered while there that I was Expecting, so that was something to look forward to. Of course we did not have any furniture, and not much money, Martin made a nice oval table with two drop leafs and stained them. He also made a kitchen cupboard, baby bed, a nursery chair, a magazine rack, quite a number of little articles about the house, this was all made out of an old hay rack, all of this had to be planned, planned and sawed lengthwise, etc. quite a job. This is the way my Grandfather Davidson got his furniture, after his folks came to this county from Scotland. He made some lovely pieces of furniture. Marjorie has a table he made. I got up a Larkin Club out there and I got one new chair from them.

My mother was a born nurse and had worked in hospitals until it became the law to have a license, that put her out. She was called to deliver about 15 babies out there on the prairie and they were all a success, so the time arrived for me to have my first baby, Marjorie. I had quite a time, in fact, I think I almost died. Martin went in town on horseback to get a doctor. He had a car and came out, but my mother smelled liquor on him and would not let him in, told him that she had done what was necessary and I was going to be alright. My mother was a real W.C.T.U. woman. My mother said never again would she deliver any of her own children's babies, and she didn't. My mother bought a good supply of drugs when we went out there and people used to come for miles to get help from her. The baby was kept spotless clean and sometimes it would be weeks before I would see anyone. I always listened to what my mother told me to do about the care of the baby, and her information was simple, lots of things to do that we had right in the house. To-day, they don't listen, it's foolish, so they call the doctor and pay. It's wonderful...what you can do, if you have a little faith and try.

In the meantime and in between time, we had to get some work horses and machinery to work the soil, get a garden in, a cow for milk, etc,. These were all very expensive and we had to go into debt and mortgage all this and that was not hard to do. The Bank was willing, and they got 10% interest on their money, that is, if we would get a crop. In 1916, they had a great crop, but we had not started yet. They had so much grain, the elevators in town could not take it all, but that was the last of the real good crop, sometimes they did not even get their seed back. Everybody had sunk what they had and a little more so we were stuck and the Bank was willing to stake us farther so we stayed on, just hoping and praying for RAIN. It was a very hot year and no rain. We still must press on. We had bought a dozen chickens and so that gave us some eggs, then we raised some young chickens and that gave us meat. All the fresh meat we had was chicken, then we had ham and bacon. Everyone had to build a root cellar, that's a big room underground with a roof over it and then sod on top, otherwise we could not have kept any food. We used a lot of cheese, bought it by the 10 lb. head. We went to town once a year for groceries, generally took four horses so we could bring back anything else we might have to have. It took all day to get there. We stayed all nite and came back the next day.

Everyone had to try and get some water. I could not begin to tell you the number of wells Martin dug, helping others too. These were all dug by hand, and the dirt was brought up by a windlass, had to go down 40-50 feet and sometimes very little water. In the winter, we melted snow to use for washing, but we always had a couple of barrels on a stone boat which we took to the creek for water. During the day we put a canvas or burlap bag over the top to keep bugs, etc, out.

By this time there were quite a few youngsters who needed schooling, so the neighbors got together and discussed it, finally got a small shanty built and a teacher, but it caused a lot of trouble. It would set one place for awhile and then a fight would come up and they would move it. Finally, I decided to give 5 acres on the corner of my land, so it was deeded for a schoolhouse and is recorded at Fort Benton. They built a nice little schoolhouse, called it the "Eagleton Schoolhouse". It lasted for quite a few years and then children had to go to High School. It still stands there, I am told. No school there anymore.

Next we had to have a church. My mother was chairman of the building committee, She got a lot of donations from the East. It had a nice red carpet coming from some friends in Chicago, that really made it nice. There were circuit preachers who came out, one came on horseback. There were quite a few interested but not enough, and after my mother and brother left it sort of faded away, and then people were leaving the country too. Someone bought it later I heard and used it for a house. Marjorie was baptized here. Once one of the preachers stayed all nite with us, I can't remember where he slept, no doubt on a hook. Our house had a small attic which was very handy. We kept putting in a crop, once in a while we would get enough (money) to live over the winter, with what money Martin could work and earn. Sometimes he would go to another section and help thresh.

We had two good work horses and two good mules, they were buckskin, with a brown streak down their back. They were nice to use on a buckboard, if you had one. We did manage to get a second hand one seater, then we could fly over the prairie. We had dances every two weeks, people just set the furniture out on the prairie and put corn meal on the floor. I sometimes played the piano. Martin was a fiddler. He had been playing for dances in Iowa since he was twelve years old. Then we had another fellow from up in the mountains who played the guitar, and once in awhile someone would come with a horn. We did have some good times. Once in awhile we would take Marjorie along, she played with other kids and then later, we packed them off to bed. Sometimes people used their grainery for a dance hall, then we had the house to lay the kids on the bed. It was an all nite affair because we could not find our way home until daylight. I always hated to hear the "HOME SWEET HOME" waltz. They took up a collection to pay for the music, we sometimes made $5 each for playing all nite.

Martin was a good hunter, so we could get jack rabbit for food, and then there was the sage hen. We used corn meal a lot, and I made bread and biscuits, no bakery out there. We had company for Sunday dinners, I have had as many as 20 people to eat at one time. We had to do a few things for recreation, so we just went back and forth to each other's houses for Sunday dinner.

I guess I had better devote a few lines to some of the experiences that I had. We had this nice pair of buckskin mules, one of them had very sensitive ears. Martin always kept them neatly trimmed. Every time they were trimmed, Martin had to put a twitch on his nose and every time he started to bite and jump, the twitch was tightened and that hurt the mule. I was the one who had to operate the twitch, I was in front of the mule in the manger and shaking like a leaf. This twitch is a long stick with a leather loop on the end, and this loop is put around the mule's nose. This did the trick but it was another thing I had never had to do.

Then one day, my brother Will had a horse that was sick, so he came to my house and asked if I could come up and help him. Well, he was going to give the horse an anenoma, so he had the horse down on her side, and I had to sit on her head. She had a burlap bag over her head, while he was at the other end. I was pretty scared at this but the horse was very sick and she lived.

We had quite close neighbors, a half mile or so. Well, this neighbor's wife was expecting and my mother had gone East. Her husband came over and asked if I could come over and help, a nurse was supposed to come but she had not arrived yet. This was really something I had never done, but I took along my shears and some linen thread and went over. Things were coming along good, so was the baby, just then the nurse came in, I ran to her, took her coat, gave her the thread and shears and she took over. I was sure glad of that. Out there one had to be prepared to do most anything. I don't think any of them ever appreciated what my mother did for them.

We had a dance once or twice at a neighbor's, about two miles away. We loaded my piano on a wagon and away we went to the dance, we had fun. We used to have box social and dance. Auction off the lunch and you ate with the party that bought your lunch. That was fun. We decorated the box with crepe paper and made it look as nice as we could.

When we arrived in Big Sandy in 1912, there were about a 100 people living there, but after these homesteaders kept coming in, it was soon built up, with several different businesses. There were several saloons, red light district. This had a high board fence around it and quite a popular place.

I went with quite a few young cowboys. They all wanted to get married and most of them had a "claim" somewhere. They would take me for a ride to their homestead, but I was having too good a time when I was single to even think of marrying, and I wanted some day to come back East. I always had that in mind. These boys would never leave Montana.

After I married and Marjorie was born, I was very busy making garments for her. I made all my garments, hemmed the diapers, and I had never sewed before. Mother had her sewing machine that was 50 years old, a White machine. I used this for all my sewing. Friends in the East would send me parcel post good old coats that I could make over into snow suits and such. I would send to Montgomery Wards and get some material, get it in the mail next day, go down to mother's to show her what I had done and Marjorie would have the dress on. No one could understand this. I had fun doing this and I always wanted to keep Marjorie looking nice and clean all the time. She was a pretty baby and I took pride in keeping her that way. People who came to the P.O. would remark how nice she looked. I liked that too. I did not even have a pattern. I would lay the material on the floor and just cut it out. They don't do that today and I think they miss out on a lot of pleasure.

Rodeos were a great sport and fun, they had some really wild horses. They used to have them always on the 4th of July. Generally they were held up in the mountains or down toward the Missouri River, ten or fifteen miles away. They roasted a large beef, out in the open. It was an all day affair. Then they would build a dance platform right out in the open and we danced under the moon and stars. There was no liquor in all these simple go goings on. Everyone had fun.

In 1917, Martin was called into the service, World War One. He got exempted from that since he had crops in for grain and that was important. This looks like a good year. Martin was getting anxious to get a car. So he went in town and bought a new Maxwell Touring, just on the strength that it would rain and we would get a crop. It did not turn out that way. We promptly took the car back, with no loss to anyone. I learned to drive out on the prairie. We made a couple of trips to the mountains but that was all.

In this same year a couple of my friends from Minneapolis got married and decided to come out where we were. This was Bill and Lucille Bergman. She lived on the same street I did in Minneapolis, rode on the street car every day, that's how I met her. We went to a few dances in Minneapolis, she and Bill, and I went with a brother of Bill's. So after they got out on the prairie, they lived about 3 miles from us, so we got to see them real often. She went back to Minneapolis to have her first baby.

It was quite a job to keep in stove wood for our stoves. We would take a four horse team and drive 10 to 15 miles over in the Badlands. There we got pitch pine roots and any kind of stumps that had lain there for years. It made a hot and quick fire but very hard to get in shape for the stove. Then we had another place over that way where we got soft coal right out of the ground, and some candle coal. This coal lay very near to the surface of the ground, but it was a job. I would go along, take our lunch and call that a dirty picnic. But it was an outing. This went on all through the years there, but it was a job that had to be done during the summer and fall. In the winter time, Martin was busy keeping the wood ready for the stove and kindling to start the fire. Fire went out most every nite. We could not keep chickens over the winter, we tried one winter and they froze right on the roost.

When I went out there I just had a little box camera, it took pretty good pictures, but Martin got interested and said he would sell one of his guns and buy a good camera, and he did. That got us started taking pictures. We used to send them away to be developed and then he and I would make the prints. That was something for us to do evenings. We used to put a red flanne[l] over the lamp chimney so as to have the light just right. It's quite wonderful what you can do, if you don't have much. My brother Clair used to ride over and have dinner with us a lot. He was a bachelor, he did not marry until be was 45 years old. We met a lot of nice people out there. There were some that were better fixed than we were, but eventually they ended up with nothing.

The sun shone every day during the summer and fall, and one sort of longed for a cloudy day. It would cloud up and thunder and a few drops of rain come down and then the sun was out. During the war, we were rationed on sugar, flour, coffee, etc. but being so far out of town we were able to buy 25 lbs. coffee and sugar. I learned to bake sugarless cake and not much shortening. It was not much good but we ate it. It was cake. This was the year my brother Will decided he better get out where crops were more sure, since he had three children, Thomas, Marcia, and Evelyn. He got a chance to sell his property and got some cash down. The people who bought it were from Iowa and I guess after they got home they changed their mind. The crop was not good that year so Will sold off his stock and took the down payment and left for New York State. He bought a farm near Walton, N.Y. and lived there for years and then went to Florida, where he died in 1967.

It is now about 1917, the war is still on and we are still here. My mother, Will, and family had left for the East. I could look over the prairie and could see no lights at nite, I could always see mother's light from our house. We were still hoping for a crop and that we would get a good rain. If it would rain once a month we could have gotten a pretty good crop of winter wheat. We had very little money, but our credit was still good[.] The Bergmans had left, gone back to Minneapolis, on a small lake, where they had cabins they rented to fishermen and hunters. Bill died a few years later, Lucille married his brother, and then he died, so she still lives alone in McGregor, Minn. We had lots of fun together in Montana. Martin's cousin Irve and his wife left, and took up residence in another part of Montana, she went to teaching school, he was a mechanic.

The winters were long and very cold. It seemed to be healthy, as we never had the doctor out there, just used the old home remedies. We enjoyed printing pictures and music, I still played the piano and Martin played his violin. This was a blessing for both of us. In 1918, it was time for me to have another child, so we decided we would not stay out on the prairie and take such a chance again, mother was not here, so we did not go to Great Falls until November. Martin had got hold of a second hand motorcycle. I can't remember what he traded for it. He used to ride a lot as a young man. He thought that would be just the thing, but he soon found out that cost money and only room for him, although I did take a short ride on the back across the prairie. He went into Big Sandy on the morning of the 11th of November and the town had suddenly gone NUTS, yelling and just whooping it up, he asked someone near, "What happened?" and they said the war was over. He had just recieved his second draft call, so had the war not ended then, he would have been in it.

Now, we had to begin to get ready for the new baby, clothes and the expense. Martin got a little work to do in other parts, where they had a crop or two. I used to go and cook for a bachelor, who had a fairly good crop, this was at threshing time. I would have 15 men to cook for, dress chickens and bake biscuits, this was a job in its self. We had some good friends, Jess Kessler, who lived about 10 miles from us. They seemed to always have company and good food. They decided to go to Great Falls for the winter, so they went ahead and got themselves a few rooms, and also got three rooms and bath for us, and it was near them. Martin had to get a job, he was a good carpenter and he got a job very soon. Oneday, a Union man came along and asked him if he belonged to the Union, and he didn't and could not anyway, so he lost that job. He had two or three jobs and lost them on account of the Union, but he finally got a job at the flour mill. Our baby Robert was born December 22,1918, in a Great Falls hospital. I had quite a time. Then the flu was really getting people, they were dying like flies, could hardly get an undertaker to bury, they were so busy. Martin got a slight case of it, so they brought him in the hospital for a few days. Marjorie had ear trouble. They kept me there a day longer so the house could be fumigated. I went home, and they soon decided Martin better go home, so he could be with his family. He felt terrible but he did wash diapers every day and sweat. He was sick. Robert had a cold, was born with one. He cried many nites, even the next door neighbors asked what was the matter with him. He just wanted to be tended all nite and rocked, so I decided to let him cry this out and he did get over it. There were a lot of men out of work so Martin finally got laid off from this job and we just had to go back on the prairie. In February, we took the train for Big Sandy and hired a car to bring us out, went in a cold house, for the rest of the winter none of us caught cold in this either. We went back to eating corn bread, corn mush fried and all the simple things of life. No potatoes, no butter, canned milk, but we all survived I am afraid the young folks today would not make it. Christmas didn't mean a thing out there, we just all put together, like a tureen dinner and got together. No presents.

This was a cold winter, sometimes it would get to 50 degrees below with a lotvof snow, so all we could do was stay in and keep the fire going and that was quite a job. Martin did make himself a pair of skiis, this was quite a trick, as the wood they were made of had to be put in a boiler of hot water and brought to the stage of bending for the tips of the skiis, then all the waxing etc. but he did get over the snow a little.

He did get a small job doing carpenter work, about ten miles from us, he took his skiis, hammer, saw, and square, and away he went over the snow. He did get odd jobs helping at other ranches, etc. We put in some crop and a garden but it did not rain, so now we had decided we must earn some money and get out of this country.

Life was pretty dull with the neighbors all gone, my brother was still there, he lived alone and on sour-doughs. He used to come and see us real often; he liked my cooking better than his. After Robert was born we sent away and got a washin machine, worked by hand, that rub-a dub stuff got my back, this machine cost about 16.00, that was a lot of money out there but it sure helped me a lot. I was very particular about keeping my children clean, although it might be weeks before I would see anyone else but my family.

In 1921, in the fall, we decided we had to get out or starve, so Martin took his four horses and hayracks and another man went with him, they went to the Judith Basin, down on the Missouri, about 100 miles overland. He got a job helping thresh wheat. He was gone about two months and came back with $200, that was to be ou[r] trip back East. We hid it in the back of the piano. I was home alone all this time with the children. One day the wind got to blowing real hard and I thought for sure we were going to be blown away, so I took the children and went down in the root cellar and stayed there until it died down. The thistle weed was blowing all over, and the coyotes were howling every nite, they even came up in my yard one afternoon and took one of my chickens right before my eyes.

We are now getting ready to make the last leap to get away from this and earn some money. We just left our house and everything, told the bank and said it was all theirs, they took most everything, I guess, we really never knew what did happen to our household things. We never heard any more, so guess they were satisfied. My house was still standing in 1960, then an old rancher bought it and made it into a garage. Our good neighbor, ten miles away, brought us to town in his "flivver" Ford model T. It was a cold day, but we soon got on the Great

Northern. When we got to Minneapolis we stopped over to buy a winter coat and some warmer clothes. When we arrived in Jamestown, it was raining, and we had a lot of it so we decided we had come to the right place. We left Montana on Tuesday and arrived in Jamestown on Saturday. I had written to my cousin Murray Davidson to see if he could give Martin a job, and he said he could and would, so Martin went to work for the Jamestown Ice Cream Co. on Monday. He was doing carpenter work but mostly driving the ice cream truck. Later he worked for Warren Oil driving truck, and then later he worked for Standard Oil about 14 years. Then later he went into the trucking business on his own, called Sturm Trucking Company.

With all the hardships in Montana, I have many pleasant memories, I still think of them. I have been out there twice since we came East, both times were to see my brother Clair, who was very sick. He finally married a Montana girl after 45 years of being a bachelor. He was a good brother all my life. This is not a pleasant ending to this life in Montana, which lasted 9 years. A lot of lessons can be learned from that experience, even if we didn't make any money. I learned the value of a dollar. I wore castoffs and made over things for my children, friends sent me things from the East and I was grateful to get them, today people can't do these things. The government owes them more, and they seem to get it, somehow.

I had a saddle horse to get me around while Martin was gone, I put one child behind the saddle and the other in the saddle with me, and away we went. So many things have happened since I came East, I could write a story on that, I am 80 years old plus 7 months so I don't know, from now on.

Adelia Elizabeth Hawkins Sturm Glover

Chapter Three

"IN MY OWN HOME AT LAST": METTA M. LOOMIS

METTA M. LOOMIS' LIVELY ACCOUNT tells the story of how she and another female teacher, along with the help of her brother, homesteaded near Fort Benton, filing on her land in 1909 and proving up in 1915. There are few clues as to who Metta M. Loomis was beyond what she shared in this article in the January 1916 *Overland Monthly.*[1] She is not identifiable in the Bureau of Land Management records, which means that she married and changed her name, used a pseudonym, or didn't "prove up" on her homestead. In the article, however, she claims to have "converted one of Uncle Sam's homesteads into a flourishing farm." The article may be a fabrication, but the details on homesteading costs, property values, and assets seem authentic. The original article also features photographs of her first shack, her brother helping her with her team of horses, her in the field while her hired man cut her first crop of flax, her picking up coal along the railroad lines to bake pies, and her more substantial home that replaced the shack, with the caption "In my own home at last. I am sitting in the doorway." Loomis notes that she came to Montana from an Iowa farm, and census records reveal that a Metta M. Loomis was born on an Iowa farm in May 1866.[2] There is also a younger brother, William, who may be the

This photograph of Metta Loomis appeared with her article "From a School Room to a Montana Ranch" in the January 1916 Overland Monthly. *According to the article, Loomis filed on her land near Fort Benton in 1909 and proved up in 1915, although she is not identifiable in the Bureau of Land Management records.*
OVERLAND MONTHLY, JANUARY 1916. UNIVERSITY OF WASHINGTON LIBRARIES, SPECIAL COLLECTION, UW 28589Z.

younger homesteading brother who helped his sister and her friend establish their homesteads.

Historian Dee Garceau used this article as one example of the woman homesteading genre that appeared in popular literature in the early decades of the twentieth century. The "brash, kinetic flapper replaced the Victorian matron as a symbol of womanhood" and "in this context, homesteading became a compelling metaphor for female transformation," Garceau wrote.[3] Loomis touted the advantages of homesteading and thus property ownership and economic autonomy for single women.

FROM A SCHOOL ROOM TO A MONTANA RANCH
Metta M. Loomis
January 1916 Overland Monthly

"I wish that we were safe on some good farm."

How often one hears the wish from those who are noting the advancing price of farm products and the shifting business vales of war times. This condition produces a feeling of uncertainty that is serving to awaken a new interest in farming, and increase the number who are trying to find a way "back to the land."

It is an undertaking for a man to cut loose from the anchorage of a comfortable salary and stake his future on a homestead, but for a woman to venture such an undertaking requires more than ordinary fortitude. When a woman is successful in making one of Uncle Sam's farms pay her in money and health and happiness, the knowledge of her work becomes a source of inspiration and encouragement to those who are wishing for the security of a farm. It was in the hope of furnishing such encouragement that a woman who has converted one of Uncle Sam's homesteads into a flourishing farm has been persuaded to tell her story—to report her efforts, and furnish statistics of her work—to blase a trail of personal experience that may be some guide to others who may be trying to find a way "back to the land."

"My story starts on an Iowa farm," began the narrator, as she looked with satisfaction over her own farm, so beautiful with spring's promise of autumn's harvest. "My farmer kin all enjoyed the rural life, but they all assured me that farming was drudgery, and congratulated me on my great good fortune in escaping from the labor of the farm for the easy work of teaching school.

"Some way, I don't seem to be made to live within doors, and the enthusiasm with which I began teaching very soon began to wane and was slowly but surely replaced by a longing for horizons instead of walls...a longing which must be felt by thousands who chafe against the ceaseless grind and close confinement of the school room, the office, the shop and the factory.

In the Overland Monthly *photo caption, Metta Loomis stated that her brother "helped her with her very big team."* OVERLAND MONTHLY, JANUARY 1916. UNIVERSITY OF WASHINGTON LIBRARIES, SPECIAL COLLECTIONS, UW 28590Z.

"I happened to be teaching in Montana at the time the bench lands near Ft. Benton were opened to settlement. My nerves were out of tune, and I felt that life was pretty much of a squeezed orange, but I had enough energy to react to the land fever excitement, and it was not long before I was planning my return to farm life with all the eagerness that I had felt in leaving it.

"The lone man is much handicapped when he becomes a homesteader, but the lone woman is almost incapacitated for homesteading, and her first move towards entering a claim for a homestead should be to induce some other woman to join her. Two women taking up adjoining claims can build near enough together to utilize the same machinery and to save expense in hiring help, and also to provide mutual protection—protection not so much from physical danger as from that sense of loneliness that comes when one lives without companionship amid the overpowering forces of nature, in the rough, unsubdued by civilization.

"I broached my farm scheme to a kindergartener who assured me that she would just love to have a farm, because it was such fun picking flowers and she loved fresh vegetables. I knew something about the work and care needed to make a success of a farm, and I desided it would be folly for me to try to make such blissful ignorance wise to the realities of the farm. Next I tried some of our older teachers, but they refused to commit themselves except to say: 'If I were only a man I would do it in a minute.'"

"I felt that I had every qualification for farming that a man has except the brute strength, and I argued that that was the cheapest commodity to hire. As long as our Uncle Sam would allow teachers the privilege of proving up on a claim while continuing their school work, I proposed to work for a vine and fig tree of my own, rather than to content myself with the cheerless prospect of an old ladies' home or a teacher's pension.

"My enthusiasm finally became contagious enough to induce our drawing supervisor to join me in my plan to take up a homestead. She had health and one hundred dollars in the bank. I had a brother who was making good as a homesteader, and four hundred dollars in cash, besides we both had positions, good for fourteen hundred, and one thousand respectively. Thus equipped, we proposed to take up a claim, engage in dry farming, and use our salary to convert our three hundred and twenty acres of wild grass land into a prosperous farm. Our plan was to raise all the varieties of grain that are adapted to the climate, keep as much stock as we could feed, besides raising garden truck and poultry to supply our living, and to sell if there were a market for it.

"The filing of our application and the drawing of our land was quite as conventional as securing a teacher's certificate, but conventionality ceased September 27, 1909, at precisely five-fifteen in the afternoon, when the Great Northern train stopped at a lonely watering tank and two school teachers who would a-farming go, clambered to the ground. As the engine puffed the train into motion, and the teachers saw the coveted horizons, surrounding the grazing lands where were uncounted numbers of horses, sheep, cows and antelope, our undertaking suddenly looked terrifying. A loud 'hello!' soon broke this spell, and we were restored to enthusiastic ranchers by the greeting of our agent. 'You don't look very husky, for farmers, but you are getting the pick of some of the best bench land in the State. There is a big spring in that coulee yonder besides the immense reservoir belonging to the railroad, both of which show that you will be dead sure to strike water when you dig your wells. This bunch of grazing cattle proves there is moisture in the ground, and it only needs cultivating to raise good crops. You ladies are sure plucky, and here's good luck to the pair of you.'

"In half an hour we had set our stakes and were being driven back to Ft. Benton. We filed our claims the next morning, and returned to our work in the proud assurance of our new possessions.

"That winter we read the free documents furnished by the United States Agricultural Department for our diversion. We made sunbonnets and bedding rather than fancy work, and we bought lumber and nails instead of dresses and hats.

"Early the next March we sent the rancher brother to build our shacks, a mere box car of a house with two small windows. The cost was one hundred and ten dollars for each.

"March 28, 1910, we started for our first taste of real ranch life. Unfortunately, the only train that stopped at our watering tank would land us at our destination at 11:30 p.m. The night happened to be pitch dark, and our furniture was lying in heaps where it had been thrown from the freight car, caused many a groan and many a bruise as we groped our way to our shacks.

"As the light of the train disappeared in the distance I would have given my ranch, shack, sunbonnets and bank account for a large sized masculine shoulder and a scratchy coat, where I might have buried my head and wept comfortably, but such luxuries are not for the rancher novitiate. While each was protesting against the enthusiasm that had brought her to this desolate plight, our eyes accustomed themselves to the dark sufficiently to discover two black specks, which we knew must be our shacks. Gripping hands and tugging at our suit cases, we at last reached the nearest shack.

"For that first twenty-four hours it seemed a case of 'cheer up, for worse is yet to come.' By the sense of feeling we found the matches in our grips, and then it was an easy matter to locate our candle and to find some blankets, in which we wearily rolled ourselves up and lay down on the floor to await the daylight. In the dimness of the early morning we went to the spring for water and picked up bits of coal along the track. We soon had a fire and cooked one of the best breakfasts I ever ate.

"Fortunately, a Japanese section boss had left a rude push cart near the watering tank, and with that we managed to gather up our scattered 'lares and penates,' and by a combination of shoves and pushes, groans and jokes, we succeeded in getting enough furniture into our shacks so we could luxuriate in chairs to sit on, a table to eat on, a stove to cook on, and before night-time a bed to sleep on. I assure you it was two tired farmers that four o'clock quit work and went to bed.

"Every rancher and farmer remembers that summer of 1910 as the hottest, dryest ever known, and we shall always consider it as such. The buffalo grass withered and died. The sheep and cattle were driven northward for pasturage, but the two teacher-farmers were left in their little box car houses with the sun beating down at the unspeakable degree of 108 in the shade, for days at a time. We devised several methods of making life more bearable, one of the most successful being by baking lemon pies. I never think of that summer without being thankful that I knew how to make good lemon pies, and also for the correlated fact that two men liked lemon pies, and one of those men had charge of the refrigerators on the trains that stopped at our watering tank, and the other was the fireman on the same train. It is certain we never had occasion to complain of our ice man, and we never had to go far to find coal to bake our lemon pies.

"At last the summer was over, and we went back to another year of teaching school, saving money and planning for the next season on the farm.

"My fall shopping was mostly done at the hardware store. It is surprising how wire fencing and farm machinery will use up pay checks.

"Although the season had been so dry, I hired a man to break forty acres for me that fall, and early the next spring had it sown to flax, which yielded seven bushels to the acre and netted me one hundred dollars as my share, which was one-third of the profits.

"During the summer of 1911 we made vast improvements on our farms. Our shacks were transformed into homes. The price was just $150, and consisted in adding a bedroom, shingling, ceiling, and best of all, we built in a real cupboard, a closet and bookcase. A well was dug at a cost of $100. A garden had been planted in the early spring, and we raised an abundance of peas, beans, onions, cabbage, potatoes, etc. Oh, this summer was spent in the lap of luxury in comparison with the previous season.

"That fall I decided to have another forty acres broken. By this time, we could count sixty shacks in our valley, and there were plenty of farmers who were anxious to work on shares. The following spring I planted wheat and raised fifteen bushels to the acre.

Our Uncle Sam is continually looking after the interests of the farmers, especially those who carry on dry farming. An appropriation was made by Congress in 1912 to secure and distribute the seeds adapted to the needs of those sections which have scant rain fall. We hope to have special types of sorghum, wheat, oats and grasses which the experimenters predict will increase our harvests and add greatly to the land value of all this region.

"It has cost me about ten dollars per acre for improvements and to prove up on my land. I have put about $3,000 on my place, and it has produced about $700, of which $400 was paid for help. At least $500 of my salary has gone to my ranch each year, and every penny which the place has produced has gone right back into improvements, and I have had to borrow $500.

"I proved up on May 22, 1915, under the five year act. At that time I owned my farm, which I value at $30 an acre. The land is all fenced and cross-fenced. I have 170 acres planted to wheat, twenty acres to oats, eight acres to alfalfa, and twenty acres to summer fallow. The prospect is that we will have record crops. I have four fine brood mares, a riding pony, a two year old colt, three one year old colts and two spring colts, a cow and a calf, besides some fifty chickens. I have a fine barn, a chicken coop and a root cellar. I also have a wagon, a carriage, harness, and farm implements. I am enjoying my home, and teaching our country school, which is half a mile from my house.

"Our watering tank is now surrounded by an enterprising little town, and look in any direction as far as the eye can see, the land has all been converted into thriving farms. Loss of position and fear of prolonged illness have lost all terrors for me. One couldn't be sick in this glorious air.

"I started in with the disadvantage of health none too good and nerves none too steady, and the advantage of such general knowledge as most farmers' daughters absorb and a position worth $1,000 a year. Aside from these, I have had no special handicap and no special qualifications for my undertaking. I have done nothing but what any teacher could do. There are still homesteads to be had, and Uncle Sam allows the teacher to draw her checks while proving up on her land. The farms that Uncle Sam has to give away need very careful management in order to make them into paying propositions. They are merely opportunities, not certainties.

"I advise most teachers to stick to their job. Those who have a longing for the simple life can buy a few weeks of that kind, which consists of picking flowers and eating vegetables fresh from the garden, but for those who have the real farm hunger, there is a way 'back to the land.' As for myself, I know of no other way by which, in five years' time, I could have acquired such riotous health, secured much valuable property, experienced so much joy in living, and infused so much of hope and buoyancy into life, and no other way to provide such cheering prospects for my old age.

"Uncle Sam's farms are a land of promise, but the promises are fulfilled only to those who are willing to give hard work and continual study to those farm problems which confront every homesteader."

Chapter Four

THE SUMATRA ADVENTURE:
GRACE BINKS, INA DANA, MARGARET MAJORS

IN 1911 THREE SINGLE WOMEN, Grace Binks, Ina Dana, and Margaret Majors—members of a party of landseekers from Ottumwa, Iowa—filed on "Big Dry" homesteads approximately 30 miles north of Sumatra in Rosebud County, Montana. Ina Dana brought her mother along for the adventure.

The settlers in northwestern Rosebud County were generally from the upper Midwest, where by the early twentieth century there were few opportunities for land acquisition or expansion. They were also lured by the advertising of the Chicago, Milwaukee and St. Paul Railway Company—a 1912 brochure showed a farmer plowing in the eastern section of a map of Montana, and instead of sod, the plow is turning over gold coins.[1] Sumatra, in 1911, had a brand-new grain elevator and two hotels and was described, in a 1913 Milwaukee Railway brochure, as a "thriving young town" where "nearly all classes of business are represented."

Grace Binks was a thirty-nine-year-old bookkeeper when she filed on her homestead in March 1911.[2] Ina Dana was fifty and Margaret Majors was twenty-nine.[3] When they applied for final proof, they used each other as witnesses. Margaret Majors, for example, swore that she knew Grace Binks all her life, and saw her on her land every day, as her land adjoined Binks', except for a ten-day holiday in the mountains.

The Sumatra women homesteaders did not linger long in Montana—they stayed for just a year, then left right after they established legal proof to their land. The Sumatra women purchased, or commuted, their homesteads. When she paid two hundred dollars (one dollar and twenty-five cents per acre) for her patent to the land in November 1912, Binks had a 12-foot by 12-foot house and 10 cultivated acres, valued at two hundred dollars. Ina Dana paid the same amount for her land where she, too, had 10 cultivated acres and a one-room frame house, a storm shed, chicken house, and cellar. Both described their land as "rough and broken."

There is a photograph of Sumatra women homesteaders arriving, and a photograph of them leaving. Aside from what can be gleaned from the land files and census records, we know little about them except the record of these photographs and clippings kept by Grace Binks in her album. In 1917, Grace Binks married Wallace M. Price of Seattle, Washington. She must have put the album together and written the captions sometime after her marriage, as she refers to herself as "Grace Binks Price."

The album provides a rare glimpse of the material conditions of the lives of women homesteaders both inside and outside their shacks. We see, for example, the "kitchen corner" as well as the "parlor corner" of Grace's shack. There are photographs of neighbors, including other homesteaders such as Grace Mandel. They sightsee, swim, and pose for the camera "in the old corral." A clipping from a local newspaper and the notices they were required to publish to acquire legal proof are included. The album conveys a sense of adventure as well as pride in what they accomplished, although the photographs of "Grace's Land" could be meant to convey the bleakness of the landscape. The album also provides a glimpse of the "thriving" young town of Sumatra, that is today "no longer Sumatra but only its ghost, a mere skeleton" of what it had been during the homestead boom that this album documents.[4]

THE SUMATRA ADVENTURE:
SELECTIONS FROM THE SCRAPBOOK OF GRACE BINKS PRICE

Courtesy of the Montana Historical Society Research Center

Grace Binks (later Grace Binks Price) assembled this album about her homesteading adventures with Margaret Majors and Ina Dana, who brought her mother. The three single women were members of a party of landseekers from Ottumwa, Iowa, who filed in 1911 on "Big Dry" homesteads approximately 30 miles north of Sumatra in Rosebud County, Montana.

MONTANA HISTORICAL SOCIETY RESEARCH CENTER, PAC 92-62 A1.

Grace Binks Price arriving at the train station in Sumatra, Montana in 1911.

MONTANA HISTORICAL SOCIETY RESEARCH CENTER, PAC 92-62 A1, PG. 1.

The main street of Sumatra as the women homesteaders first saw it in 1911.
MONTANA HISTORICAL SOCIETY RESEARCH CENTER, PAC 92-62 A1, PG. 1.

Grace Binks described this photograph as "A band of 'woolies,' exploring their new surroundings." HISTORICAL SOCIETY RESEARCH CENTER, PAC 92-62 A1, PG. 1

Binks simply titled this "Grace's House" in her scrapbook.
MONTANA HISTORICAL SOCIETY RESEARCH CENTER, PAC 92-62 A1, PG. 5.

Binks labeled this photograph "Grace's Land." The Sumatra women
homesteaders described their land near Sumatra as "rough and broken."
Located on the plains, it was terrain that was treeless and dry.
MONTANA HISTORICAL SOCIETY RESEARCH CENTER, PAC 92-62 A1, PG. 5.

Grace Binks was a thirty-nine-year-old bookkeeper from Ottumwa, Iowa, when she filed on her Montana homestead. In her scrapbook, she kept this clipping announcing the arrival of the Iowa settlers.
MONTANA HISTORICAL SOCIETY RESEARCH CENTER, PAC 92-62 A1, PG. 5.

Grace Binks outside of her 12-foot by 12-foot homestead shack.
MONTANA HISTORICAL SOCIETY RESEARCH CENTER, PAC 92-62 A1, PG. 6.

Photographs of the interiors of women homesteaders' shacks are rare. This is Grace Binks' "Parlor Corner." Binks tried to recreate the comforts of home with her lace curtains, her carefully arranged pictures, flowered wallpaper, and books.
MONTANA HISTORICAL SOCIETY RESEARCH CENTER, PAC 92-62 A1, PG. 6.

Margaret Majors in front of her cabin feeding her chickens.
MONTANA HISTORICAL SOCIETY RESEARCH CENTER, PAC 92-62 A1, PG. 6.

*Grace Binks' "Kitchen Corner." Note how she tried to create a cozy atmosphere,
with her curtains, her cooking pans hung neatly on the walls, and her
polished tea kettle on the woodstove.*
MONTANA HISTORICAL SOCIETY RESEARCH CENTER, PAC 92-62 A1, PG. 6.

This is probably the homestead shack of Ina Dana. When Dana "proved up," she valued her improvements at two hundred dollars: "One room frame house with storm shed, chicken house, cellar, ½ mile two wire fence, 10 acres cultivation."
MONTANA HISTORICAL SOCIETY RESEARCH CENTER, PAC 92-62 A1, PG. 8.

This interior shot of Ina Dana's cabin includes her mother, who accompanied her on this adventure.
MONTANA HISTORICAL SOCIETY RESEARCH CENTER, PAC 92-62 A1, PG. 8.

ABOVE AND BELOW: *The interior of Ina Dana's homestead shack, featuring her mother (below) circa 1911.* MONTANA HISTORICAL SOCIETY RESEARCH CENTER, PAC 92-62 A1, PG. 8.

Grace Binks' original caption read: "3 Sunbonnets."
MONTANA HISTORICAL SOCIETY RESEARCH CENTER, PAC 92-62 A1, PG. 27.

The Sumatra Homesteaders (from Left): Grace Binks, Ina Dana,
Margaret Majors. MONTANA HISTORICAL SOCIETY RESEARCH CENTER, PAC 92-62 A1, PG. 27.

Homesteader Ina Dana's mother.
MONTANA HISTORICAL SOCIETY RESEARCH CENTER, PAC 92-62 A1, PG. 27.

Grace Binks' original caption for this photograph was "first crop" in 1911: potatoes.
MONTANA HISTORICAL SOCIETY RESEARCH CENTER, PAC 92-62 A1, PG. 27.

ABOVE AND BELOW: *Binks' original caption was "Going Home." Grace Binks, Ina Dana, Dana's mother, and Margaret Majors returned to Iowa after "commuting" or purchasing their homesteads in November 1912. Binks paid two hundred dollars for her homestead.*
MONTANA HISTORICAL SOCIETY RESEARCH CENTER, PAC 92-62 A1, PG. 38.

This postcard of Sumatra Station is included in the album beneath the photographs of the women "going home."
MONTANA HISTORICAL SOCIETY RESEARCH CENTER, PAC 92-62 A1, PG. 38.

Sightseeing near their homesteads. Grace Binks is on the right. The others (from left) Bess and Josie, may have been neighboring homesteaders.
MONTANA HISTORICAL SOCIETY RESEARCH CENTER, PAC 92-62 A1, PG. 41.

In this picture, friends pose in the wind atop rock formations near the original homestead. Binks' identified them as: Elizabeth Frisbee, Stan, Grace Price, and Josie.

MONTANA HISTORICAL SOCIETY RESEARCH CENTER, PAC 92-62 A1, PG. 41.

Stan sits near Josie's house.

MONTANA HISTORICAL SOCIETY RESEARCH CENTER, PAC 92-62 A1, PG. 41.

More picture-posing on the rocks. Binks' original caption reads:
Grace Price, Josie, Grace Mandel, Bess.
MONTANA HISTORICAL SOCIETY RESEARCH CENTER, PAC 92-62 A1, PG. 41.

This photograph, taken in what Grace Binks' terms the "old corral" features:
Grace Mandel, Elizabeth Frisbee, Josie, Bess, and Viola.
MONTANA HISTORICAL SOCIETY RESEARCH CENTER, PAC 92-62 A1, PG. 41.

Grace Mandel, who was a neighboring Sumatra homesteader.
MONTANA HISTORICAL SOCIETY RESEARCH CENTER, PAC 92-62 A1, PG. 41.

Every homesteader had to publish a "notice of intention to make proof" for five consecutive weeks at the newspaper nearest to their land. This is Grace Binks' notice that she intended to make final commutation proof to establish claim to her land. It was published in the Forsyth Times Journal.

MONTANA HISTORICAL SOCIETY RESEARCH CENTER, PAC 92-62 A1, PG. 39.

(Non-Coal Serial No. 011917.
Notice for Publication.
Department of the Interior, U. S.
Land Office at Miles City, Montana,
September 24, 1912. Notice is hereby
given that Ina Dana, of Sumatra, Mon-
tana, who, on March 29, 1911, made
Homestead Entry No. 011917, for
SW¼, Section 12, Township 15 N.,
Range 34 E., M. P. Meridian, has filed
notice of intention to make final com-
mutation proof, to establish claim to
the land above described, before D. J.
Muri, U. S. Commissioner, at Forsyth,
Montana, on the 30th day of October,
1912. Claimant names as witnesses:
Grace Binks, Margaret Majors, Cloyd
Foster, Thomas Gordon, all of Sum-
atra, Montana.
            A. KIRCHER, Register.
First publication September 26, 1912.

*Ina Dana's notice. Grace Binks neatly clipped and pasted the notices of each of
the three homesteader friends, with the caption "Legal Proof."*
MONTANA HISTORICAL SOCIETY RESEARCH CENTER, PAC 92-62 A1, PG. 39.

Non-Coal Land—Serial No. 012394.
Notice for Publication.
Department of the Interior, U. S.
Land Office at Miles City, Montana,
September 24, 1912. Notice is hereby
given that Margaret Majors, of Sum-
atra, Montana, who, on May 11, 1911,
made Homestead Entry No. 012394,
for NE¼, Section 12, Township 15 N.,
Range 34 E., M. P. Meridian, has filed
notice of intention to make final com-
mutation proof, to establish claim to
the land above described, before D. J.
Muri, U. S. Commissioner, at Forsyth,
Montana, on the 30th day of October,
1912. Claimant names as witnesses:
Ina Dana, Grace Binks, W. A. Van
Buskirk, all of Sumatra, Montana; Art
Heisel, of Jordan.
            A. KIRCHER, Register.

Margaret Majors' notice.
MONTANA HISTORICAL SOCIETY RESEARCH CENTER, PAC 92-62 A1, PG. 39.

Nan Pritchard Francis (standing at left, next to the horse) and her mother (seated at the front of the wagon). Francis moved from California to Montana with two small children in 1910 to homestead; she was joined by her cousin Lulu West and uncle Frank West, who were also homesteaders. Francis and her party sailed north from Redondo, California, to Seattle, Washington, then took the train east to Stanford, Montana. OVERHOLSER HISTORICAL RESEARCH CENTER, FORT BENTON, MONTANA, 1995-RP-593-7.

Chapter Five

LONE TREE, MONTANA:
NAN ("NANNIE") PRITCHARD FRANCIS

NANNIE P. FRANCIS, A MOTHER OF TWO small children, was living with her own mother in California when she decided to homestead at Lone Tree, Montana, in Chouteau County. She traveled with her uncle Frank West and cousin Lulu West, who were also homesteaders.[1] She was thirty-two years old. In 1910, they sailed from Redondo to San Francisco and then Seattle, where they boarded the train to Stanford, Montana. Her experience is a reminder that not all homesteaders moved west—she moved east and sailed the Pacific, rather than the Atlantic, to arrive in Montana.

Francis' vivid chronicle of the challenges of homesteading—the cold, wind, hunger, and the difficulties of travel that made each trip to the homestead "dreaded"—provides a valuable description of the variety of ways women homesteaders made a living while they were proving up, especially during the years when there were no crops. Nannie and Lulu successfully proved up, while Uncle Frank got discouraged and left Montana for good. "But we women didn't give up so easily," Francis wrote.

It is unclear when Francis wrote her memoir, but it illustrates some of the puzzling discrepancies between homesteading memoirs and land

Francis' homestead shack, which was considerably more substantive than most. She acquired a patent to the land in 1914. Although Francis eventually returned to California, she found herself "longing to go back to Montana." OVERHOLSER HISTORICAL RESEARCH CENTER, FORT BENTON, MONTANA, 1995-RP-593-4.

records. Francis began her memoir by writing that her husband had died six months earlier. Elsewhere in the memoir she refers to herself as a widow, but in her homestead entry she describes herself as a deserted wife.[2] In 1914, when she applied for final proof, however, she states again she was a widow.

Francis ends her memoir by writing that as soon as she got her patent she leased her land. At that time she had improvements on her homestead worth $1,600, including a house, barn, and well. She moved back to California and built a bungalow on the edge of her mother's orange orchard. Yet "with the fruit, flowers and wonderful climate I find myself longing to go back to Montana." It appears that she answered this longing; in the 1920 census, she is listed as living in the household of a family in the Square Butte Bench area of southeastern Chouteau County.[3]

MY EXPERIENCE HOMESTEADING
Mrs. N. P. Francis
Overholser Historical Research Archives

Since my husband[']s death six months before I was feeling so lonesome, and unsettled at mother's, that when my Uncle Frank West and cousin Lulu West came out on Monday, March 14th, 1910 to bid us goodbye as they were leaving for Montana to take homesteads, having reserved berths on the Steamer "Queen", sailing the following Thursday, I felt I would like to do something like that for a change. So after much thought and prayer for guidance, I decided to take my children Donald, aged 3½, Muriel 1½ and go with them. We just flew to get ready, but were at Redondo and sailed with them on St. Patricks day 1910.

We were a little sick the next morning in Frisco, but changed boats there and took the "President" a much larger boat from there on to Seattle[.] [W]e all felt fine physically, but the mental anguish I underwent was almost dispair, in fact I felt desperate, it wouldn't have mattered to me if the boat had sunk to the bottom of the ocean. Nothing mattered since Mr. Francis was gone. It was this state of mind that nerved me to go on to an unsettled wild, cold country with two babies.

We went by rail of course from Seattle to Montana and as we neared our stopping place, (Stanford) we felt so anxious for it to be a homey sort of place, on the contrary it was a very small town setting on the bleak prairie. We stopped at the only hotel but were pleased to find the people real pleasant and like us so many of them were strangers there looking for homesteads. We went from Stanford to Dover and stayed there until our cousin came in from the country (fifty miles) to meet us. One morning before daylight having put everything in the big lumber wagon that is seemed possible to load on, we got on and found a place to sit down, but oh so crowded, my knees rubbed against the trunks in front of me all the way. Just as it began to get red in the East, Muriel said, "Mama there comes the day". We traveled ever so

Under this photograph, Francis (standing at right in the white blouse) scrawled in her loopy handwriting: "Fred Brunskills—his son and daughther, Don and me."
OVERHOLSER HISTORICAL RESEARCH CENTER, FORT BENTON, MONTANA, 1995-RP-593-8.

slowly, it seemed hundreds of miles, towards night I supposed we must be nearly there when my cousin said the horses were tired so we better stop at a little deserted shack they called the half way house, so here we stopped.

[We were] a party of seven and stayed in this little eight by ten shack no floor and no accommodations but a mattress and a small stove. We enjoyed a lunch after our tiresome ride. Before we retired a thunder shower came up something unusual to we Californians, but we rather enjoyed seeing the big black clouds roll up over the hills as we were in a beautiful place at the edge of the Bad Lands. We women and children slept or tried to, on the mattress and the men in the other corner on their "road beds", one of the necessities of frontier life.

The ride next day was wonderful, in spite of sick headache, crossing the "Bad Lands". The road was nothing but a trail the freighters had used years before on a ridge, part way very little wider than the wagon with great gapping canons or coulees on either side. I think my hair would literally have stood on end [if] it had not been tied down so tight to keep it from blowing away in the awful wind they have most of the time in Montana. Then for variety we would have one of these coulees to cross, no bridge, and of course the steep bank on the opposite side to ascend. We would all get off and the men would lash the horses into a run to keep the wagon from miring. We crossed on logs or anything available.

After traveling over the worst roads I ever saw, what seemed thousands of miles, we came in sight of the end of our journey. A small shack 16x24. My cousin did not have their things unpacked yet and we had to run a regular boarding house for two weeks, with very little to cook except dried fruit, canned corn, tomatoes and of course, beans, beans, no end! Our dinner would usually consist of a big pot of beans in the center of the table and maybe some dried peaches, but oh how the men did eat and how interesting it was to we tender feet, or pilgrims as they called us to hear the old timers, [who] would stop there when they were out locating homesteaders, tell of their early experiences of their hardships, etc. It would make us almost shudder when we would think we might have some of the same experiences as we realized the country was yet new.

At the end of two weeks this cousin[']s wife came, which helped matters a great deal. We unpacked things and lived more like civilized folk although there were eleven of us in this small place. It kept we women busy trying to keep something cooked. With our limited means and 45 miles from town it was no small task, and especially for us Californians coming from a land flowing with milk and honey.

This proved to be a very dry year, nothing was raised. One of the worst features of the country is the terrible wind which blows almost incessantly when there isn't a cloud in the sky. One day Uncle Frank, Lulu and I were building a pen for some calves, when it was completed imagine our consternation, as the children and I went into the barn to get the calves, to see the barn roof up and sail off over our heads like it might have been a feather and dropped to the ground some 100 feet away. Our nearest postoffice was Lone Tree 18 miles. There was joy in camp when some of the crowd would make the trip for our mail and bring back a grain sack full.

Well we continued to live like this for three months. We could not live on our homesteads, which were 4½ miles from our cousins, as it was too dry to plant anything. Lulu and I having a little money bought a team for $150.00 of a cow boy, borrowed wagon and harness got Uncle Frank's consent to go with us and [journeyed] back to Stanford. Our cousin and family had been very kind and hospitable but we felt it an imposition to stay there any longer. We hadn't the remotest idea what we would do in Stanford, but [knew] we must try for something. We could not find a house to rent anywhere, but we found a man who let us have his tent. It was anything but pleasant with the wind and thunder showers we had so often.

We looked everywhere for work but could find none. At last we found a room we could rent and with the advise of some of the business men of the town we started a bakery[.] Lulu and I still had enough to buy our supplies. This proved to be pretty good as we supplied both stores and quite a few families with bread. By this time Uncle Frank came down with a sick spell got discouraged and left the country for good. But we women didn't give up so easily. We continued with our bakery until two young men members of the family circle at our cousins came to town to get work, but could find none, so they persuaded us to go to Dover, and rent the hotel there, as that would give us all employment. We gave up our business sold our bakery supplies at a great sacrifice. Moved bag and baggage to this small town. Nothing but a grain elevator, lumber yard, saloon and our hotel[.] Our patrons were all men from the country who hauled their grain to this elevator. For a week our prospects seemed fairly good. Then I came down with typhoid fever, was in bed three weeks. What a burden I felt when Lulu had me to wait on and the children to look after. How lonely I felt no one will ever know and how I longed for Mr. F! I gave the last cent I had to the

Doctor. Well I got up as everything seems to come to an end in time. We stayed with the hotel another month, but it was awful the drunk men we had to contend with, etc. We found out the hotel business was not our calling as we came out $200 behind. I did not leave until I had given the saloon keeper a temperance lecture.

In the meantime Lulu got the position of Governess in the home of an old time stockman, at a place called Lone Tree, a country P.O. [T]hat left the children and I with these two young men who were not much help to us. We moved our things into an old tumble down building, next door to the saloon, that had been a store in some prehistoric age. Our stay here was anything but pleasant as I had only a heating stove to cook on, and these boys required about 20 hotcakes a piece each morning made of water and flour and baking powder. After we had been here a few weeks they went back to the country to my cousins to be gone several days this left the children and I alone. There was no way to lock the doors in this big barny house and at night I lay there with sickening apprehensions of drunk men coming in and all sorts of terrible things. The snow would sift in through the cracks on our bed and I thought, O, you sunny California with the posies bloomin. When the boys came back I left the children with them and went to Stanford to look for work. I went into every place of business except saloons, and asked for work but could find nothing. I [felt] rather blue and the only thing left to do was write home for cash. I did and of course had word to come home. They sent more than I actually needed for my fare home and I was foolish enough to lend these boys enough to go home. And to this day very little of it has ever been paid back.

This was the last of November 1910. We waded through snow to our knees to get to the train to go to California. I felt so discouraged I think I would have sold my homestead for 50 cents had I been offered that amount. During the summer Lulu and I had some shacks built on our claims. The children and I arrived in California December 3rd, 1910, and really it seemed like I had died and gone to heaven, California never seemed so perfectly lovely before.

A Mr. and Mrs. Kennedy neighbors of my mothers had two boys on homesteads near Stanford, Montana. It hapened that these boys or young men came down to visit their parents this same winter that I came home. I felt very skeptical about Montana but they were loud in their praises and said great things were in store for Montana. Their mother finally persuaded me to go back and keep house for them. They promised to help me prove up on my homestead, which was afterward abundantly fulfilled. So on March 27th, 1911, the children and I start out again. The day was one of those ideal California days that can't be described. It seemd a terrible thing to leave this delightful climate for the northern windy cold one, but I thought it was best to hold onto the homestead. We enjoyed the beautiful scenery all the way. In northern California the fields were golden with the California poppy[.] In Oregon everywhere the fruit trees were just beautiful with their blossoms. The rest of the trip consisted largely of grand mt. scenery[.] After a journey of five days and five nights we arrived in Stanford thoroughly tired out April 1st at 4 p.m. and oh the change of weather from what we had left five days before. It was snowing and one of those raw cold winds from the east was blowing a gale. We waited until eight o'clock for our cousin, then five of us rode cramped in a single seated buggy to the little town of Dover. The experiences of the previous year hadn't endeared the place to us. We stayed all night in the restaurant and imagine, our bed as a single bunk without springs or mattress. The lady who owned the restaurant weighing some 200 lbs occupied it with the children and I, we only had one comfort under us and one over us, sleep of course was out of the question and I lay there wondering if a homestead in Montana was worth the hardships that it seemed necessary to undergo to secure it. After hours and hours of restless, almost agony daylight brought more cheerful thoughts. It seems almost unblieveable but the rest of the party in our bed slept well. After breakfast we start[ed] on our journey in a big wagon loaded with wheat in sacks, the team hardly able to haul an empty wagon on account of scarcity of feed during the past winter, the weather was even worse than the night before...At 9 o'clock that night we arrived at my cousins covered with snow, cold and hungry. The children and I were sick for two weeks. Then my cousin Lulu came who had been teaching at Lone Tree and we went over to hold our homesteads down. During this time we had another awful spell of weather what seemed to me almost a blizzard. There were great cracks in the walls and floors of our shacks so it was rather difficult to keep warm with our fire made of cow chips. We could hardly keep a lamp lighted on account of the wind blowing through the cracks. Our beds consisted of comforts spread on the floor. The team Lulu and I had bought the summer before were nearly starved and we could only get a small supply of oats. It was so pitiful when they...during the blizzard would look in through the windows at us and nicker for oats which we couldn't let them have. The nights were dreary enough so deathly still with only an occasional howl of a coyote, the pararie dogs were thick on our claims, they made plenty of noise during the day. We became so hungry for fresh meat we ate some of the dogws with a relish. A great deal of our time was taken up hauling water some four or five miles from an old sheep ranch.

After thinking I had stayed on my homestead (or Happy Home as Muriel always called it) long enough to satisfy "Uncle Sam", I decided I better go over to keep house for the Kennedy Bros. about 50 miles away on Coyote Bench. I was at my wits end to know how I would get there, but about this time cousin Lulu was going to Fort Benton 45 miles away for supplies, and although it was in the opposite direction to the Kennedy's ranch, I decided to go with here and take the train from there to Stanford, so on May 1, 1911 Cousin Lulu a young man, who was looking after Lulu's place, the children and I start out on another long journey. Getting started fairly early we thought we could make the trip in one day so didn't take much lunch, in fact we didn't have much to take. We didn't make such rapid progress as we had supposed we could and night was upon us and the horses very tired when we arrived at an old deserted building that had at one time been a hotel where the freighters from Lewistown to Great Falls, had stopped to rest and change horses, Clarence, our driver unhitched the horses fed and watered them and left them there to graze on the grass, we waited for him as we did'nt like the idea of going into this sppokie looking place with out him. Very follishly we had come away without matches or lantern, so we had to grope around through those large rooms wondering if we could find a place to sleep, but there wasn't an atom of furniture or anything to be found, we made our bed of a lap robe under us and one over us. We girls of course couldn't sleep on such a bed with the weird noises the rats[,] wind and bats made. Cousin Lulu and I arose about four o'clock and went out to see what the horses were doing. We couldn't find them so came back and called Clarence and from that on all day we wandered over those hills (taking turns, one of us staying with the children) looking for those horses, with nothing to eat but a crust of bread for breakfast. About dark we gave up as it seemed they had literally dropped out of sight. Lulu and I kept saying this must be "One of the all things that work together for good to them that love the Lord". We didn't know how far it was to a ranch so decided there was nothing else to do but stay there another night without food. It was doubly hard for me to think of the children being hungry, but imagine our joy after hailing a passer by (the only one so far during the day) and telling him our troubles he gave us a loaf of bread and a can of tomatoes which we ate with a relish. Then later we decided if there was another passer by we would ask them to take us to the nearest ranch. It seemed Providence sent one more man and he took us some five miles to a ranch house, where we stayed all night, everything was extremely untidy the beds full of bu gs, etc, but we were thankful we didn't have to spend another night in the "old hotel" when we afterward learned a cattle rustler had been hanged on the front proch. It was a good thing we didn't know it the night we were there. We hired a saddle horse of these people and Clarence went back to hunt for our team, which he found nearly back to our homesteads, 25 miles. In the meantime we found conveyance into Fort Benton (20 miles) in a lumber wagon with a man who happened to be passing. It wasn't a very comfortable ride as we were obliged to stand or sit on the bottom of the wagon as we might prefer. After securing supper and a nights lodging the children and I start out again enroute the Great Northern R. R. for Stanford. Arrived there at 2 p.m. Kennedy Bros didn't happen to be in town so we rode out with the man who carried the mail to Coyote P. O. some 12 miles or more from Stanford but near Kennedy's ranch. It seemed a relief to get to a place where I expected to stay a while at least. I was so t[i]red and had no idea what this new home would prove to be. They had been baching for some time so they were glad to see us and gave us a hearty welcome. From past acquaintance I knew them to be fine [C]hristian boys. But they went beyond my expectations and proved to be just splendid in every sense of the word. It seemed a Haven of rest after all our hardships. We had such pleasant times here as they had a piano and were splendid singers.

Donald now being 5 years old I started him to schoold, which was one and one half miles away in an old homestead shack 12 x 14. But it served the purpose until a larger one was built. I rather disliked the idea of sending him so far away amoung strangers. Muriel and I missed him so much during the day. Muriel never failed to go out to the field to meet the boys at meal time as she was sure of a ride to the house on one of the horses.

Everything went along smoothly until it would come time for those dreaded trips to my homestead 50 miles away.... We enjoyed our stay on the Happy Home Ranch as each time it seemed more and more like home. After a stay of two weeks Rob Kennedy came for us. Phil was glad to have us return as he didn't like baching alone.

The children and I helped the boys pick up potatoes and do most anything to help along, such as holding down the ranch, doing the chores etc, while they would be away to the Little Belt Mts. for logs some 70 miles away....

The day before Xmas we made dandy and prepared a little pine tree the boys had brought from the Mts. Some poor neglected children across the way had never seen an Xmas tree so we invited them over.

We arranged the tree behind a curtain turned out the lights and when the children came in it was dark, then Rob began to light the candles, how their eyes did sparkle and the exclamations of joy did us all good. After giving each their little tokens we felt indeed paid for our trouble and decided Xmas was a happy time even away up in Montana. We realized more than ever before that helping others brings real happiness to our selves.

A few days later the Jones baby died. It really seemed a blessing as there were so many and they were so poor. Everything was in a deplorable condition. They had nothing fit to bury the baby in so Phil and I put one of Muriel[']s dresses on it. The funeral was a pitiful dragged out affair by the babies grandfather and elder in the Latter Day Saints Church.

Although behind time the children enjoyed an Xmas barrel from home gifts galore and nuts, and candy in abundance. In spite of the cold stormy weather the thermometer sometimes hovering around 30 below we enjoyed the enving with a fire roaring in the big heater, reading[,] popping corn, making candy and playing various games. Sunday evening we had a little religious service would sing, one of us would read a sermon then we would all pray. It was very helpful to us all.... As spring came we enjoyed the firs[t] meadow larks, the green grass[,] the first mess of rhubar[d], etc but I dreaded the thoughts of the trip across country to the homestead. Rob took us this time, we had several speriences going over. First we got stuck in a creek (Wolf Creek) we had to ford. Then Donald took sick, hand't been well for several days but grew worse as we journed on. We persuaded the foreman of Milner[']s ranch to let us have a nights lodging, all that night Donald was so ill I though[t] he was taking pneumonia, there we were among entire strangers (save for Rob Kennedy) 35 miles from a Doctor. Nothing will ever efface that nights experience from my memory. I was so pleased to find him better the next morning, so we went on, had a pleasant stay on the claim. The trip back to Kennedy's was made in safety.... [Some months later] I went to my homestead and stayed two weeks. Lulu and

I put a new tar paper roof on my house, made cupboards, etc, although it was small it seemed cozy and like home. It gave me a strange glad feeling to look out over those broad acres to realize in a few years I would have a deed to it all....

When spring rolled around again, I decided I better spend the rest of the time on my homestead. Just the day before we started Rob came back from California laden with oranges and presents from mother. It required two sets of sideboards on the wagon to carry all my belongings and a four horse team to haul us. It seemed so strange to sit up so high. We stored the children in the back among the comforts. I really felt sad to leave so pleasant a home, had been there two years. My stay at Kennedy's Ranch will always be a pleasant memory. It was a beautiful day and gave promise of a pleasant journey but it was entirely the reverse, the roads were very soft as the frost was just coming out of the ground. When we would come to a low boggy place, Phil would lash the four horses into a run to keep from miring. I would be so frightened perched up on such a high seat with the wagon swaying to and fro that I nearly had nervous chills. I couldn't get off and walk as it was too muddy. In spite of all of Phil's efforts to prevent we mired to the hubs of the wheels three times[.] Had to unload the furniture and get some ranchers to bring his teams and help pull us out. We were so delayed we had to stay one night at a ranch house. Had another soft ? bed on the floor. I didn't close my eyes alnight. I felt so sorry to have the Kennedy boys have so much trouble getting me to my homestead....

The children[']s bravery and Kennedy Bros. patience through all these experiences were marvelous. When we arrived at my cousin[']s at eleven o'clock that night, I had to mount her steps on my hands and knees as the wind was simply howling. My nerves were shattered I was completely exhausted and my brain seemed scrambled[.] I vowed I would never make that trip again till I could go on the train. A R.R. [railroad] was about completed through there at this time[.] It was such a restful feeling to be settled in our little Hapy Home[.] We made a fine garden, I hired a steam plow to break 20 acres. The year before I had a neighbor break 20 acres. One of my neighbors rented it on shares and he planted wheat and oats. How proud we felt of our first crop. We watched it daily from the time it sprouted until it was threshed[.] Had a fine crop[.] At this time the R.R. was completed and we had a town only 14 miles away[.] During the summer I cooked at a nearby sheep ranch to make expenses. One of the sheep herders fell desperately in love with me and I had a terrible time getting rid of him. Another old batch heard I was a widow and walked 20 miles to see me proposed marriage that night[.] I found it a difficult thing to stay single....I got a loan on my place and the following winter Kennedy Bros. came over and built me a fine little bungalow painted and all. We felt real dressed up. Had such a lovely view from our front porch of Old Square Butte and the High Wood Mountains in the distance. In the summer acres and acres of waving grain in every direction.

The next spring in order that the children might go to school I rented a house five miles away. I boarded the teacher and in this way the children got three months of school[.] Although we hated to be away from our place with the new house and all, but enhoyed it as the teacher was very pleasant.

We drove 20 miles to the land commissioner to make final proof[.] Then on July 1914 I received my patent or deed. I was so proud and felt with all my hardships I had earned it. I rented it and with the remainder of the loan I came back to California and had a little bungalow built in the edge of mother[']s orange orchard. But with the fruit, flowers, and wonderful climate I find myself longing to go back to Montana.

Chapter Six

CROSSING THE BORDER FOR LAND:
LAURA ETTA SMALLEY BANGS

AS THERE WERE NO HOMESTEADING opportunities for single women in western Canada, many crossed the border and homesteaded in the United States. In 1910 Laura Etta Smalley, known as "Etta," originally from Ohio, was teaching school near Edmonton, Alberta, and boarding with the Woods family, which included two daughters. When Mr. Woods and one of the daughters, Sadie, filed on homesteads near Inverness, in Hill County, Montana, Etta decided to join them. She filed on 320 acres and proved up while continuing to teach, at first in Alberta and then at Inverness.

Etta earned her patent to her land in 1914. That same year, she married a neighboring homesteader, Will Bangs. They ended up with four children. They lived at first on Will's homestead and persisted through drought, grasshoppers, and World War I—even as Inverness and nearby Joplin were "all but abandoned."[1] Will Bangs lost his homestead to the bank in 1926, but Etta retained hers. The family moved into her original homestead shack, as she describes in her memoir. In 1943, they bought a larger house and had it moved to her land. They lived on her homestead until 1954, when they retired and moved to Havre. Etta Bangs died in 1973 at the age of eighty-seven. In 1980, her homestead was turned over to her grandson, Tom.

In the early twentieth century, people hoping to homestead flooded the Canadian prairies, particularly the province of Alberta. Many single women who arrived on their own or with their families were surprised to learn that they were not permitted to homestead, as they could in the United States. In Canada, a woman was eligible only if she was a "sole" head of a family and had a minor child or children to support. Consequently, dramatically fewer women homesteaded on their own north of the forty-ninth parallel.

This situation generated a petition that asked that the right to homestead be granted to unmarried women over the age of thirty. Published under the headline "Spinsters Want Homesteads," it originated in Edmonton, Alberta, in 1910.[2] The petition was organized by a woman from the United States who had been lured to Alberta because she had read the advertisements about "free land," but when she applied, she was told she was ineligible. "Well I was surprised, just having refused to join another single woman, who with her father was filing on 160 acres of choice land in Arkansas."[3] Among other things, she argued that unmarried women who had cared for aged parents "should be rewarded, not looked down upon and called 'old maids' on the bargain counter." It was soon reported that this woman had returned to the United States.[4]

A homesteads-for-women campaign was organized in the years leading up to World War I, and a petition asking that homestead rights be granted to women either born in Canada or Great Britain (excluding women from the United States and other foreign countries) became the central strategy. But it failed. In Canada, homestead rights were never available to single women, except in Alberta after 1930, when there was little homestead land left.[5]

MY HOMESTEADING DAYS
Laura Etta Smalley Bangs
Montana Historical Society Research Center

In March 1910 I was teaching the home school about 80 miles east of Edmonton, Alberta. There was a family 8 miles south of us at Warwick that I knew very well. In fact, I felt almost as much at home with the Woods' as with my own folks. They had two daughters, one slightly older than I, the other a few years younger. The oldest daughter married. Mr. Woods and the younger daughter came to Inverness about the middle of March and filed on a homestead. While there, Sadie, the daughter, wrote me begging me to come down and file too.

I came down during Easter vacation. The train on which I came was simply packed with homeseekers.

There were locators, men who would take you out and show you the land available, take you to the land office and help you file, for a fee, of course. The locator at Inverness was a Mr. Gesche. I got off the train there at eleven o'clock p.m., went to a hotel that was in the process of construction and spent the night. I arose very early the next morning and went to see Mr. Gesche. I told him I wanted a homestead near where the Woods' had filed.

I heard him giving instructions to his brother-in-law, John Kindschey, who was to show us the land. There was a party of four from Missouri who were to go too. I overheard Mr. Gesche tell Kindschey the half-section to show me. Kindschey said, "That land is no good or the land would not be taken all around it." Mr. Gesche explained that a young man had chosen that land, but changed his mind when he got to the land office and filed on another half-section to be near friends.

Mr. Kindschey took the Missouri folks in a democrat and had a young boy, Ervin Zorb take me in a buggy. After we left Inverness we did not see any houses till we got to the Selmyhur Ranch, except some small homestead shacks being built some 3 miles out. It was the 31st day of March. We drove to Sage Creek. We stopped and ate lunch on the north

Laura Etta Bangs' graduation photo from Normal School in Ohio sometime before 1910, when she emigrated to Edmonton, Alberta, to teach school. That same year Bangs filed on a homestead near Inverness, in Hill County, Montana, and proved up in 1914. COURTESY OF THE BANGS FAMILY ARCHIVES.

bank and were perfectly comfortable. It was so warm that spring and that summer was extremely hot and dry.

After lunch Mr. Kindschy took the horse and buggy and drove me a mile and a half west to show me the land. He drove the length of the half-section. I decided to take it.

We rejoined the others. He proceeded with the Missouri folks to the Goldstone neighborhood where they camped for the night. I went back to Inverness with Irvin Zorb. Mr. Gesche sent his secretary with me to Havre to file on the land. His secretary was a Chicago woman. I believe she took a homestead south of Inverness.

We came in on the night train. It too, was packed. We stood near the door and as soon as the train stopped were off and running to the land office. It was after midnight. We were the first ones in to Mr. Pyper's, the land commissioner's office. He had just returned from a dance. He threw off his coat and began to take my registration. In a short time the office was full. After we finished we went to the Oakland Hotel and spent the rest of the night.

In the morning we returned to Inverness. At Rudyard all I could see was a watering trough and some buildings in the process of construction where Ledin's store later stood. I hear there were a few buildings further west that were later moved to the town-site.

I went home and resumed my teaching. School closed for summer vacation about the middle of June. We taught 10½ months in Canada at that time. Now it is 10 months.

I came back in August to establish residence. I bought a house 14 x 20 from a Mr. Knight in Joplin. He agreed to make arrangements to have it moved to the homestead. He hired a Dane, Mr. Hans Hendrickson to move it. This man had homesteaded south-west of Inverness bringing with him several large Percheron horses expecting to get work breaking land. The weather was so hot and dry that he had had no work. He took 6 horses and two wagons and loaded the house on the wagons. I had put everything into the house that I needed. My bedding, dishes and cooking utensils I brought from home. The rest I bought in Joplin. My furniture consisted of a bed, table, a few chairs and a small fourhole coal cookstove. The table was a home made one that Mr. Knight had made and the cupboard consisted of 4 or 5 shelves nailed in the corner. I hung white muslin curtains up to it. I bought groceries and coal, loaded these and my trunk and suitcase in the house and we were ready to start.

Miss Nancy Adams rode out with me and Mr. Knight came along to help. We had packed lunch. We rode along all day, Nan and I in the house, the men outside. Things went smoothly till toward evening. Mr. Hendrickson got worried because he thought it time we came to the Selmyhr ranch and he could see no sign of it. He got excited and starting cursing. About that time Miss Adams looked out across the prairie and said, 'Oh, there is our place' and left me. It was about two miles to the homestead shacks of her brother, sister, mother and herself who had come earlier that spring from Chicago.

Well, I was not used to profanity and it bothered me. However, Mr. Knight seemed a fine man. After a little, the men found the trail leading to the ranch and all was right again. On arrival there, I found Miss Constance Selmyhr, later Mrs. Boucher. She was housekeeper for her uncle. I cooked supper for the men and they ate in the house with me that they were moving. I spent the night with Miss Selmyhr. She is widowed now and lives here in Havre.

In the morning we started out again. We did not have so far to go but it was well in the afternoon when we reached the homestead. The men unloaded and started back to Joplin. I was left to spend my first night alone.

In the few weeks I was there that summer I hemstitched curtains for my windows and cupboard and picked rock. Yes, I dug part of my cellar, too.

During the summer quite a number of folks had come in and were living on their claims. I met a lot of these folks that summer. Mr. and Mrs. Roy Phifer lived about 7 miles from me. They came on Sunday and had lunch with me. They live now on the hill just east of Havre. The day they were there Mr. McNeil and his family of Inverness called on me. The Lembcke's lived about a quarter of a mile from me.

I went back to Alberta and taught in the same school from September till Christmas when I resigned, intending to come back to the homestead as soon as the holidays were over. My doctor brother had finished his internship at the Indianapolis General Hospital in the spring of 1910 and had taken over Dr. Houtz' practice for the summer at Spearfish, S.D. while Dr. Houtz attended clinic in the east. He had visited us in Alberta for the holidays and was returning to South Dakota where he was employed by the Homestake Mining Company as company Physician for 4 years. I intended to come this far with him but my younger sister was ill and my mother wanted me to stay home till she recovered. Before I got away our house burned. The shock was no great for my mother that I stayed on to help her get the family settled in a small house nearby.

Consequently it was toward the last of February before I got to the homestead. I stayed a few weeks then went back and taught a summer school. It was a new school just being opened. It was in a Rumanian settlement. Only two of the pupils could speak a bit of English. I finished the term and returned to the homestead the first of September. I brought my 15 year old sister with me and taught her high school subjects. She had spent the summer with me, too.

I took the teacher's examination here in October under Mr. T. J. Troy, who was then superintendent of the Havre high school. We expected the [to] spend the whole winter on the claim but in mid-December the Inverness school board offered me a position as teacher of the lower grades. The teacher whose place I took had been teaching on a permit and failed in her examination.

At Inverness there were two school houses that had been built for country schools. Mr. Fred Leslie taught the 6th, 7th and 8th agrades. I taught from the first to the 6th. I had 38 pupils and received $50 monthly. I held this job until Christmas 1912 when I resigned, thinking I was not putting enough time on my homestead.

My mother came to visit me in February. Again I was offered a position as teacher in the Oriana school. A teacher from Canada had been teaching there and had failed her examination. Here the school was held in a homestead shack that spring. I was the first teacher to teach in the new school house the following fall. This time the school was nearer so I could spend all my weekends at home.

In the summer of 1911 I hired the rock removed from 40 acres and the land broke. Two homesteaders did this work: one used horses for the breaking, the other a yoke of oxen.

I hired this 40 acres seeded to flax in 1912. I had difficulty getting threshing done as soon as it should have been done, consequently under each pile of flax the mice had shelled out quite a little causing a loss. However, I got 11 bushels per acre. The next year I rented the land. It was seeded to wheat and yielded 17 bushels per acre. In the summer of 1913 I had a 3 wire fence built around the half section.

A Sunday school was organized in the spring of 1911 in the Grace Church neighborhood. In the fall they organized the church. A Sunday school class was formed for the young folks. Miss Louise Phifer, now Mrs. Al Suckow, suggested the name of Yoke Fellows for the class, thinking of course, of its spiritual meaning. In looking back the name seemed quite appropriate as 8 couples from the class were married. None of these unions were dissolved by divorce, but death has dissolved all but three. These three couples are all retired and living in Havre.

In the spring of 1912 they were building the first part of the church. The women were to furnish the lunch. Mrs. Lembcke and I had walked three miles carrying our contribution to the lunch when we were overtaken by a Mr. and Mrs. Bangs in a buggy. Mrs. Bangs walked the remaining half mile with me while Mrs. Lembcke rode with Mr. Bangs. This was my first meeting with any of the Bangs family. In September I brought a young girl out with me from Inverness to spend the weekend. On Sunday we attended church at Grace. Mrs. Bangs introduced her son, William. He held the hymn book for me and I thought him a very gentlemanly man.

In December at our class party we played checkers or pretended to play. I think we talked more than we played. After that no party was quite complete if he were absent. We were married in Havre June 8th, 1914 by Rev. Poole of the First Presbyterian church.

We had four children, two boys and two girls, all born on Will's homestead.

For so many years we lived in a small house. Finally in '43 we bought a larger house and moved it on to my homestead. We had wonderful neighbors. They came and helped to pour cement for the basement, then helped with the moving of the house. They never quit till the house was on the foundation. Then Will hired a carpenter. Will, the carpenter and our son Kenneth worked on the house till spring. They changed the windows and some of the rooms, relathed and plastered it. In April we moved into it. We had three bedrooms. Later we added two more bedrooms and a bath. We got electricity in '49 when REA came in.

We retired in 1954, came to Havre and had Mr. Davidson build our house for us. Our son, Kenneth, lives in the house on the farm. As he has 7 children he needs a big house.

Janet ("Jennie") Williams, a young homesteader who staked her claim in 1907, with her horse, Zip. Williams was informally adopted by the Camerons, who treated her as a daughter. When Evelyn Cameron died, she left Williams her Eve Ranch and her work: 1,800 negatives, more than 2,700 prints, and 35 diaries.

PHOTOGRAPH BY EVELYN CAMERON. EVELYN CAMERON COLLECTION. MONTANA HISTORICAL SOCIETY RESEARCH CENTER, PAC 90-87 49-2.

Chapter Seven

EVELYN CAMERON PHOTOGRAPHS OF JANET ("JENNIE") WILLIAMS AND OTHER MONTANA WOMEN HOMESTEADERS

IN 1978 DONNA M. LUCEY, an editor at Time-Life Books and *Look* magazine, was working on a series on the "Old West," when she learned from a curator at the Montana Historical Society Research Center that "there was an old farm woman in the eastern part of the state who was hoarding a cache of glass-plate negatives made by a woman during the frontier days."[1] The "old farm woman" was Janet Williams, a homesteader who had staked her claim in 1907 at Fallon, Custer County, at age twenty-four. The photographer was Williams' close friend and neighbor, Evelyn Cameron. Evelyn and Ewen Cameron, from England, were among the early ranchers in the district. Williams had resisted all previous efforts to make the collection public, but Lucey gained her trust. On the first day of Lucey's visit to Terry, Williams "proudly showed me her vast fields of wheat, which were being "thrashed"—harvested by an enormous threshing machine—and then she told me tales of her pioneering days at the turn of the century."

Williams still had her own original homestead, and she had inherited the Cameron ranch with all its contents when widowed Evelyn Cameron died in 1928. These included treasures such as Evelyn's thirty-five

This female homesteader of German-Russian descent is "discing" her field behind a team of horses in 1912. PHOTOGRAPH BY EVELYN CAMERON. MONTANA HISTORICAL SOCIETY RESEARCH CENTER, PAC 90-87 65-3.

diaries and her photo albums and over a hundred boxes of fragile sixty- to eighty-year-old prints, glass-plate negatives, and film negatives. The Camerons' clothes, scrapbooks, letters, and other documents were also stored in Williams' basement. But the stunning quality and quantity of the photographs, as well as the diaries, put Evelyn Cameron "in a class by herself," wrote Lucey. "Hers is perhaps the most complete portrait we have of one woman's pioneer experience—a virtual home movie of life on the frontier."[2]

Janet Williams (who signed all of her homestead documents "Jennie"), her sister Mabel, and their brother all filed on adjoining homesteads, and their parents bought land nearby from the Northern Pacific Railway. Janet was born in Wisconsin, but was living in Minneapolis when her family pulled up stakes and moved to Montana. Janet's 10-foot by 14-foot tar-paper shack was built the following spring and she settled in with her possessions, which included a piano.[3] She received

Jennie Williams (left) and Evelyn Cameron (right) sit closely together—a testament to their friendship. Williams lived on an adjoining homestead, and the well-worn path between her and the Camerons' properties was dubbed Williams Boulevard. PHOTOGRAPH BY EVELYN CAMERON. EVELYN CAMERON COLLECTION. MONTANA HISTORICAL SOCIETY RESEARCH CENTER, PAC 90-87 59-1.

her patent to the land in 1911, having purchased her 155-acre home-stead at the rate of two dollars and fifty cents per acre.[4] Williams de-scribed to Lucey how she found the dry Montana air to be the perfect cure for her asthma: "When we came out here…I felt as if I was just lifted up out of the air; things were so light. It was just lovely. You could run for a mile and not breathe hard."

All the Williamses became fast friends with the Camerons, but, as Lucey wrote, "Janet in particular became a kind of surrogate daugh-ter to the childless couple, living a good part of the time at their Eve ranch." The Camerons were from privileged backgrounds, and they had elegant accents and manners. They taught Janet to ride, took her along on overnight trips herding cattle, and encouraged her musical talent. Janet "Jennie" and Mabel Williams are, as a result, probably the most photographed solo women homesteaders in Montana. A sample of these photographs are included here, along with some Cameron took of other women homesteaders of her district. As Lucey wrote, Cameron "took obvious pride in the robust life of the western woman, and was anxious to sing her praises."[5]

[Editor's note: The following poem was written by Evelyn Cameron for Janet and Mabel Williams and was published in the Miles City Messenger *of Custer County.]*

Montana Historical Society Research Center

Verses

Written by a Homesteader in Despair at the Exclusive
Attitude of Two Lady Dry Farmers

I

NO Fairy dancing on the green
Nor sea-washed Mermaid fairy
Can pierce the breast with dart so keen
As capitivating Jenny.

II

NO fur-clad child of woods or moors.
Not deer, nor moose, nor sable.
Has liquid eyes that melt like yours,
Most fascinating Mabel!

III

THEN, Sirens, pray forbear to screen
Such charms from sighing Misters.
Your were not "born to blush unseen,"
Incomparable Sisters!

IV

NO need, Sweet Maids, to fire the grass
And set the prairie blazing,*
Your cold disdain precludes a pass
From any neighbor's grazing.

V

ADORED by all, you favor none:
We fain would turn the tables
And bask enraptured in the sun
Of Jenny's smile or Mabel's.

[Editor's note: The following is Evelyn Cameron's note that appeared when the poem was originally published.]

An allusion to another lady dry-famer who accidentally burned off a large portion of the range.

On April 10, 1911, Cameron (center) and the two Williams sisters (Janet at left, Mabel at right) straddle Dolly the horse for a portrait advertising Cameron's photography business. MONTANA HISTORICAL SOCIETY RESEARCH CENTER, PAC 90-87 49-9.

Evelyn Cameron published an article in the November 22, 1911, issue of Country Life, *which included this photograph of Janet Williams with the caption "Intervention by Force of Arms." The article, entitled "Jealousy in a Turkey Tom," was about how Janet's male turkey, which she fed in this position, displayed intense jealousy when she held another fowl the same way.*

Formal portrait of Rosina Roesler's homestead. Roesler (seated at right) filed a claim in 1912 and proved up in 1915 on 320 acres. In her book on Evelyn Cameron, Donna M. Lucey notes that each day after Roesler finished her chores, she walked 6 miles to the town of March to earn extra money washing clothes and doing other housework. MONTANA HISTORICAL SOCIETY RESEARCH CENTER, PAC 90-87, 68-1.

Surrounded by her threshing crews, homesteader Mary Whaley (right of center) sits proudly next to the sacks of grain harvested from her homestead. Whaley proved up on her 160 acres in 1909. PHOTOGRAPH BY EVELYN CAMERON. MONTANA HISTORICAL SOCIETY RESEARCH CENTER, PAC 90-87, 224.

Homesteader Mabel Williams brings water to the threshing crew at work on her family's farm in September 1909. PHOTOGRAPH BY EVELYN CAMERON. MONTANA HISTORICAL SOCIETY RESEARCH CENTER, PAC 90-87, 4-3.

Chapter Eight

A HOMESTEAD NEAR THE LITTLE CROOKED: MIA ("MAY") ANDERSON VONTVER

MIA "MAY" ANDERSON WAS BORN in 1892 in Tranas, in southern Sweden.[1] She was the fourth of nine children born to Anna Lovisa Bolling and Anders Johan Anderson. According to her memoir, life in Sweden was difficult; her father was profligate and her mother "raked hay in our landlord's meadows and tied grain-bundles in his harvest field to keep a roof over our heads. The hard labor did not seem to trouble her, but I hated our poverty and grieved over her servitude." At age twelve, May immigrated to the United States with her oldest brother, John, since her "only prospect was to take service somewhere as a nurse girl." When a sister-in-law wrote Vontver's mother, "How can you bear to send Mia to America when she is just twelve? My little Hilder is just twelve and I would never think of having her go so far away," Vontver's mother replied, "Your little daughter has prospects for the future. You have only two children, Hilder has a dowry and your son will inherit the farm. Mia has no prospects whatever in this country."

In the United States, Vontver and her brother worked for an uncle in New Hampshire who had advanced them money for their passage, and then she lived with an aunt in Nebraska. She attended Normal School in Kearney, Nebraska, during the summers, where an English teacher

Mia "May" Anderson Vontver in Kila, Montana, in 1916, one year before she began to homestead. Vontver noted on the back of the picture that the horse was named Jim and the rifle was not hers. COURTESY OF THE VONTVER FAMILY.

first noticed her literary skills and published her compositions in the school paper. The trouble was that she had to "scrub, wash, iron and cook to earn my board while going to school; there was never an opportune moment for beginning the masterpiece that I contemplated." By the time she was seventeen, she had enough credits to teach in a country school, which was the beginning of a lifetime career in teaching. In 1913, she moved to Montana where she taught and homesteaded near Roy. She began living on her homestead in 1917 and left in 1920, but in those three years she spent seven months, plus summer vacations, on her homestead, leaving to teach school in Kendall, Montana.

May Anderson married Norwegian homesteader Simon Antonson Vontver in 1920. They had a son named Louis. She graduated from Normal School in Dillon, Montana, in 1927 and from the University of

Minnesota in 1947. While she was a superintendent of schools in Petroleum County in 1929, she attended a creative writing class taught by H. G. Merriam at the University of Montana–Missoula and wrote a short story, "The Kiskis," about her teaching in a homesteaders' school near Valentine. The story has been widely reprinted.[2] She also wrote a novel in Swedish, based on the life of her grandmother, *Utvandare till Nebraska (Emigrants to Nebraska)*. Vontver died on January 10, 1990, in Seattle, where she lived with her son, Dr. Louis Vontver, and his family.

The "Memoirs of May Vontver" were recorded and transcribed by Ester Johansson Murray between 1971 and 1973 for the Historical Memoirs Project of the Billings Branch of the American Association of University Women. The document, however, reads as if it were written rather than spoken, and it is possible that Vontver or perhaps Murray edited the oral interview. For Vontver, homesteading was not a happy or rewarding experience. But it furnished her with material for a moving account and a unique perspective that focuses on the destitution of the people and the land.

Vontver told her son, Louis, of a coulee near the Missouri River that contained numerous fish bodies that had been replaced by clay. When they were exposed to air and sun, the bodies disintegrated. When Dr. Vontver visited the homestead in 1982, he verified her story by finding clay replacements of fish that did, indeed, disintegrate. The only evidence he found of anyone having lived on her 40 acres of cleared land was a small depression in the earth that was her root cellar and a rusted door hinge.

MY HOMESTEAD EXPERIENCE
The "Memoirs of May Vontver"
May Vontver

Montana Historical Society Research Center

My uncle had homesteaded in eastern Montana in Judith Basin near Denton and he had become wealthy growing wheat. Maybe if I took up a homestead I could eventually sell the place and help finance my higher education. So in 1916, I began to look around for free government land that I could prove up on. However, my venture never made me rich and turned out to be a mistake financially.

I went to Lewistown to the land office there. I found out all the good land had been taken up, but there was a relinquishment available which I could have by paying a certain sum to the original owner, or filer. Then I filed on the land and went out to take a look at it. I could see why it was the only land left. The 320 acres were crossed by a very deep ravine, so deep that the tops of the tallest spruce trees growing in the bottom could not be seen. The ravine was perhaps no wider across than 30 feet, with very steep sides. To me it looked like there might be a possibility of finding water in the bottom because the vegetation was greener there than anywhere around. This would be a great incentive because if one could find water it would make the place valuable despite the barrenness on either side of the ravine. So at first I was not sorry I had gotten this piece of land and I did not have to take possession until New Years of 1917.

My homestead was near Roy, Montana. At that time there was a little post office to the east of Roy called Little Crooked. And this is where I got my mail when I taught the Kiskis school.

The government soon came to realize that it was impossible for the homesteaders to make a living on this homestead land, so the government allowed a dispensation. Homesteaders would not have to stay on the land. We could leave and make our living somewhere else. So all in all I spent only seven months, plus my summer vacations on my

Vontver sitting in front of her "homestead hut," as she called it. She began living there in the winter of 1917. Because of the ongoing drought, the government released homesteaders from their obligation to live part of the year on the land. Vontver lived a total of seven months on her homestead, working elsewhere as a teacher and returning for summer vacations. COURTESY OF THE VONTVER FAMILY.

homestead. To fulfill the other requirement I had a small cabin built with a cellar underneath and I had forty acres of land broken up and planted in flax for linseed...

Before I went on my own homestead there was a four month homesteader's school that had not, by August, been able to get a teacher. The poor pay and short term discouraged many applicants, but because I had to be on my homestead by the first of January it would fit in nicely with my plans. The pay was $60 per month, $20 of which had to go to my landlord. However, I took the job and I have always been glad that I did because there is where I found the Kiskis children and when they brought me the gift I thought at the time I must write this episode down, but it incubated in my mind for eleven years before I finally got it written down. In a later section I will elaborate more fully on the writing of the Kiskis story, but first I will describe the type of people I came in contact with when I took the homesteaders school. These people were quite different from any I had encountered before and made a deep impression on me....

The first thing that struck me in this community where I had taken up my homestead was that the people were so poor, and this poverty seemed to bring out a strange quirk in their nature so that they tried to scheme to get money from one another. For instance, one child lost a mitten which was found by another child and taken home, and the mitten would not be given up to the owner unless he paid the finder the cost of the mitten, a price that was figured out carefully to come to slightly less than its cost in the Montgomery Ward catalog. Such an action struck me as being downright dishonorable. Another action I had never heard of before was that one man would hide his neighbor's horses and the owners would search and search, then eventually the first man would state: "If you pay me I will take you to the place where your horses are." I had never seen people who were so un-neighborly and so unkind to each other.

Those of the people who had cows and could make butter to sell in the town of Roy would also sell to their neighbors if they got a tiny bit more than they were paid in Roy.

I boarded with the family who had the biggest house. These people had come from Indiana and I have never in my life had so little to eat...The man had come to get me at the railroad station in Roy, and on the way he told me the reason they had gotten permission from the school board to board the teacher was because they had the largest house and I would have a room to myself (which I thought was nice). As it turned out I did get along all right with them despite the fact that they fed me so poorly and were so stingy, but the worst thing that happened was when I finished my term and the man was driving me back to Roy, he said, "I will not take your trunk unless you pay me a dollar and a half." Of course I had to pay him, but I half way expected him to stop on the way to Roy and say, "I will dump your trunk off here unless you pay me another $1.50." Because that was the way these people were to one another. The one exception was the Clark family.... They knew how scanty the food was that was doled out at my boarding place and since I had to pass their home on the way to the school they often stopped me and asked me in to eat with them. The Clarks were the only family in the area who did not indulge in the dreadful treatment of their neighbors...

MY HOMESTEAD

There was a stagecoach that came out to the post office from the railroad at Roy, and the stagecoach driver took me from the post office out to my place which was a distance of seven additional miles. He helped me to unload the stuff I had taken with me. I had a little cot, a small stove, and the carpenter had built a fold-up table. I had a couple of folding chairs and the carpenter had made some shelves, and he had made a hole in the ceiling and roof so I could put the stove pipe through. There were enough stunted pine trees growing nearby so I could have fuel. Among my tools I had an axe, hammer, saw, and tools for most any emergency. At this time there were homesteaders on every half section so there were neighbors all around me. How this changed before three years had passed!

There were no requirements in the law as to the size of the building, as long as it was habitable, and as I was alone, my shack was only ten feet by ten feet. When spring came I had a cellar dug out under the house, almost as big as the house, just leaving enough foundation so it would not cave in. It was about seven feet deep and it made a very cool place for me to stay in greatest heat of the summer days. The entrance was with a ladder down from a trap door inside the house.

When I moved in on January first I had no worry about summer heat, but instead had the freezing winter weather to contend with. Nevertheless, I had a feeling of home-coming, this my very first own home here in America. Although I was all alone and didn't know any of my neighbors, it was pleasant to spread out my belongings and set up and make up my bed. The carpenter had left a big supply of wood so I did not immediately have to go out and chop down trees for fuel. I had brought such foods as would not freeze, because everything froze solid at night. I sometimes got up at three o'clock in the morning to build another fire in my little iron heater because as soon as the fire went out it became the same temperature inside as it was outside.

My neighbors came and called on me and they were pleasant and I got along fine with them. It has never been difficult for me to like people if they were at all likeable.

When spring came, I was not required to plow up the forty acres to plant this first year, so I started out by having just enough land broken for a big garden. I hired a man to do this. As he did the breaking I worked it down and planted the vegetable seeds I had sent for. We had late snows and all the things I planted came up, but after the spring rains, it never did rain a drop again all summer. The plants all came up and grew four or five inches, then withered back onto the ground. All the neighbors experienced the same misfortune because that was the first year of the Drought in that locality—the beginning of the bad years. I only lost a large garden, but those that had had their forty acres or more put into flax or wheat or corn, lost all their crop. Most of them were family people, they had cows and horses with nothing to feed them. The dams they had built held nothing more than mud puddles which soon dried out. These families had to leave their homesteads in order to make a living, and only bachelors or school teachers like myself who had taken up land, but had other sources of income, could stay on, so the first summer I was not all alone in the area.

After I had my cellar dug, I would go down there to escape the heat of the sun. When it wasn't too bad outside, I would follow the shade of the cabin around, sitting and reading, crocheting and doing fancy work. In those days I had excellent eye sight. I was very fond of reading which passed the time pleasantly and I carried on a great deal of correspondence with friends and relatives. The mail was received twice a week at the post office and twice a week I walked the seven miles in to get it, fourteen miles round trip. The postmaster there was a gentleman by the name of Montgomery Marshall. He was a Zionist from the Chicago area and was the only person with any interest in culture in the whole vicinity. I had many interesting conversations with him and remember one of his quotations: "The cultured person wishes to do things in the right manner and say things in the right way and the uncultured doesn't give a damn."

Mr. Marshall was also an enterprising man. He had gotten the people together to construct a communal dam which held water covering an acre or more, and after the drought struck, those people who stayed on could haul water from there on a stone boat or wagon. I had no horses so I had to pay a man to bring me two barrels of water every two weeks. Later on I will relate a rather harrowing experience I had when the man failed to bring me the water....

THE CANYON ON MY HOMESTEAD

The very first spring I was on the homestead I chose a little plot for a garden which was described earlier. I hired a man to plow up this quarter acre plot and he said to me, "I have never found in so tiny a breaking as this so many arrowheads, when I was harrowing it." I thought this was quite interesting although I had never bothered to look for arrowheads, since they were so common before the 1920s. But I did ask him if he would give me a couple which he did.

Between the steep, perpendicular cliff of the canyon and my cabin lay the plowed garden. One day when I was down in the canyon I came to the steepest side of the canyon which rose like a precipice. For some reason I poked around at the foot of the cliff and I found two or three arrowheads, not far beneath the surface, and I compared them with the ones Max had found on top, and they were exactly the same kinds. I decided to take them over to Montgomery Marshall at the post office, since he had quite a collection of arrowheads. I told him Max had found more in my patch than he usually found in forty acres and they matched the ones I found at the bottom of the cliff. Mr. Marshall felt the similarity was significant and when I queried him as to why there should be so many in those two places he suggested that there might have been a little buffalo jump there. This was all new to me. I had never even heard about buffalo jumps before. He explained to me how the Indians would drive a small portion of a herd of buffalo, very, very cautiously close to the brink, then suddenly they would wave blankets, hollaring and shooting arrows at them, scaring them over the edge of the cliff. Although it was but a small jump in comparison to other jumps in Montana, it apparently was effective and I accepted that explanation by Mr. Marshall. On the seven mile walk back to my cabin, I pictured for myself how these Indians had carried out their strategy and I could imagine it very clearly.

Another phenomena of my little canyon is worthy of note. I had noticed damp spots in the bottom of the canyon. Some of the areas were greener than other places and it seemed to me that if there were to be any water found on my homestead, the floor of the canyon would be the most logical place to look for it. So one day I took my post hole augur, my shovel, a pail and a tin cup and went down into the canyon and walked until I came to what seemed to me a likely spot to dig. The black top soil came away easily. After that I struck clay and sand and the deeper I dug the wetter it got, which seemed very encouraging. I lost track of time and the damper it got the more excitedly I augured and dug. After I had excavated to the depth of about three feet, I scooped out an extra little hole and sat down and watched the beautiful, crystal clear water seep very slowly into this bowl-like depression. When sufficient water had gathered in the hole so that I could dip my tin cup in and partially fill it, I did it with high hopes, raised it to my mouth and took a swallow. But what a shocking taste and terrible disappointment! This liquid was just like a very strong solution of Epsom salts. This water was full of alkali and of no value whatsoever....

SLOW ELK AND POVERTY
One young neighbor used to bring his wife and two little girls over

to visit me whenever he was going "hunting." It was revealed to me only after I had lived among these homesteaders many months, that what he called "hunting", was simply going out and butchering some creature belonging to the big cattle ranchers whose herds grazed all over the vast prairies. These animals were branded and belonged to the cattle barons. The homesteaders didn't know whose brand belonged to whom in every case, but would get together with the other homesteaders, go out and rustle an animal, butcher it and divide the meat and take it home. If it hadn't been for these "slow elk," none of them would have had any meat to eat. They were very careful not to tell me what their hunting actually consisted of, because I was a stranger and they suspected that I might think what they were doing was against the law. They felt they were justified in doing what they did because they were keeping their families from starving.

Perhaps the first time the poverty of my neighbors struck me was when the young mother and the two little girls first called on me. I was busy making a patchwork quilt. It was not a crazy quilt but was made of square blocks from my dress remnants. Although I was not adept at dressmaking for myself, I still had my dresses made for me as one did not buy as many ready-made dresses as now. So I was working on these many pieces of material left over from the dress-making, the pieces being about eight inches square. I was nearly finished and there were two small squares left over. The young mother asked, "May I have them?"

"Why of course," I answered, "but what use can you find for two little patches like that? They don't even match, one is blue and one is green."

"Well," she said, "they are big enough so that they would make two sleeves for a little dress. When I get hold of another piece of material I can use them for sleeves."

I must have shown how flabbergasted I was. She said, "You know with us, it isn't a matter of how a garment looks, just to keep them covered is what we are worried about!"

I realized that although I had grown up in poverty in Sweden, it was not of the sort that was found in the drought striken areas where the homesteaders had taken up dry land farms. In Sweden they could have garden patches, pick wild berries in the woods, fish in the many lakes or ocean. It wasn't the absolute destitution you found in this dry land farm area.

LAST SUMMER ON MY HOMESTEAD

By the last summer, my third, the drought had driven everyone away. The only one left was the postmaster seven miles away at Little Crooked. The bachelors had been called into the Army for the First World War, and the families who had left the first or second year had no reason to return.

So I was all alone, and in order to get water I had to make arrangements with a man who lived on the other side of the post office in what was called the "Missouri Breaks", and he promised to bring me my water. However, he said he would have to charge more since he had to make the trip for me alone rather than for several customers. So knowing it was absolutely necessary for me to have this water, the man promised that he would come without fail every two weeks. And he did keep his word and come punctually every two weeks, except for one time.

On that particular occasion the man did not come on the appointed day, so I boiled the water left in the barrel, which I usually had to do anyway towards the end of the two weeks. And neither did he show up the following day, but I thought, "I am in not too bad a shape, I still have some of this boiled mess that I can use in an emergency, and I have some canned tomatoes and some canned milk, so I did not worry." But when you are afraid you are going to run out of water you get thirstier. I drank my canned liquids and I drank the boiled dregs of water although it was nauseating, but I got through the next couple days. It was not until the water was absolutely gone did I think I had better do something about the situation.

The first thing I thought about doing was going down to the abandoned farm that was at the mouth of my canyon where it opened out into the valley. I would see if there would be any water left in their cemented dams. They also had drilled a well on their place. Now the main reason so many of the homesteaders had left is because their horses had laid down and simply died. The owner of the valley farm had opened up one of the dead horses to see what had caused its death. He had found the belly of the horse full of gravel. The horses had eaten the roots of what little grass there was until they had also filled their stomachs with gravel. Such was the case of my neighbors, the young couple with the two little girls. They had had five horses, four for hauling and one for riding. The last time I saw the husband he had come riding over to my place. He sat bowed down in the saddle like an old man, his four draft horses had died of the gravel and he saw no way except to take his family away. They were the last to leave.

I took a bucket and a rope and set out to see what I could find in the valley. Previously I had not ventured down there, the people were gone and I had no wish to face the oppressive heat down there. At least up on the bench where my place was, there was, at times, a slight breeze to cool the air. When I got down to the dams, to my horror I found the dams were completely dry, so I went over to the well. I threw a pebble in and heard it "splash" so I was quite encouraged and lowered the pail. I could tell the water was not very deep, but I swished the pail around, got as much water in it as I could and pulled it up. In the stagnant water I had drawn up floated a dead mouse.

The well had been left uncovered and animals in search of water had come to it, so it was not only thick and unappetizing but seeing the dead mouse in it too, I knew very well I would have to be terribly thirsty before I could drink anything like that.

There was nothing to do but go back to the house. I began to think I would have to walk to the dam at the post office where Mr. Marshall had a filter for the water found there. The only trouble, if I went for water, I would drink up, probably, what water I could carry on the trip home. It was late in August and very hot. I considered walking in the cool of the evening when I could carry the water better. But when I thought of that I remembered that the rattlesnakes had a liking for stretching out in the wagon ruts and if I walked in the dark, and the snakes were over-nighting in the tracks, I couldn't see them until I was upon them, so that did not seem to be a good idea either. There was nothing to do except wait just one more day. I had nothing except some of that boiled water, which was so horrible, I would just barely moisten my dry lips with it.

Finally I went to bed and I slept fitfully and I had dreams. Dreams all about water and all extremely vivid. The first dream I had was that I was at a banquet table, there were chandeliers hanging over the table, there were goblets at every plate and lackeys went around with crystal pitchers pouring water into these goblets and I was so anxious for this lackey to come and fill my glass with water, but before he reached me I awakened. What a nightmare! I resolved not to think any more about water and finally went back to sleep.

I had another dream, this time I was by a waterfall and the water came down like the pictures of Niagara Falls and a river flowed away from the waterfall. I hurried to the river, leaned down to drink and woke up again.

Again I slept and I had a third dream. This time I was back in Sweden and I was on the way to a little spring that flowed into the lake by which we lived. This spring was noted for having exceptionally good water. As children we went there with our water pails, following a path along a field, then the path cut down to the spring which was quite close to the edge of the lake. It had a sandy bottom and the water was so clear you could see the two holes where it bubbled up. In my dream I was on the path along the oat field, hurrying to the spring. I was so thirsty and I leaned over to drink, but again I awoke. Those three dreams about water I had in succession that night, were a sort of psychic experience to me.

(In 1971, I was home in Sweden and remembering how the spring figured in my dream, I again took the path to see if the spring were just like I remembered it but through disuse it had become overgrown with water plants and the sandy bottom was no longer visable.)

The next morning I had no choice except start out for the post office. I wore high laced elk hide walking boots, a wide brimmed hat and long sleeves as protection against the merciless August sun. Just as I started out, in the distance I saw the water man coming. Words could not express my relief.

I was anxious to learn what had detained him. He explained his horses had gotten lost and all these days I had been without water, he had been out hunting his horses along the Missouri River. Among the horses' hoof marks along the river his horses were shod and he was able to track them down that way.

RATTLESNAKES

The very first time the agent had taken me around to show me the markers and corners of the land, he had stopped short as we were walking along, turned and ran to his car and got his revolver and shot a rattlesnake. This is the first time I had seen and heard a rattlesnake.

My most memorable experience with a rattlesnake came during my very last summer on the homestead, and whether it was before or after my experience with the thirst, I do not recall. I was sitting and crotcheting by my one window in my ten foot square house, in the forenoon before the day's oppressive heat was upon me. I heard something on the outside of my house, as if someone were scratching their fingernails along the rough surface, a scratchy sound on the bottom shiplaps. Out here in the silence where I was aware of every sound, I was instantly alerted. I looked out the window and I could see coming over the raised platform that was my doorstep, a huge triangular snakehead. I immediately got up to see if I had my screen door latched, and it was. So I sat down again and just watched. And this huge flat three-cornered head, which I recognized at once as a rattler's, was followed by a thick, thick body. Very, very slowly he wriggled across the door step, right gainst the threshold, went down the otherside, close to the building, and I saw he was going to go under my window, so while he passed under the window I didn't see all of him, but I was startled by the thickness of his body. I had read up on rattlesnakes in the encyclopedia and according to what I had read, it was seldom that they were more than three or four feet long. So I kept thinking that after awhile I would see the tail of this one and see his rattlers. He did not rattle, the only sound was the scratching, scraping noise. He just continued to slide along, so slowly and so majestically, taking his time, and I kept looking for what should be the end of him but I didN't see an end. He just came and came and came, still unbelievably thick. I thought to myself, "There are no rattle-snakes like this, there are no such rattlesnakes as this one. They can't be this big according to what I have read." But the thick body kept com-ing and coming, and finally I saw the rattlers coming, but by that time I was so stunned I didn't think of counting them.

This snake just went on and on and his tail never came in sight until he had turned the corner and his head was out of sight. He must have been longer than the ten foot house. He was so regal and so awe-inspir-ing I thought to myself, "This is the king of all the rattlesnakes, and with all the people gone he is just surveying his domain again." The incredible size of the snake, the slowness with which he crawled along left me weak. From all I had read and from those I had seen, I was not prepared to believe there could be such a monstrous one. When he disappeared, I did not dare to go out. It was frightening thought to imagine encountering him outside. I stayed in a long, long time before I dared to venture out to look around, but by that time he had com-pletely disappeared.

I don't think I have ever been so shaken by the sight of any animal as by this stupendous snake and the majesty of his movements. I realized I must not keep this fright, I must not let it keep me from walking around as I had always done, so towards evening when it cooled off I forced myself to walk around outside. I never saw him again and I never knew what became of him. Needless to say, when I later told people about my encounter with this mammoth snake, it is doubtful if they believed me.

END OF HOMESTEADING

Then when fall came, because of the drought I had permission to leave my homestead. Ordinarily, the law stated you had to live there constantly for three years. But every summer the drought persisted and I was permitted to leave to teach during the following two winters. I taught in the gold mining town of Kendall. It was there I began working with primary grades only, enjoyed it and was successful in it. I taught in Kendall for four years and in 1920, I married S. A. Vontver, who had been one of my neighbors, six or seven miles distant from my homestead.

Several years afterwards, the Government, realizing what an injustice had been done to those who had lost three years of their lives and wasted whatever they had borrowed to live on, offered to buy back the homesteads from those who wished to sell them. So I listed mine, but the official who replied to my letter said they only bought back homesteads from those who had families. I, who had a profession, was not in need and they would not buy it back. So I still own the land. I have not been back for years and years and I have no desire to go back. The shack eventually blew down and fell into the cellar underneath, so there are no remnants of it. The huge trees that grew in the canyon were subsequently cut down for lumber and fuel, so they also are gone.

The "twin shacks" of Mildred B. Hunt and friend Sophie Maude Jefferson, with the property line running between the houses. OVERHOLSER HISTORICAL RESEARCH CENTER, FORT BENTON, MONTANA, 1995-RP-535-A.

Chapter Nine

2 LETTERS, 5 FEET OF SNOW:
THE MILDRED BELLE HUNT DIARY

IN 1910, MILDRED BELLE HUNT, from Berlin, Wisconsin, filed on a homestead of 320 acres on the Highwood Bench near Fort Benton. Her right to homestead was initially challenged by an official at the Great Falls Land Office because she provided insufficient evidence of her marital status.[1] The official wrote that "it does not satisfactorily appear that you are the head of a family as claimed. In view of the fact that you claim to be the head of a family, you must satisfy this office whether or not you are married or single, widow, or deserted wife, or anything in fact that will show that you are the one upon whom your family depends, also please show what your family consists of."

Hunt had thirty days to furnish this evidence or lose her claim. She had been reticent to admit that she was married to Fred S. Hunt, and had been married for six years at the time of her homestead entry. To be eligible she had to gather sworn statements from two male citizens of Berlin. One was her employer, F. J. Trickey, and one her physician, Dr. B. E. Scott, who stated that her husband had not "in any way contributed to the care, support, or maintenance of said Mildred Belle Hunt," and in fact she had "contributed to the support of her husband during the marriage." The physician explained that Fred S. Hunt "is physically incapacitated from supporting his family by reason of his habits of excessive use of intoxicating liquors and the resulting diseases of the stomach and nervous system." He further added that Mrs. Hunt had lived apart from her husband for most of the marriage. Because her husband was a "confirmed drunkard," Mildred Hunt was considered the head of a family, and was permitted to file on a homestead.

The sworn statements of her employer and physician were required in her case since married women normally were not permitted to homestead. She also had to swear that her husband had never taken up a homestead and that he "has not in any way furnished or provided her with any of the necessaries of life, and that she has had to rely upon her own efforts for her support; that [she] on numerous occasions furnished and provided money for her said husband, to care and maintain him, out of her wages, which is earned by her own labors."

Born in 1876 in Lena, Illinois, Mildred Hunt was the daughter of Jacob and Theresa Bossung Dietrich.[2] In Berlin she worked in the bookkeeping department of the Luther Glove Company. In 1905, she was a boarder at the Jefferson home in Berlin, when several members of the Jefferson family, including siblings Lulu, Harry, and Sophia Jefferson, decided to homestead in Montana. Mildred Hunt decided to homestead, too, perhaps to start again, far from her husband, and likely as an investment in her own future. She had a claim and shack next to Sophia Jefferson, age thirty.

Her diaries from 1912 and 1913, held at the Overholser Historical Research Archives in Fort Benton, document the presence of other homesteaders from Wisconsin, possibly part of the same party. Hunt was part of a busy settlement where the homesteaders helped each other by dividing up some of the tasks and visiting often. She also experienced loneliness and homesickness. Her marital status appears to have been kept secret from her neighbors. As she wrote in her diary on October 18, 1913, when a neighbor asked if she was married yet, "She did not find out. I will not have my affairs pried into."

When the time came to apply for her patent to her land, Mildred

Hunt was concerned that she might not qualify, once again, because of her marital status. She wrote to the General Land Office in Washington, D.C., asking if she had to be divorced in order to make final proof. She explained, "I am a Catholic and on account of my faith I have not procured a divorce but we are as much separated as though a divorce had been granted." She must have been very relieved when she was informed that her entry as head of family was accepted in 1910, and "In the absence of other objection it will not be necessary for you to be divorced in order to submit satisfactory proof upon said entry."

She was also concerned because she was absent from her homestead from December 1910 until April 1912 (except for April and October of 1911). The explanation was illness, which once again required a sworn statement from Dr. B. E. Scott of Berlin. In December 1910, Dr. Scott wrote that it was "necessary to perform a very extensive and serious abdominal operation and throughout the whole of the following year she was constantly under my care for observation and treatment." During this time, he wrote, Hunt could not have performed her homestead duties and it would have been unsafe to travel. "It was under my orders that she remained quiet and nearby so that she might receive the care and observation that her condition demanded."

This testimony was acceptable, and Hunt successfully proved up in 1914. She had approximately 100 acres of wheat and flax under cultivation and a one-room, 10-foot by 12-foot frame house. As her diaries document, Hunt was absent from the homestead each year as she proved up. She'd stay on her homestead until the wheat was sold and hauled in late October, travel back to Berlin for the winter, and then return to the homestead in late April. Although she noted in her diary that she was happy to "go home" each year, Hunt became a permanent resident of Fort Benton in 1916. She rented out her land and made her home in the Harber household (possibly W. K. Harber, the editor and manager of the *River Press*). Hunt belonged to many organizations, including the Fort Benton Woman's Club, of which she served as president for three terms, and as Montana's District II president. She remained a devoted member of the Immaculate Conception parish. She worked at the Fort Benton Sanitarium and for the Rudolph Insurance Agency until her retirement in 1929. The house on her Highwood Bench homestead was destroyed by fire in 1947. She died in Fort Benton in 1953 at the age of seventy-five.

The excerpts are transcribed from Hunt's original diary. Although she wrote in her diary almost daily, I have selected entries that most colorfully illustrate life on her homestead—her dependence on her neighbors for plowing, food, baking, and just plain company; the importance of news from home; and her pride in her potatoes, beans, and wheat. Although I have capitalized sentence beginnings to make the text more readable, I have not corrected other errors in grammar or punctuation. I am grateful to Ken Robison for the original additions and explanations in the 1912 text and have followed his identifications throughout.

The diary begins as Mildred was returning by train to her homestead after being absent from December 1910 until April 1912 because of her illness. She was thirty-six years old.

MILDRED BELLE HUNT DIARY, 1912–1913

Overholser Historical Research Archives

Transcription by Ken Robison

1912

[TUESDAY,] APRIL 30[, 1912:] Left Berlin [Wisconsin] for the West warm sunny day had head ache.

MAY 1: Eight crying babies on Sleeper not a very pleasant trip.

MAY 2: Raining. No one to meet me...

MAY 3: While getting breakfast Mrs. J. [Sophia Jefferson] and Frank [Frank Messenger] came. S. [Sophie Maude Jefferson on adjoining claim; daughter of Albert C. and Sophia Jefferson] went to town. House looks like the remains of a cyclone. Cleaned up and baked bread. Mrs. J. [Sophia Jefferson, mother of Sophie Maude Jefferson] came to dinner later set out strawberr[y] plants. Took a walk down in coulee. Wrote several letters & postal. Had good bread. [Sophie Maude Jefferson] bought Groceries.

2 years ago we came out to build and live on our claims.

MAY 4: Messenger [Frank Messenger] came while we were eating breakfast there Mr M. [Fred Moldenhauer; Fred and Bertha E. Moldenhauer were from Wisconsin] and boys on way to town. Unpacking trunk, which brought to mind very pleasant memories. And a very homesick feeling. Must "sit on the lid" and not give in.

The little cupboard looks mighty good. Harry [Jefferson] and Frank [Messenger] came to spend the night.

MAY 5: After breakfast went to work in my cabin then took a both [bath] dressed and rode up to Jeffs [Albert and Sophia Jefferson] with Fred [Moldenhauer] who was on his way back from Benton with a load of coal gro[ceries] etc...

Will sleep in my own house to night. Sandy, the cat went away this Sunday night—and he never came back.

MAY 7: After work was done made my curtains H. [Harry Jefferson] &

F. [Frank Messenger] came down to work. Got dinner for them Jacobys [John Jacoby] cattle got out S. [Sophie] put them back and fixed the fence I worked in the garden quit about 5 P.M. Got lunch put the dishes in my cupboard it looks mighty fine and I'm very proud of it. Later F. [Frank] Messenger came with bunch of letters for us to give postman. Then we three called on Ida. Set sponge.

No letters to day. Mr. Reynolds brought wood we may build the road Hurrah!

MAY 8: Was so tired couldn't sleep. Got up early and mixed bread. Out of gas [?] so must take it up to Jeffs [Albert and Sophia Jefferson] to bake. Warm day. Baked the bread and had a chance to ride down to Moldenhauer with Frank [Messenger]. Called then got butter and eggs. We toted six loaves bread 2 doz. eggs 2 # butter a kettle basket bread two shawl and sweater. Nearly dead when we arrived washed up and had a lunch fresh bread and cold meat. Bread fine.

MAY 9: Rec'd 2 letters and a postal one letter just filled a long felt want.

Great news. Mother is better.

Made garden. Planted radish, lettuce, onions, peas, carrots, beets and corn. Mighty hard work on new breaking....Sis. sent me a sunbonnet.

MAY 16: Up at 4 30 planted 900 hills of spuds. Killing work quit a 10 A.M. Rested balance of day....Very warm and mosquitos bad.

MAY 17: Up at 5 00 A.M. Finished planting spuds about 1200 hills in all. about 5 P.M. went over to coulee for dandelion greens saw team near cabin proved to be Mr. & Mrs. Tobey of Benton [Mr. & Mrs. Marshall W. Tobey] to call. Stayed to Supper and had delightful visit on their way to Grange meeting at Vaughns....

MAY 19: Went to Maurers [Otto Maurer] to Dinner. Good dinner but glad to get back to my own little cabin we rode home from Schwarks [John and Anna Schwark came from Wisconsin] with Hans hired man. Asked us 'were we at the Ball Game' No. Did we go the Dance the other night. No. Looked at us in astonishment saying 'Dont you go any where?'

JUNE 3: Baked two lots of bread S. [Sophie Maude Jefferson] ironed her dresses after dinner she [we] hauled stone of[f] her land with old Jeff and stone boat I had several funny experiences trying to stay on the boat. Later fixed other end of pasture fence got Supper, etc and to bed by 8 30 most dead.

Hanson digging stone @ $1.50 and meals.

3 Meals. [presumably for hired men]

JUNE 4: Hansen digging stones and two Boys working on Culvert. S. [Sophie Maude Jefferson] at the other place helping build fence. Walked to Moldenhauers for Eggs. Letter from Mrs. B. Scrubbed kitchen floor then hunted bugs in S. garden.

My Birthday.

Weather fair and windy.

7 Meals.

JUNE 9: Nice and wet. Fixed netting on door then Mr. Woodcock came with load lumber, cut fence in Milners pasture. Would not stay to dinner.

Went up to wheat. Stood in mine up to my hips found several pretty stones.

After Supper went to M. [Moldenhauers] for butter retd 9 P.M. discovered cattle near wheat at 9 30 S [Sophie] went up. I to M.[Moldenhauers] for help got lost. Found road went up to Jeffs [Albert and Sophia Jefferson] got Boys. Hunted them until 12 15 A.M. nothing doing. To bed.

JUNE 10: Up at 3 A.M. found cattle about 5 A.M. run 36 head thru fence. Home by 5 45 A.M. Tired to death.

Boys working on Culvert.

June 11: Working on culvert broke plow [h]andle and quit at noon. Worked for [Sophie] a while.

Hauled water from Milners with stone boat

Very warm.

Recd 5 letters.

2 Meals

JUNE 16: S. [Sophie] went over to Rays place I kept house at home. Had company all afternoon.

Mr. S. [John Schwark] says My wheat is best of his fields also made me proposition for next year if Haus boys do not plow.

Fine day.

JUNE 21: Men finished at Noon. Hoed my garden in the morning then after dinner S [Sophie] and I pulled mustard and tumble weed out of wheat which is nicely headed. Looks fine....

JUNE 26: Up at 5 A.M. after the everlasting potato bugs.

Mrs. Calleo down to Supper

Extremely warm last night's rain did not help much chased cattle from my wheat this A.M. Casper running theirs thru the fence into Jacobys

Wheat looking fine never saw anything like it....

JULY 7: Busy as usual went to Jeffs [Albert and Sophia Jefferson] late in the afternoon.

JULY 8: Too busy to write. Washed.

JULY 9: Ditto. Ironed....

JULY 28: ...Cutting my wheat today.

Very warm.

14 to dinner.

JULY 29: Cutting my wheat Very warm

JULY 30: Finished cutting my grain to day <u>looks</u> <u>fine</u>

Prairie fire broke out near field at noon every one fought with all their might.

Walked 4 miles to borrow Kodak.

JULY 31: Took pictures of wheat field. Mrs. J. [Sophia Jefferson] down to do her washing.

AUG. 1: Cleaning house am happy once more to be in my own cabin...

AUG. 2: Did an immense washing then cleaned up thoroughly looks like Twin Shacks again.

Chased horses off oats twice.

AUG. 25: Finished threshing at Schwarks after dinner then move on mine [?]

Mrs S [Anna Schwark] and I drove over after dinner to see it work.

Mr S [John Schwark] got 21 bu[shels] wheat per a[cre]...

AUG. 26: All threshed by 3 P.M. 24 1/s bu[shels] per a.[cre] 98c[ents] in all....

SEPT. 3: Still it rains. Am baking bread. and sewing. Letter from Sister have had my wheat on display at Bank in St. Cloud.

SEPT. 4: Too dark and threatening to put out clothes Mr S. [John Schwark] called and we settled plans for next year crop. Am to have 80 a.[cres] broken.

Mr Moldenhauer also called

Did not sleep well lack of exercise I guess. I must take a tramp I guess.

SEPT. 9: F. [Frank] busy disking all day. I baked bread and then sewed all afternoon. After Supper we walked up to Lone Shack also visited at Schwarks.

Finest day I ever saw in Mont.

S [Schwarks] are raking my field will start seeding tomorrow....

SEPT. 14: Found snow on Mts this A.M. Very cold and dreary...

Six weeks from to night I want to start East.

Sept. 16: Went up to Jeffs [Albert and Sophia Jefferson] quite early to stitch stayed until 5 P.M.

P. Halbo the herder said my bread was best he had had between Chicago & Seattle.

SEPT. 17: Waited for the mail then hurried up to J's [Albert and Sophia Jefferson's] to chicken dinner. Bird was to meet me and take me home with her. She failed to put in an appearance. Started home at 5 P.M. Mr. Cook over took and gave me a ride in the two wheel gig....

Rec'd gun —hurray! and two letters from Berlin....

SEPT. 18: Mr Halbo brought Jack, the collie pup over this A.M. for Harry he is as broad as he is long and the cutest little "dogy"—want him myself. Had first choice but cant keep a dog and be away too. Baked bread and sewed all day.

Bird came about 8 30 P.M. will stay all night.

SEPT. 22: Went to Jeffs [Albert and Sophia Jefferson] for dinner. Had fried chicken. Was very good. Reached home about 4 30 Smokey all day is raining now.

Had offer to lease my place for $200 per year. Refused....

SEPT. 30: We are digging potatoes. Turning out well but terribly hand [hard] work for me. Quit at 4 P.M. bathed and rested on my couch.

OCT. 2: Finished my potatoes by 11 A.M. then got dinner....Getting ready to go home. Hurray!

OCT. 9: Snowed all night ground was covered when I got up this A.M. puttered around there started to Emb.[embroider] on gown. Herder came for bread and gave me glove order [?] He talked about mental telepathy, palmistry and several other "isms" later Mr S. [Schwark] came with load straw to cover my spuds.

Mr J. covered S[puds] with dirt.

OCT. 11: Mr Schwank called to let me know that wheat is sold @ 70 c[ents]

Cleaned up my house and I found my coral broach. Oh! but I'm happy.

This must be one of my lucky days.

OCT. 12: Baking bread and cleaning garden herder called. Bread not baked but gave him biscuit for his supper....

Men started hauling wheat today.

OCT. 18: Packed my trunk then threshed beans Mrs S. [Anna Schwark] came over and helped finish the job. Got flour sack nearly full...

Men loading my grain.

OCT. 20: Did not get up till 8 30 packed and later walked up to J's. Had fried chicken for dinner.

Entered order for Mrs. S. [Anna Schwark] then call at Moldenhauers.

Franks [Messenger's] bill for labor is $8.00

Men loaded last of my wheat today.

Recd letter from D. was given to Fred G. by stage driver yesterday.

[LAST ENTRY DURING 1912]

1913

[WEDNESDAY,] MARCH 19: Nearly froze last night and our car is very cold this morning. Storming in N.D. can hardly see out of the windows

Never met a jollier bunch on any of my trips.

MARCH 21: Yesterdays trip was frightful reached Schwarks about 8 P.M. nearly frozen. Very little coal at Twin Shacks.

Called on Mrs Mold'r [Moldenhauer] and stayed to tea.

Very cold.

MARCH 22: Went to Twin Shacks for the day washed windows dishes girts [?] and hung a few pictures....

Very cold....

MARCH 24: Am still at "S" too stormy to go to town for my coal. Am getting anxious to get settled in my own house again.

Went to Bauers this after noon. Was treated to ice cream & cake glory! But I was cold—cold enough with out that.

Have had several twinges of homesickness it seems so dreary out here. I miss the bustle and daily change in my work.

MARCH 25: Letters. What a treat what would I do without mail.

Took my work and spent the afternoon with Mrs. J [Jefferson].

Snow is drifted badly.

MARCH 27: Mr S. [John Schwark] has gone to town for my coal. It looks as tho I'd soon be home again.

He got home about dark. Brought me 2300# @ 20 c[ents] per 100 for hauling. Coal cost 6/05 +

Rec'd bundle Berlin papers.

MARCH 28: Reached here [Twin Shacks] about 10 A.M. started fire and went at my cleaning. Was busy and happy for a while. Decided to write a letter then my homesickness got the best of me fought it out with myself. It had to come has been picking up for a week. I felt better after it was over with.

MARCH 29: I feel quite cheerful today. Cabin is so neat and cosy as can be.

The snow is disappearing fast.

No mail.

MARCH 30: Wind is blowing a gale cannot go anywhere as walking will be too hard. Am trying to busy myself with magazines and letters, but it is hard work.

MARCH 31: Found it was a nice day when I got up. So hustled my work. Schwarks drove up before I had breakfast drank a cup of coffee then started for town.

Laid in a supply of Gro. Met Mr Muern [?] who urged me to see about proving up called on Mr Schmidt and fixed up the papers. Am glad it is started.

Mr Schwark, F. Moldenhauer, Sophie & A C J. will be my witnesses...

APRIL 12: ...am visiting all I care to now while people are not so busy in a little while we'll all be working....

APRIL 14: Set out currant bushes Mrs. E. gave me then cut up an old dress into aprons. Am doing a lot of odd jobs.

It is very warm

Sent two letters by Stage.

A large coven of prairie chickens flew by this evening.

APRIL 15: Heard my first curlew this morning.

It's cloudy and some cooler than for past few days. Am mending an old waist.

5 P.M. It has started to rain and the wind still blows a gale. The Mts are dim and Old Baldy is entirely gone.

Its dreary.

My 'chimbly' [chimney] blew down don't dare to have a fire in this gale without it.

Rec'd nice long letter from Maud B told me all about her claim.

The month is half gone can't move any too swift to suit me.

APRIL 16: Wind blew a gale all night long. Couldn't sleep. Was fearful the cabin might go over.

Worked on my waist nearly all morning. It cleared off about noon went to Schwarks and then over to 'J" spent the after noon and stayed to supper. The walk home was delightful every thing was so fresh and clean and could see so far.

The Bearpaws are covered with snow.

APRIL 17: Fine day. Carried snow from the Coulee to replenish my supply of water. Rec'd Berlin papers but no letters which has sort of taken the ambition to work out of me. Mrs Smith called had a nice visit with her. Is a bright woman.

Saw a lone coyote & just other side of Milners fence east of cabins. Stopped several times and looked at us. Can see plow out working on Frenchmans Ridge

Was a wolf.

APRIL 19: A beautiful morning can hear Hams plow at work on Messengers who will have 100 acres broken then they move on mine.

Rec'd card from Walter Mother is gone. passed away Sunday night, 13th and buried at S. C. Wed. 16th. My little world seems to have caved in around me.

Letters and magazines from Berlin which help some today.

Tried to storm this P.M. later took a walk to No Coulee Found a few yellow bells

APRIL 24: Stage came this way but no letter only bundle Berlin papers. Started work on my garden Oh but it is hard work so dry & lumpy.

Quite cool today.

APRIL 26: Such a time as I have had baking in that horrible little oven. Its windy and disagreeable. Fred G. says that was a wolf and not a coyote I saw just inside Milners fence....

APRIL 27: A Lovely day warm and quiet. Fred helped me set the broken rain barrel in cement. If it's a failure I'll blame him but on the other hand if its successful I'll take all the credit. Guess that's the way to do it. We need rain badly.

Took a "buggy" ride with Fred over to S. [Sophie's]. Must have made a picture. Me in my sunbonnet sitting on a box in the big wagon. The seat is broken hence the box....

APRIL 28: Worked in my garden until 11 A.M. in a few moments Mr

Braithwaite called to see about plowing refered him to Mr S. [John Schwark] after dinner went over there for eggs found Mr B. there and then made agreement with him for 80 a.[acres] in case Hams let us off for 40 a.[acres] promised.

Came back and walked over the North part to be broken then filled Mrs S. [Anna Schwark] barrel with snow in my coulee started to snow then rain Mts are white again.

Mr S. [John Schwark] walked down past Sch. Sec. [School Section] to head off Frank [Messenger] who was taking load coal to Hams. Its on my place now.

I feel quite happy to night...

APRIL 29: It rained last night. Got up a 3 45 A.M. to see if tubs were full. Found ground covered with snow and storming hard this morning. Did some baking then after dinner Fred G and I drove over to S. J to see him about coal for Mr B. Fred went home. It started to storm harder so I stayed all night. We played whist until 12 30.

The Men beat us....

SATURDAY, MAY 3: Mr. S. [Schwark] and Frank [Messenger] went to town with 8 horses for coal. I scrubbed and cleaned my cabin slick as a whistle. Then settled down with my sewing. The stage brought me the Berlin papers, a letter from Mrs Callings and a box from the Woods. Six big rosy apples in it. My but they do taste good.

Have had a variety of weather today hail, rain sunshine and now it is snowing. Three years ago today I left Berlin to live on my homestead.

Wish could see my friends and homesick this afternoon.

The herder brought his sheep into Milners today.

MAY 6: Am baking. Wind in the East which means rain.

Fred brought Maurers R.J.R. [Rhode Island Red] rooster which was at their place in a crate and there was no such thing as sleep for any one after he started crowing about daylight.... Mr R. brought me a good letter, magazines and finished pictures I took at Evers. are much better than I expected.

Have three big loads of coal and two more on the road for my breaking....

MAY 10: Nice bright morning. Started plowing about 9 A.M. and are busy at it. After dinner went after butter & eggs started to rain so Mr S. [John Schwark] couldn't seed. Hitched up and bro't the Mrs [Schwark or Miller??] & I over here and then to the Plow. Doing fine work even on gravel knolls. Mrs Miller is pleasant and has a cute little kiddi was on the engine all morning and looked a little darky.

Enjoyed being in the rain was so warm and smelly....

MAY 16: Finished my ironing during the P.M. it rained & hailed had quite a storm. Right after dinner the men broke camp and moved over to S. [Sophie's]. Frank [Messenger] brought my gas & oil Mr B. stopped told me my plowing was 5 acres short had no coal to finish.

MAY 17: Baking bread and cake. Rec'd good letter which boosted my spirits considerably during P.M. went to S. [Sophie's] visited with Mrs M. [Moldenhauer?] who is cooking in the house. got home after 6 P.M. fixed my fire and took a good swim.

MAY 19: Clearing up. But snow is on the Mts. and its cold...
Sent Com.[missioner] Schmidt a letter to see if he knows why delay in final proof....

MAY 23: Worked in the garden this morning until the heat drove me in. Took a cold sponge bath and discarded my long under wear...

MAY 24: No letter. Feel as tho was deserted by everyone. Not very happy to day. Will go up to "J" this evening to see if any of my mail is there....

Not a word yet from Land Office am getting nervous to say the least....

MAY 25: Stayed all night with Mrs S. [Anna Schwark] and hardly slept a wink The plow men hitched up and took us 3 women over to Bottomleys to see the Gas o [gasoline] outfit work. Mrs Miller invited us to dinner in the tent helped her get it. After ward we played cards. Mr S. [John Schwark] retd from Sand Coulee about 6 P.M. then I went home by way Moldr's and carried two pails of water.

Warm day.

MAY 26: Up about 5 A.M. am going to town with the S.'s and Mr Moldr. S & Weber prove up today. Met Mrs Evers also Mrs McDonald in town.

Had good dinner at the Overland Hotel.

Very warm in town Saw a blue vasu [?] in the Canyon the first I ever saw. was about a yard long.

Talked to Mr Schmidt about my final proof.

MAY 27: Started to hoe my garden then planted beans.

Rec'd finished postals from Berlin also magazines <u>no letter</u>. And notice from L. O. [Land Office] can prove up July 14. About 3 P.M. Sophie drove up with two men. One was the inspector.

It looks as tho it was no go for us. Am too heart sick to write.

Questioned me as to length of residence on the place. Paid no attention to any thing else. We will undoubtedly have to make up the time.

Some one out here on the bench "set" him onto me.

MAY 28: Planted spuds, squash and cukes. Am all in and about sick over the situation I feel as tho I'd like to go some where and "jump off" and end it all. Life is nothing anyway but one hard long struggle and very little of joy or happiness in it for some us to make the struggle worth while.

We have so many black birds here this spring. are busy with their love making they sing two or three sweet notes drop their wings stick their tail up in the air and bow to the "lady" very gallantly.

JUNE 4: A warm day but thunder caps are hanging about the Mts. We need rain badly. Schwarks are sending flux [?] here and Mrs came to spend the day.

Its my birthday mercy but I am getting old. But some how I cant feel that way.

JUNE 5: Rec'd a letter and birthday box which I like very much. S. [Sophie] sent down letter from Mr Nash which about broke my heart. Told Mr S. [John Schwark] my troubles

JUNE 6: Looked like rain but we started for town any way. Saw Schmidt and he advised me to withdraw for the present rec'd letter from Mrs B. also from Mr Jenks. Signed the deed and ret'd at once.

I'm pretty blue and homesick today. Mr S. [John Schwark] will investigate my record at L. O.

Found radishes in my garden for my supper.

JUNE 8: A nice day. The S [Sophie] & I [or J] started to Evers about 8 A.M. had a dandy time. Met Mrs Williams and after dinner we four women took spin in Auto, to Alkali Lake took 2 pictures of queer rock formation we also went to Milners. Oh but it's a beautiful place. Interesting part of house locked but was in kitchen and smoke room. Also bunk house. Yard full of trees shrubbery and flowers. Did not start home until after Supper. We planned to leave early and go round by foot hills but they wouldn't hear to it. Reached S [Sophie] at dusk found Moldr's [Moldenhauers] then staid all night as it was late.

JUNE 14: Nice day. Fried down my meat. Baked doughnuts and then took my swim. Later went over to S. [Sophie's] with my provisions for picnic baked two cakes for her and "did" the dishes then helped get Supper for plow men who came back to work.

JUNE 15: Lovely day. Got up at 4 A.M. and got ready to start. Had the men for Bkft too. No one went but the S. [Sophie], Mrs M. [Moldenhauer] and my self. Had a fine trip and the scenery was grand saw 4 tunnels and went thru one.

On one spot on Savage ranch could see Bearpaws, Highwood Little Belt & Big Belt also several peaks of the Rocky Mts.

Ate our lunch just across the bridge at Peck and Lacy crossing. river very high and swift just now.

Got home about 8 P.M. just ahead of a shower.

JUNE 18: Heard a cow bellowing at 4 A.M. called S [Sophie] and we flew down the lane met about 50 head at the culvert. They were more afraid of us and away they went tail "hiner" S. [Sophie's] boot rubbed a big blister on her heel. We got bkf't and then I worked in the garden....

JUNE 20: Had a fine big rain last night, heard it thunder so got up and fixed the boards and tubs and then it started to hail lay there in fear and trembling for our grain. but it didn't last long. But it <u>rained</u> and <u>rained</u> and we are happy.

The men hauling R.R. timber and camped at foot of lane must have had a nice time last night. I chased 5 head of cattle down the lane this A.M. then we walked up to J's. they are building their road across the coulee.

JUNE 21: S. [Sophie] went to town with John. I baked and scrubbed and later went to Moldr's [Moldenhauers] for water bro't back 2 pails of water and jar of butter. never again Too much to tote.

S. [Sophie] did not get home until 9 P.M. a big storm is raging in the Mts.

S. [Sophie] brought box berries "for my birth day"....

JUNE 24: Cool and Cloudy. Started to crochet lace for a waist is very fascinating can hardly leave it alone.

About 5 P.M. I went to the garden and hoed the potatoes. No letters today but living in hopes for Thursday.

The light and shadows were beautiful on the Mts today.

We walked up to the wheat. My heart sank when I saw how short and burned it looked. Flax coming fine and wheat is tall and thick where choff [?] has mulched it. Pulled a lot of tumble mustard near my granary also Sophies.

JUNE 26: Cool and cloudy. Took a tramp thru Miners over to coulee near Black Butte for mushrooms brought back load of kindling and large bunch of blue bells instead. Ret'd just in time to meet the Stage Recd post, papers and 3 letters....

JULY 6: It's very warm and windy a disagreeable day. Haven't much to read and am having difficulty in killing time. Storm clouds blew up about 5 P.M. Then I started for M. for water. Rained a very little here. Wrote four letters.

JULY 7: Nice day. Nothing much doing here today. Some days are very long.

JULY 9: Got up about 5 A.M. Then went over to S's to help Mrs poison potato bugs. The heat was terrific and I was sick before we quite finished was too much for me. Seemed as tho every drop of blood was in my head and things looked black.......

JULY 11: Sent letter to Gt. F. L.O. [Great Falls Land Office] to day in regard to sickness [this refers to her abdominal surgery as discussed in introduction] also to Gen L. O. about separation.

JULY 15: Mr S. [John Schwark] started cutting my grain this P.M. Went up to see how the machine worked.

JULY 22: Warm day. Ironed and baked bread. then rec'd word that Jess would be out on night train. Later the Girtons came. got supper and went back with them for the night to get good start to town. They were going in for groceries.

JULY 23: Reached town about 9 30 went to the Hotels at once. No one there. Went back toward Choteau House. Met Jess and Mr McD. on the street. Did one errand had dinner then started for home. Got here about 6 30. Mr McD. came too.

Jess was delighted with every thing is same jolly girl she always was.

SATURDAY, AUG. 2: Started for Benton about 6 A.M. Met Maurer on the road seemed rather put out that we had his horse. Reached B. [Fort Benton] at 9 A.M. and started back about 3 P.M. got caught in a storm but was not alone a young man on horse back rode bridle the rig all during the worst of it. Reached Twin Shacks at or a little after 6 P.M. and Maurers at 9 P.M. O.M. [Otto Maurer] pulled a long face and informed me the horse was all in.

Mr Mac kissed me good bye. His mustache was terribly "prickery" nuf sed.

AUG. 9: Got up at 5 A.M. hustled my clothes out but it looks stormy so will not go to town finished my washing then scrubbing and run an ugly big splinter half way up under my nail hurt terribly toward night so held in hot water. only remedy I had.

It rained nearly all day. Got postal and best letter including the one that was lost.

This has been rather a pleasant day for me.

AUG. 12: Busy about the place went over to S. [Sophie's] during P.M. got home just before the terrific looking storm thought sure we were in for a twister. Stood on the prairie and watched it until the sand began to pelt m[y] face then I went in.

Was sorry I had been in such a hurry to get home.

Heard late it blew Fogdens granary down.

AUG. 16: Warm day. Made the trip home from Moldr's [Moldenhau-er's] after bkft and then right back to S. [Sophie's] and hustled into the work.

Have 22 men besides extras.

Staid all night at Moldr's [Moldenhauer's] but hardly slept a wink guess was too tired.

AUG. 18: Rained enough last evening to delay them this A.M. moved onto mine after dinner. We walked over alter and snapped the machine twice. Wheat looks good.

Mr S. [John Schwark] took me home last night it got so late before the work was done.

Mrs. S & Mrs G. rode home in Fogdens rig looked to frail for another passenger so I walked.

I lifted a bu. [bushel] of wheat up to the wagon. Failed at first attempt & split my sleeve doing it.

AUG. 19: Four loads to finish on mine then start threshing Franks grain did not expect them for dinner but got partly ready they came at 12 M. hustled around and gave them what we had. Rested all P.M. and rode over with the Girtons after Supper.

Nice bright day Mr R brought me good letter to Schwarks.

Mine went 534 bu [bushels] on 40 a. [acres].

S.M.J. [Sophie Maude Jefferson] 340 bu [bushels] on 30 or 33 a. [acres].

Oats 164 bu[bushes] to 10 a. [acres].

AUG. 20: Nice cool day. Did not get up early for felt "all in." Hung my bedding out to sun and air then got bkft. Later Halbo called for bread but had none for him. gave him spuds and cukes instead.

Mr S. [John Schwark] called later was considerably "fussed" because I should have said I didn't like to see the rakings wasted.

Set him right as quickly as I could.

He acts like a Kid and must be handled with gloves or gets edge wise.

AUG. 21: Warm and windy am baking bread and fixing up under wear getting things ready for "home" Oh I can hardly wait for the day to come when I can start.

L.H.J. Post. B papers and card from L.O. [Land Office] came in to-day's mail.

Can prove up Oct 9....

AUG. 30: Very warm out in the sun but cabin is delightfully cool. Fin-ished trimming my hat. Worked on the neckbow and made noodles for my dinner. Thought I'd get some kind of mail but nothing came.

The sunset last night was lovely. Mts were bronze with pink clouds over head and rain bow in background.

AUG. 31: Nice and cool today but wind blows a gale looks as tho it might blow up a train. Have written two letters and fussed around some besides reading still the day seems endless I sure am getting anxious to start home but must have a little more patience.

SEPT. 1: Baked bread and cake and finished my third Susette bow

SEPT. 2: It is cool and cloud today but all signs seem to fail here.

Pulled and stacked part of my beans.

Hams kicking Sorrel ran away about noon tore past the cabin the lugs beating it at every jump. Fred Erwin finally caught it.

No mail am much disappointed. Will go over to S. [Sophie's] later in the day.

Mr. S. [John Schwark] has stated cutting my flax is so short can only get about 2/3 for it.

SEPT. 3: Finished pulling my beans to day in upper patch.

SEPT. 4: Threshed one pile of beans this A.M. Mr J. brought down barrel of goods for S. [Sophie]. Rec'd the best letter and one for G. F. *Tribune* my first ad was Sept 3.

After noon or while eating dinner I smelled smoke saw a prairie fire west of us and high N. W. wind blowing hustled things into my trunk & suit case and tied my bedding in a bundle ready to haul it across the road but Webers plowing stopped it from coming this way.

SEPT. 10: Cleaned up around and then buried myself in my cabin dur-ing the P.M. Mrs Weber and children came. She wants to engage S. [Sophie] for her coming sickness finished by asking could I come if S.

[Sophie] did not. Heavens! what good would I be at a time like that.

SEPT. 11: Baked bread and waited for the mail Went over to S. [Sophie] after baking was out of way. Very warm day. Mr. S. [John Schwark] broke small wheel on binder and hurried to town for rpr's.

Heard last night that Mr S. [John Schwark] said he wasn't going to seed my 70 acres. That when he told me "I went off a bawling" if he told what he's a big ___

Thought some thing was wrong when both S. [Sophie], J. and Mrs W. asked "Wasn't I going to have any crop in this year"

SEPT. 12: Helped Mrs S. [Anna Schwark] chop mixed pickles to day. Is very warm out in the sun.

SEPT. 15: Was going to help Mrs S. [Anna Schwark] make corn relish but pulled and gathered flax instead. Mrs helped with the stacking.

We found spot on mine where buck weed and rose bushes are growing....

SEPT. 24: Started to town about 8 A.M. went directly to Choteau House then called up Mr Ball.

S. [Sophie] called me up am invited to Supper at Sanitarium. Want me to help them a few days they are short of Nurses.

Bought a house dress apron & slippers and will start work in the morning.

Mts are covered with snow.

SEPT. 25: Lovely day. My case was heard at 10 A.M. Through a misunderstanding another notice must be served case is postponed until we hear from F. H. [Fred S. Hunt, her estranged husband.]

Am about frantic.

SEPT. 26: Another lovely day. Mr B. wants me to stay in town if possible as Judge will hear my case Sat. 5 inst if ret'n card is rec'd from letter to F. H. [Fred S. Hunt] Have decided to stay all of next week.

SEPT. 27: Busy doing all king[d]s of thing. can't say I admire this kind of work

OCT. 6: Hustled with my work then witnessed operation on little 5 yr old boy

I "assisted" by mopping the Dr's brow and swatting flies. the roads are terrible will go home on stage to morrow.

OCT. 7: Miss H. S [Sophie Jefferson] M J & my self went down town then over to picture show. Last evening was a good rest and I slept fine....

OCT. 8: Came home [to Twin Shacks] yesterday on stage thru slush and snow, a terrible trip on the horses. Had a big swede for driver who tried to fill me full of "hot air" about how he hated whiskey after I'd seen a bottle and jug. He used to drive stage across the Mts to Shoshone also was on the round up.

Reached home about 2:30 started my fire and got dinner late Mr S. [John Schwark] came on Phallis looking for stray cattle. Every thing is covered with snow have 8 in[ches] here.

Went up to S. [Sophie] & J's [Jeffersons'] today.

OCT. 9: Went into town today with Mr S. [John Schwark] and made proof had Joe Ham as other witness.

Took dinner at the San. [sanitarium] later sent up sweet potatoes and fruit to the Nurses.

We got a late start home. Brought out a lot of groceries for Joe which delayed us. Did not get home until about 8 P.M. Nearly frozen.

Schmidt asked a lot of questions of Mr S. [John Schwark] about my claim his looking for a chance to contest according to his reputation.

OCT. 10: A Chinook is blowing and the snow is about gone except on the Mts.

I heard there is 5 ft of snow So. of Gt Falls.

Went over to S. [Sophie's] yesterday and settled up. It made me "see stars" for a while when I realized how deep in I was.

OCT. 12: Wrote letters and did a few odd jobs also burned about a bu[shel of] letters that had accumulated in my trunk.

OCT. 13: Did a big washing and dried 'em in the house. Then I cleaned S. [Sophie's] floors & windows and did a number of other jobs.

OCT. 14: Ironed and cleaned and packed some more put up clean curtains & cushion covers in S. [Sophie's] cabin and then mended stockings am mighty busy getting ready to leave.

OCT. 15: Dug my spuds and sold 'em to Halbo about 2 P.M. while picking them up Dr Porter's car came bringing Miss Higgins to stay a week. Is worn out with the work at San.

OCT. 16: Rec'd 5 letters and word my proof is accepted. I'm so relieved and happy that have no comment to make.

Price of wheat is way down 58 c & 57 c.

OCT. 17: Mrs J. [Sophia Jefferson] & O M. [Otto Maurer] & Mr J. [Albert Jefferson] were here this A.M. the latter to take in a load of my wheat.

Will go to dinner at J's to morrow.

Went to M's [Maurers] for water and over to S. [Sophie's] helped Mrs S. [Anna Schwark] gather her spuds.

OCT. 18: Last of our wheat was taken in this A.M. Mrs S. [Anna Schwark] was here after helping the men load up.

Had a nice chicken dinner at J's [Jeffersons']. Mrs J. asked me if J. was married yet. She did not find out I will not have affairs pried into.

Rec'd check for 7 00 from Halbo for pickles beans bread and spuds. "Every little bit helps."

OCT. 19: Was to go to Grays for Dinner but they did not send for us. Is cloudy and windy.

I'm going home

[DIARY ENDS]

Chapter Ten

DEAD, PLUCKY, OR PROVED UP: WOMEN HOMESTEADERS IN THE MONTANA PRESS

EVIDENCE OF MONTANA'S SOLO WOMEN homesteaders can be found throughout the newspapers of early twentieth-century Montana. The most frequent mention is in the newspapers' "Notice of Publication" section where homesteaders published their notice of intention to make three-year proof to the land to establish their claim. Often their names had changed between filing and proving up, as in the example of "Sadie Hall, formerly Sadie Belzer, of Glasgow, Montana," who filed her notice of intention to establish proof to her land in September 1916.[1] Local news sections recorded the travels of women homesteaders, including their absences, usually in the late fall, and their springtime returns. Wedding notices often mentioned that the bride and groom would reside on the bride's homestead. It was rare to have a feature article about a woman homesteader, such as the one about Catharine Calk (see Chapter Twelve). Aside from these occasions, women homesteaders appeared in the news when misfortune or a death was reported. Two examples are provided here.

In May 1916 Nora Nereson, from Gary, Minnesota, filed on land near Saco, in Phillips County. She built a shack and lived on her claim

Nora Nereson's death was reported via this handwritten affidavit stamped October 27, 1920, from Greve, Montana. UNITED STATES NATIONAL ARCHIVES AND RECORDS ADMINISTRATION, MTGLS0050707.

until July 5, 1916, when she was "killed by wind storm."[2] Her mother, Thilda Nereson, also of Gary, Minnesota, entered on the land as heir of her daughter and proved up in 1921, without performing any residence requirements, although she had a frame building and 23 acres under cultivation at the time of her application for patent.

YOUNG LADY KILLED
Hinsdale Tribune, *July 14, 1916*

Alone in her little homestead shack five miles west of Greve, late the night of July 5, Miss Nora Nereson, a school teacher, was killed when a cyclone picked her house up and tore it to pieces on the prairie, says the *Saco Independent*.

When found she was clad in her night gown and it was evident that the storm struck the shack while she was asleep. Neighbors early the next morning seeing this and another homestead shack completely demolished soon came to the scene of the tragedy. Her body was brought to Saco and Coroner Tucker was called but decided that an inquest was not necessary. The remains were shipped to Gary, Minn., her old home. She had left home but two months ago after having finished a term of school.

She was twenty-two years of age.

Similarly, teacher and homesteader Irene Van Kleek, came to public notice because of her untimely death in 1910, as shown in this article from the Lewistown newspaper, December 30, 1910, edition of the *Lewistown Daily News*.

TRAGIC DEATH OF IRENE VAN KLEEK WELL KNOWN HIGH SCHOOL TEACHER FATALLY INJURED

Thrown From Horse While Riding to Homestead

Sad Affair a Great Shock to Her Many Friends
Lewistown Daily News, *December, 1910*

Miss Irene Van Kleek, in charge of the commercial department of the Fergus county high school, met with a tragic death Tuesday when she was thrown from a horse, sustaining injuries from which she died a few hours later without having regained consciousness.

Miss Van Kleek took up a homestead last October on the south fork of McDonald creek about ten miles southwest of Grass Range. She went out Monday last, intending to spend a portion of the holiday vacation on the place, stopping at the John Single ranch. Mr. Single had been building a house on the homestead, and had it nearly completed. Miss Van Kleek was anxious to have it finished and Tuesday morning left the Single ranch with Mr. Single and three men, who were to assist in the work. Miss Van Cleek wanted to go out on horseback, although the wagon went along and would not accept Mr. Single's advice to ride in the wagon. Instead she rode a horse belonging to Mr. Single. The animal is neither wild nor vicious and had been ridden ten miles by Mr. Single on the morning of this trip.

Miss Van Kleek was not an experienced rider and found it easier to go on a gallop or a walk and generally led the party a considerable distance then walking her horse until the others caught up with her.

THROWN FROM HORSE

The party had gone about four miles from the Single ranch and coming to a gate, one of the men dismounted to open it. Miss Van Kleek was the first one through and rode on ahead at a rather fast rate of speed, which quickly increased. The horse did not shy, as has been reported, but the speed doubtless unnerved the girl who was apparently unable to check the animal. Suddenly she fell to the ground, alighting on her head. The others quickly rode up to her and found her unconscious. Without delay she was placed in the wagon and taken to the Walter Gooch place.

Mrs. Gooch is a trained nurse and was able to give Miss Van Kleek the best of care, while one of the men mounted the horse the injured woman had been riding and got to Grass Range in thirty minutes. He telephoned to Jack Rowley, of this city, at whose house Miss Van Kleek made her home, and at 2:15 p. m. Dr. H. M. Wilson started for the scene in his auto, accompanied by Prof. G. L. Wait, of the high school. Miss Van Kleek was beyond human aid, however, having died thirty minutes before the physician could arrive. The accident accured at about 10:30 a. m. and Miss Van Kleek breathed her last at 3:30 p. m. She showed no signs of consciousness except once when Mrs. Gooch asked if her head hurt. To this she said, "yes."

WAS ABLE WOMAN

Miss Van Kleek was about twenty-eight years of age and a native of New York state. She was at one time private secretary to Andrew D. White, former president of Cornell, and later ambassador to Germany and ambassador to Russia. Later still she was secretary to the editor in chief of World's Work and had accompanied Theodore Roosevelt on one of his speech making tours. She was especially well qualified for the position she was holding in the high school as was loved by the students and her associates on the faculty.

SURVIVED BY SISTER

Miss Van Kleek's parents are dead, but she is survived by a married sister who resides at Ithaca, New York, and a nephew, Ralph Ferris, of Binghamton, New York. Mr. Ferris sent a telegram yesterday instructing that the body be embalmed and made ready for shipment, stating that he would start immediately for Lewistown to accompany the remains to Ithaca. Miss Van Kleek was one of the new high school teachers, having come here last fall. Her work gave complete satisfaction. She was a woman of much character, self reliant, yet womanly and most gracious always. To those who knew her her tragic end comes as a shock.

The body was brought in Wednesday afternoon in charge of Prof. Wait, and is now at Creel's undertaking parlors.

Press coverage of solo women homesteaders suggests that they were not always welcome. Nellie T. Holt, a homesteader near Harlem, was editor of the *Square Butte Tribune* in Chouteau County. Born in South Dakota, Holt entered on a relinquishment she had purchased from one Stella Henderson in 1920, at the age of twenty-three. In an affidavit Holt signed on March 4, 1921, she stated that at the time of her filing there was "a habitable shack suitable for dwelling purpose." But when she drove out to the land to establish her residence on March 1, she found that "her house had been removed by persons unknown and that she is therefore unable to start her residence upon said land at this time due to the fact that her house is gone and at the present time she is not able financially to erect another and therefore asks that she be granted a period of six months additional time in which to establish her residence thereon."[3]

"[R]unning [was] not a family trait," Holt declared to a reporter in the article below and she persisted. She had already experienced considerable adversity. The April 25, 1919, issue of the *Square Butte Tribune* reported that "Editor Has Accident": "Miss Nellie Holt...was painfully burned Wednesday morning at the printing plant at Square Butte. While attempting to hurry up a slow fire by pouring kerosene on it an explosion followed enveloping her in flames. Help was at hand and the flames immediately smothered, but her face, hands and lower limbs were quite badly burned." Ten weeks later, it was reported, she could sit up a little each day but a full recovery was still weeks away.

On June 24, 1921, Holt and her coeditor, Mrs. W. E. Haller, notified the readers of the *Square Butte Tribune* that they were retiring from active newspaper work and that the paper was under new management. Holt turned her attention to her homestead. She had 10 acres broken, but finding the soil "so full of gravel that it cannot be properly broke so as to produce a crop," she applied for a reduction of area required for cultivation. In September 1924, she married Emery O. Smith of Havre. Later in 1924, when she applied for her final three-year proof, she signed her name Nellie Holt Smith. This was approved in 1925. She had truly remained undaunted by the mysterious removal of her house.

NELLIE HOLT AND HER STOLEN HOUSE

Girl Editor of Square Butte Tribune Demonstrates Her Good Nerve

Thieves Steal Her House From Off Her Homestead, So She Builds Another; All that Was Left on the Place Was the Well; Will Grow Prize Potatoes
Opheim Observer, *June 17, 1921*

Undaunted by the mysterious removal last winter of the house on her homestead near Harlem, Miss Nellie T. Holt has purchased another house and returned to the claim, determined to stick until she gets a patent "and then some."

"They didn't leave anything but the well," Miss Holt said in describing her loss. "Last fall when I started back to Square Butte to continue my work of editing the *Square Butte Tribune*, there was a shack, roughly furnished, on the place. When I went back this spring to renew my residence, there was only a rectangular plot where the shack had stood.

RUNNING NOT A FAMILY TRAIT

"Somebody must have objected to having a 'girl nester' in that particular region. But they haven't scared Nellie Holt. Just because my sister and I took first prize last year at Helena in the three-legged race for women at the picnic of the State Press association, someone seems to have got the impression that running is a family trait. It's a wrong impression. I'm here to stay, at least for the term of my legal residence."

Miss Holt says she took up homesteading as a relief from the trials and tribulations of an editor's life in a small town during the more or less unsettled period through which the nation is passing. She's had four years of it at Square Butte and feels she's entitled to a vacation—if homesteading on Montana bench land can be thus described.

"Having a house stolen 'without a trace' is a bit unusual in these days, I suppose, but I assure you there was very little excitement in it for me," Miss Holt said. "I had gone out from town in a hired automobile, carrying bedding and grub. When I got there and found no house, I debated the matter of returning to primitive methods and sleeping out in the open until I could get another house, but it was the rainy season and it didn't take long to decide to get back in the automobile.

The published rumors that two teacher/homesteaders had been found frozen to death in the winter of 1916 are examples of efforts to discourage women homesteaders by pointing out their unsuitability and ineptitude and singling them out for criticism. Several newspapers reported a story similar to this one from the *Glasgow Democrat*.

GIRLS FREEZING, PEN NOTES

Two Montana School Teachers, Alone on Ranch Write "Good-By's"—Letters Found Beside Bodies

Glasgow Democrat, *February 11, 1916*

Butte – Realizing they slowly were freezing to death in their remote homestead cabin east of Havre, in Northern Montana, two school teachers wrote letters to their mother in Ohio, telling of the bitter cold and bidding farewell to the folks at home.

The story was brought to Butte by Cliff Meed, a traveling man, who was in a neighboring village when the frozen bodies were brought in. Their names were Misses Moore.

The two girls took up a homestead a year ago. They resided with a rancher and his wife, at first, but when their funds ran low they decided to live on their own place to cut expenses. The rancher took them to their little home, and it was after he had driven out of sight, they realized they had no matches.

That night the mercury dropped 40 degrees in an hour. By morning it was 60 degrees below. The girls had few blankets. Realizing they were freezing to death, the sisters each wrote a letter to their mother. Their frozen bodies were found wrapped in blankets. The letters which lay on the table with "Good-by" sprawled by frozen fingers, have been sent on.

Although widely reported and repeated, the story was never corroborated as this excerpt from the *Great Falls Tribune* indicates, suggesting that the story was invented.

NO MONTANA TEACHERS WERE FROZEN TO DEATH

Story That Has Been Going the Rounds of the

State Press and Which Has Reached Some Outside Papers Is Evidently Without Any Foundation in Fact

Great Falls Tribune, *February 8, 1916*

A week ago Monday there came to the editorial offices of the *Tribune* a report that two school teachers had frozen to death in a cabin on their ranch "near Havre." No details were available.

On Tuesday the report was again current in Great Falls, this time a few details being added. It was said that the young women had frozen to death in bed "east of Havre." The *Tribune* at once made inquiry of its correspondent at Havre and was promptly informed that nothing of the kind occurred at Havre or in Hill county.

In the meantime inquiry came from an eastern city about the "freezing of two school teachers near Havre." Being unwilling to miss an item of news of such importance as was indicated by this inquiry and by the reports circulated, the *Tribune* again communicated with Havre and with other cities and towns "east of Havre." No one knew anything of school teachers freezing to death.

About the same time the story found its way to Butte, being carried there, it is understood, by a traveling man. It was published in a Butte paper on Tuesday, with considerable detail. The following day it was republished in another Butte paper and became a general topic for discussion over a considerable portion of Montana.

This story contained considerable detail, but many facts were wanting which a person reading or hearing it would at once want to know. It was stated that the two school teachers named Moore, first names not given, realizing that they were almost sure to freeze to death before morning, wrote letters to their parents in Ohio (name of place not given).

These women according to the story, had gone to live in their ranch cabin on a homestead "east of Havre," in order to reduce expenses. They were said to be teaching school in the neighborhood. A farmer took them to the cabin. He left them late in the afternoon, well supplied with everything but matches.

No intimation is given as to when this disastrous event occurred, but it is stated that the temperature fell to 40 degrees below zero that night. Having no matches, the two teachers could build no fire. Their cover was but slight, and the cabin was a futile shelter against the blood-chilling breath from the north.

The next morning, according to the story, when the ranchman called, the bodies of the young women were found wrapped in the two flimsy blankets, arms clasped in death. On a table was found the letter referred to. Its contents have not been made public, so far as the *Tribune* can learn.

The bodies were taken to a "little village" and shipped to the old home "back in Ohio." The name of the little village has not been made public, and the name of the place to which the bodies were shipped is also wanting.

When a report of the story as told in Butte came to the *Tribune* inquiries were again sent out to get the details of the story. Telegrams were sent to all county seat towns in Montana "east of Havre," and to many other places in northern Montana. From every place came back in substance the same reply:

> "We know nothing about two school teachers named
> Moore, or any other names, freezing to death."

From Havre, upon second inquiry, we obtained more
detailed denial, as follows:

> There is no truth in the story about two school
> teachers by the name of Moore freezing to death.
> There is no report here of any bodies of that name
> being shipped from any station along the Great
> Northern east of Havre during the cold weather. No
> women named Moore taught school in this county
> this year."

So the *Tribune* is unable to furnish further details of
the tragedy, and is forced to offer a suggestion that this
particular tragedy might not have occurred. There were
enough of them in Montana during the storm, heaven
knows, so that there could have been no good reason for
inventing one, but this one bears some of the marks of the
inventor's genius.

The last article from the *Ronan Pioneer* of December 15, 1916,
could be read as an effort to discredit solo women homesteaders and
to suggest that the homesteading legislation encouraged unorthodox
marital arrangements and deceit, although it ends on a note of
approval. The land file of Maud Miller indicates how "the story current
in Highwood" got started. From Illinois, Maud Miller filed on land
at Highwood, Montana, in December 1911.[4] Sometime before 1915,
when she filed her notice of intention to make three-year proof, she

married Royal I. Baird, and her name became Maud Baird. She made considerable improvements as she had a two-room frame house, a frame granary and barn, 82 acres broken, and all her land fenced. One of her witnesses was her brother, Lyle K. Miller. Her land patent was approved in January 1916.

In October 1918, a "complaint against the validity of this entry" was received at the General Land Office made by Ira Starr and Clara Starr. Clara Starr initiated the proceeding, writing, "Can a person hold a homestead when they filed on it as a single woman and was married at the time she filed on it? Please look this up. Miss Maude Miller filed on a homestead and at that time she was married and her name is Mrs. Maud Baird. But she posed as a single women then so she says now, she don't care who knows that she was married when she filed for she is proved up on it. She has a husband to support her. Please look this up soon. She told me this herself."

Clara Starr's husband, Ira Starr, worked for the Bairds on Maud Baird's homestead and on land which Royal Baird rented. The Starrs swore in a statement, made at the Norbert, Montana, post office in November 1918, that Maud and Royal Baird had told them on several occasions that they were married before she filed on her homestead and that "she filed under her maiden name, Maud M. Miller, as he would not live on a ranch for...he was only out there to get it broken up and then was going back to the city again. He said that L.K. Miller wanted him to come out and file on a homestead and he wouldn't do it so they got Mrs. Baird, sister of L.K. Miller to come out from the east and file. They moved out here from Des Moines, and had a child three years old called Bobbie, and spoke of having an older child, a girl, which died in the east...Mrs. Baird used to come out on her homestead in the summer time and in winter returned and stay with her husband, while Baird was only out here one season staying less than a year and running the Highwood Hotel."

A "special agent" of the land office was sent to investigate the complaint. He interviewed Maud Baird, who showed him her marriage certificate dated December 18, 1912, in Chicago, and the authenticity of the certificate was confirmed. The agent noted that Maud Miller/Baird continued to sign her land documents with her "maiden" name for some years after, but concluded, "Whatever motive Mrs. Baird may have had in concealing the fact of her marriage from her neighbors, if she did so, it does not appear that she was married when she entered the land. It seems that Baird worked at other pursuits than farming and this required his absence, and it is possible that Mrs. Baird said she was single in order to account for his absence from the homestead. However, Mrs. Baird did not admit that she posed as a single woman after her marriage, but stated she had sent wedding cards to several neighbors near the homestead, whom she named." The agent concluded that there was "no foundation for such a charge" and believed he found "motive for the protest" on learning that Ira Starr believed Royal Baird owed him money for wages. And Mrs. Starr, the agent found, "evinced some animus by making the remark in a rather emphatic manner, 'I hope they lose the place.'"

MONTANA HOMSTEADERS WHO ARE WOMEN

A Plucky Chicago Girl Wins a Home and a Husband

Frugal Couple Divorced, File on Separate Homesteads; Prove Up Land and Remarry
Ronan Pioneer, *December 15, 1916*

The 80-mile stretch of wheat country from the Highwood mountains to Chester on the north within the last five or six years has seen a big influx of women homesteaders, and intermingled with the stories of their successes are threads of romance.

There is the story of Maud Miller, who, like the Maud Muller of poetic fame, was reared on a farm. Until a few years ago her home was in Chicago and it was there, according to the story current in Highwood, that she met an electrician who proposed to join fortunes with her. This seemed all right until they compared notes and realized that the union of their capital—his earning capacity as an electrician and his meager savings and her modest bank account—would fall far short of providing them with the home of their dreams.

Miss Miller had heard of Montana and the money to be made from land to be had virtually for the asking. She suggested that he stay in Chicago and save his wages while she went to the Treasure state to file on 320 acres of Uncle Sam's domain. He consented to this and Miss Miller obtained a homestead three miles from Highwood. Three years later Miss Miller proved up her homestead and sent to Chicago for her sweetheart, who came west on the first train to claim her as his bride. For six months the couple lived together on the ranch. Then, a few weeks ago, they sold their holding for $9,800 and returned to Chicago, where it is reported that he has gone into business with a big electrical store of his own. And now they have the home of their dreams....

Then there is the story of the couple that located on a homestead near Glasgow. When they had proved up their homestead they found they were possessed of an estate that would make them comfortable for life, but they were not satisfied—they longed to be really rich. And they found the way. They were divorced and the woman located not a great way from Highwood, a homestead of her own, which she proved up in the course of time. Recently they were remarried and their joint holdings are equivalent to an entire section...

Then there is the story of Miss Jasper, who located on a homestead 10 or 11 miles north of Fort Benton, which was the nearest railroad station. For several weeks she hauled wheat almost daily all this distance to the elevators—hauled it all alone and did a good part of her farm work without the aid of the stronger sex.

Chapter Eleven

"A SURE-ENOUGH PIONEER": ADA MAUD MELVILLE SHAW

ADA MAUD MELVILLE SHAW PUBLISHED her memoir of her homesteading days in Yellowstone County, Montana—"the richest and most valuable chapter of her life"—in several installments (1931–32) of *The Farmer's Wife: The Magazine for Farm Women,* a popular monthly magazine published in Saint Paul, Minnesota, where she served as the magazine's managing editor from 1915 to 1928.[1] Born in 1862 in Montreal, Shaw moved to the United States around 1880 and became a naturalized citizen at Cook County, Illinois, in 1894. She was married in 1897 to evangelist John Barber Shaw of Chicago, who was twenty-three years her senior.

By 1910 she was a widow, a writer, and a companion to Margaret Sudduth, a journalist, and was living in Broadview, Montana. She filed on her 160-acre homestead in October 1911, when she was fifty years old, and had lived there for a year and a half when she wrote to the Department of the Interior stating that her homestead was hay and pasture land and was not cultivatable.[2] She wanted to know if the acreage she was required to cultivate could be reduced and if she could commute, or pay for her homestead, writing that "I am a self-supporting widow living alone on my ranch and there is not a male man within reach to give me any EXACT information on this point of commuting—or any other. I believe our Uncle Sam is in the service of such!—especially since some of us are beginning to vote."

As her memoir details, Shaw worked two winters at a lawyer's office in Nesterville, Montana, but by January 1914 she had a temporary position with *The Farmer's Wife*. Shaw received her patent to her land in 1915 and returned to city life, but it is not known what happened to her land. After her years at the editorial desk of *The Farmer's Wife*, Shaw continued publishing poetry and stories until her death in 1937 in Saint Paul.

The only agricultural periodical pitched entirely to farm women, *The Farmer's Wife* had well over one million subscribers by 1930.[3] The magazine's articles and editorials promoted rural and farm life as a fulfilling, authentic, and dignified existence for American women. At the same time, the magazine gave a voice to the concerns of rural women who wrote letters about their standard of living and isolation and the need for better roads, rest rooms in towns, and vacations. Shaw's memoir, among the more carefully crafted of those in this book, provides great insight into homesteaders' frustrations, challenges, fears, and loneliness. Overall, it is the story of how she was completely altered by the experience—how she won independence, learned tolerance, and conquered fears. "'Twas a great experience," she concluded, "and turned into my spiritual coffer wealth which worldly standards cannot measure, wealth that has remained with me." Shaw's memoir speaks to the importance of religion in the lives of many homesteaders, although in her case it was the "Great Mother" who was her spiritual guide.

Although she experienced drought, poverty, hail, and other misfortunes during her homesteading days, Shaw's memoir stresses the positive results of her experience. It is interesting to compare this memoir to Pearl Danniel's account (Chapter Thirteen). While Shaw's memoir was published at the same time as Danniel's, she was looking back on what was to her a happier and simpler time in the 1910s, while Danniel was actually experiencing the devastation of the 1930s in rural Montana.

The following excerpts from Shaw's memoir of her homesteading days in Yellowstone County, Montana, were published in several installments from February 1931 to May 1932 in *The Farmer's Wife: The Magazine for Farm Women.*

CABIN O'WILDWINDS:
THE STORY OF A MONTANA RANCH
Ada Melville Shaw

The Farmer's Wife: The Magazine for Farm Women

Cabin O'Wildwinds was the very appropriate name I gave to the tiny something-between-a-shack-and-a-house in which, when well past what is usually understood to be the prime of a woman's years, I settled alone, a homesteader on semi-desert land with only the snow-crowned Rockies to relieve the flat stretches north, south, east and west of cactus, sage, and greasewood country, not a neighbor close by and stores very far away.

"But how did you ever come to do such a foolish—crazy—thing?"

This question has been thrust upon me times without number by very sane friends who never could have been persuaded into any such adventure. However, while preparing to take up the new life—a vivid chapter in my hitherto well-ordered, if not humdrum, existence, I felt—though I could not explain my feeling—that I was neither foolish nor crazy; now that I can look back upon it all, weighing and measuring this with that of the total outcome, I know that the adventure was one of the richest and most lastingly valuable chapters of my now nearly seventy years of life....

Receiving an invitation to be the companion of a woman friend, who, with money in her purse, had gone a-pioneering for health's and wealth's sake, into territory newly released for agricultural purposes, I burned my city bridges behind me and struck trail from a Chicago boarding house for the Unknown, never dreaming how far afield the trail would lead....

The day I left my friend's home near the little new town of Nesterville, and "hit out" for my homestead miles across the level country, is graved deeply in memory—a picture of light and shade, of laughter and tears, of fear and high courage. I had engaged a fellow-homesteader to haul me and mine out to the waiting Cabin, up whose brick

When Ada Melville Shaw's homesteading series "Cabin O'Wildwinds" first appeared in The Farmer's Wife in 1931, it was accompanied by drawings by Montana cowboy artist Irvin "Shorty" Shope. Shope studied with C. M. Russell and Edgar Paxson and had an undergraduate degree in fine art from the University of Montana–Missoula. ILLUSTRATION BY IRVIN "SHORTY" SHOPE. REPRODUCED COURTESY OF THE SHOPE FAMILY.

chimney no smoke had yet felt its way and to whose door no friendly trail was as yet beaten out on the virgin sod: my beautiful, intelligent shepherd-collie, Lassie; my winsome and no less intelligent little black cat, Betsy Bobbett; a huge vinegar cask for water, since I had no well and no money to sink in the gamble for one; my trunk, filled mainly with books; a few simple and essential furnishings such as bed, stove, etc.; a three-months' supply of food, all canned or packaged.

It was anything but a "nice" day. Clouds hung low and the greasewood flat was dressed in tones of black and gray—a grim challenge to the tenderfoot and a very lame foot at that! While still far off I spied the Cabin, its new lumber shining against the dun background, looking very much like a carelessly abandoned pill-box which the wind would one day toss out of its path. But it was mine!

With high heart beats I climbed stiffly down from the wagon, my driver looking at the house with a wise eye.

"So you're goin' to try to make it here alone? Some guts fer a woman, I'll say! An' you aint so young neither!"

With feelings I cannot even now reveal, I put my new key in my new door and slowly turned the new knob. I was very sentimental about it—should have liked some sort of ceremonial. I looked in—I had not seen the place since the first stringers had been laid above the sod. And this is what greeted me: floors strewn deeply with shavings and other builder's litter, egg shells, bacon rinds, empty tomato cans, sardine cans, fruit cans, tobacco quids, meat bones, discarded rags. A mess where I had visualized a clean waitingness; stale odors where there should have been the clean breath of pine....

My mover and I worked hard and fast and before darkness settled down, a stove was up, the water barrel was filled from a neighboring well, lamps were filled with oil, bed ready to make, boxes of food opened, coffee simmering, bacon sliced and waiting for the pan. How I loved it all! Then my first companion at the first meal in the new home drove off, and I watched him disappear in the thick gloom which was fast settling on the land, swallowing me up. The only sign of other human habitation was a distant log barn and beside it a dreary-looking squat hut built of stone; there, I learned, sometimes stayed over night a homesteader who earned his bread—since his land had turned out to be non-arable—by hauling logs from the far distant foothills. Aside from this, empty, treeless, lightless, pathless gloom stretched away to the encircling horizon. And the rain came down.

As a matter of fact—a fact I seriously understood later on in my mad career—that rain was a life-saver to the homesteaders on the new land, that semi-arid territory on which they had cast their lot. But that night, in my ignorance, I hated it, for I had but the narrow personal outlook—what was it doing to me! After all, it is that same narrow personal outlook that is the seat of most of our miseries. A year later, rain, no matter what passing personal misery it inflicted, was matter for the deepest thankfulness and joy. So we learn—so the soul is trained!

But then, I shivered away from the chill of the elements, shut the doors and locked them, albeit there was no one to lock out, looked around and whispered to the crass ignorance of me, fool! fool! fool! I did not like the voice of that coyote "singing in the rain!" I did not like the unshaded windows beyond which lay black, impenetrable gloom! I did not like the discomfort, the strangeness, the silence! I did not like to think that no matter what might be my need, there was no human help within call! I did not like to face the untried future! In fact, for a bad ten minutes I did not like any of it and had there been way of escape...But there was none—yes, there was!—a flour sack of mail picked up en route from town to homestead. Two or three books sent by knowing friends, magazines, newspapers, letters—a fat package of them. After all, I was not wholly cut off!

Clasping the material evidences of friendship and love to my heart, I proceeded to indulge in what women understand as the relief of "a good cry." Then I dried my eyes and began to read, and as I read these messages from here and there, one even from across the sea, my courage returned. After all, this was going to be all right! I was just tired. Blow wind, out there on the flat! I'll give you fields of grain to blow over, in time....

But morning came—morning always comes! There was much to do. I was at length a sure-enough pioneer.

"But what did you get *out* of it, after all? Not money—you are not the money-getting type. What *did* you get out of it?" my loyal but disgusted friends have asked me.

Fortunately for most of us in this world of uncertain and uneven distributions, there are solid values quite apart from money. What did I get out of it? Much, every way—more than I can convey in words. It was an investment of spiritual capital, the interest from which has never ceased to accrue.

Then and there I began to lose a certain helplessness and neshness, to use a graphic word of my old grandmother's, bred of city life and a desk job. Then and there I began to work out the truth of the paradox that *it is possible for one to do what is to be done whether one can do it or not!* In other words, I began to discover within myself, power, strength, ability, which I should never have known existed in me but for the tremendous situations of need which uncovered them to me. Then and there I began the search within myself for that mental and spiritual equipment which I had to have if I were to go through with the Adventure: patience, perseverance, endurance, courage, initiative, humor, uncomplainingness, optimism, dauntlessness, inventiveness.

There was no bakeshop within reach and I must have bread! To have bread, I must have money for flour, yeast, salt, water—for even water had to be hauled and paid for; I must find someone to haul the flour and the water to my door and pay for the service; I must find someone else who would go to the timber, bring logs to me at so much per haul and then find another someone else with time from his own acres who would cut the logs up for my stove; I must know how to build a bread fire; I must learn how to make the bread and, while I was learning, eat with more or less relish my own sorry experiments. No use making a fuss about it—fussing only intensified matters.

On many a winter morning, when I reluctantly turned back the covers, the thermometer beside my bed registered 10°—15°—20° below zero, for I had neither fuel nor stove which would "keep" fire all night. As the dry air shrunk the boards of my walls and made incursions in my poorly built roof, cracks came and the snow drifted in and sometimes lay on my bed covers. There was no one to shake down the stove or turn on the steam! Whether I liked it or not the fire had to be built, the ice in the barrel broken, the bread fished out of the foot of the bed where, securely wrapped up, I had kept it unfrozen with the warmth from my feet. The frozen bacon had to be chopped out for the pan, the frozen eggs (when there were eggs!) had to be cooked in the best way for edibility—and I had to discover that way for myself. I drank my coffee clear because one thing I never did attain was a liking for frozen canned milk.

The winds that whirled across the unbroken miles shook the Cabin till sometimes I stood ready to fly for the open. When I set out to walk to the nearest neighbor's and range cattle bunched between me and my goal, it was my job to find out how to go ahead just the same. If a rattle snake gave me "good hunting!" as I passed by, still it was my job to know what to do and how to do it.

There were long lonely nights and long lonely days—and Sunday, had I permitted, would have been the worst of all. There was mental poise to sustain, inward calm to attain and preserve, fear to be turned away, laughter to be put in the room of tears, cheer to be substituted for gloom, hope to be drummed into line in place of despair. These things had to be done unless one were to be ignominiously beaten and no real woman wants that to happen....

For half a century, life—that is to say the organized, standardized manner of living prescribed by civilization—had not been any too kind to me. I had felt bruised, starved, deprived, cheated, but could not shake loose. But now here I was—free—a homesteader, a pioneer. I could work in my own way, play in my own way, learn the secrets of nature, do without what I could not get, enjoy what I had, read, think, shout, sing, pray, laugh, weep, without let or hindrance. I was independently alone with Nature, had all the absolute necessaries of life—with one exception. Water! The cup of freedom was at my lips, but the cup was dry. For the barrel my mover had filled would soon be empty and I did not know where to get more. And even the bravest, the patientest, the most inventive, cannot do without water....

Cabin O'Wildwinds was planned for a home. The requirements of the law tied one to the land for not less than five years—I hoped to identify myself with that portion of the West for even longer than that. I had therefore specified and paid out my few hard-earned dollars for good building material and good work....

Not all the tradesmen failed me but enough of them did to make my house and poor shelter against wind and cold and dust and heat and rain (when the blessed moisture came). The walls developed cracks, the roof developed leaks, the putty fell out and the poor glass splintered, the "select" flooring was of boards made from trees that had been well roasted in forest fires and very early in the year stripped up into a surface of splinters that made them impossible of perfect cleaning. I paid for good doors—they shrank and cracked until they were splendid ventilators. The little root cellar which was to keep my future garden crop safe for winter consumption, turned out to be a mere hole in the ground—the nicest kind of hidey hole for all the itinerant insects and small animals abroad, and the first consignment of vegetables, a gift from a good neighbor, froze solid. The only undesirable creature that failed to live in my cellar was the one animal which is a symbol of wisdom—the snake....

Nearest to my Cabin, of these neighbors, were the Heathlowes— Dave, his wife Mary, and a family of ten boys and girls—most of them old enough to earn and go away from home save when the heart-tug of their gentle, self-sacrificing mother brought them intermittently back. Dave Heathlowe pursued two callings—the ministry and the farm. He was good at neither. Although hard working, he was also hard-headed, hard-hearted, heavy-handed—a hard husband, father, neighbor. His young stock not infrequently died from harsh treatment and his "gospel" was as punitive as his whip. But Mary—Mary was beloved of the entire community. It was she who gave their huge barn of a house its magic air of comfort and hospitality, though actually it was comfortless in most essentials and there was but little to spare from the pantry for hospitable sharing. And Mary, pitying me in what she felt to be a foolish and certain-to-fail endeavor, took me under her wing. She cast about what she could do to help me "make a go of it" and the only thing she could think of was to set me up in the chicken business.

"Oh, you'll learn!" she assured me when I protested that I did not want animals of any kind about the place and gave her what seemed to me to be good reasons. "If you're going to farm, you've got to do something!"

So, on that memorable day when I moved into the Cabin, Mary was hot on my trail, bringing in her one-hoss hay, a shabby and old but still workable incubator and gift of sixty-six eggs. I threw up unappreciative hands! I had still to learn what it means for a woman placed as she was, broken in health, poor in purse, overworked, without companionship in her man, her older children leaving home as soon as they became sustaining, to select and spare for a gift sixty-six eggs. Oh, how much I had to learn! Of true heroism, unobtrusive self-denial, sheer pluck, genuine manliness and womanliness. Since those days, when I hear delicately sheltered women complaining about this and that and the other, I can feel only pity for them that fate has spared them the grilling processes by which largeness of soul and toleration of mind are developed. Mary with her work-broken nails, her string-mended steel bows, her shabby clothes, her ill-fitting shoes, was a real woman—and surely that is all that a woman needs to be in the final outcome of things.

I installed the unwelcome incubator in my bedroom, right beside the bed, for it needed twenty-four-hour-a-day attendance, it being impossible to depend upon the flame of the smoky lamp. For after all, when you set eggs to hatch, there is an inner feeling of responsibility toward the helpless, developing life—you must do your best by it even though later you slay and eat it. Somewhere I bought enough eggs to make up the one hundred which the machine would accommodate. But what was I going to do with one hundred chickens! I cried—for even I knew that they had to have shelter and intelligent care, water and feed, and I had none of these at hand.

"Oh, you'll learn!" said Mary again. "And there will not be one hundred chicks—you'll be lucky if you get a fifty-per cent hatch—the machine is old and you're new. But fifty chickens will give you some food and eggs."

I could not contemplate even fifty with any serenity. However, I studied the tattered book of directions and a stray Government Bulletin on how to mother motherless chicks. And as the days went by I became genuinely interested in the game....

So, while the rain came down during the first week of testing, I created my home and, on paper, laid out my first garden. I already had an enormous package of seeds which I had ordered late in the winter. I'd *show* these scoffers who wondered what "that there old woman thought she was a-doin' on a homestead!"

But despite all my resolutions to the contrary that week and many weeks that followed, tested my courage to the bottom. For one thing there was the gumbo. No one had told me mine was gumbo land and if they had I should have been none the wiser. Very soon my new floors—and my very new thoughts—were "sicklied o'er" with the sticky grey "cast" of gumbo. Both cat and dog showed their hatred of it—I had to soak their poor paws in warm water—and I could illy spare water for such purposes—to relieve them of the misery of the adhesive mass that daily got between their toes. For the first time in my life I was completely out of touch with humanity and for day following day could not discover on the distant road even a passing horseman. The stillness punctured only by the steady drip of the rain—I was not yet wise enough to be thanking God for that fall of moisture, the howl of the wind and the night song of the coyotes, stretched on my nerves to the twanging point. And I said to myself, "If I feel like this now, what is going to happen to me in the five years ahead?" And once again I would whisper to my humiliation: "Oh, fool! fool! fool!"....

My faithful water boy, Hedrick, from a nearby homestead, at last had to give up the task of keeping my barrel filled—they had found something else for him to do in his spare time at home. I hoped in time to be able to toss the dice of chance for a well but was not yet in position to take so great a risk. They had a good well at Dave Heathlowe's and I thought that at least one of their two younger sons could be spared to haul water for me once in a week or perhaps two weeks. Mary Heathlowe had the same idea and before I had said a word about the matter suggested it to me—she was ready to take the whole world under her wing and she certainly did want me to make good. "Pa may object,"

When Ada Melville Shaw first moved to her homestead, she relied on Hedrick the neighbor boy to fetch water. ILLUSTRATION BY IRVIN "SHORTY" SHOPE. REPRODUCED COURTESY OF THE SHOPE FAMILY.

she said; "he gets fussy sometimes but if he does, I'll fix it up. The boys like you and—you don't need to pay a cent. We can afford to do that much for a neighbor!"

However, I knew something about Dave Heathlowe's disposition and insisted that I would pay....

The Sunday following Mary's suggestion about water, I was able to attend service. It was a hot day and the little wooden box, filled with the odor of bodies more or less unwashed and of breath from lungs more or less unclean, and resounding to the harsh shouts of the preacher was not an inviting proposition. But one learns to bear and bear and "Be a villain still!"

After the service, which the preacher always drew out as lengthily as possible, having borne so far, I summoned all the latent grace in me and extended my hand to Dave Heathlowe to express as best I might some decent appreciation of his strenuous endeavors to set our feet in the right path. He eyed me coldly from his gaunt height and spoke first, loudly enough so that all in the room could hear.

"I understand you want us to haul water for you. Well, we can't do that. My boys' time belongs to me until they are of age. You'll have to look out for yourself. We had to when we came. You should have thought about these things before you came."...

My next and only known recourse—unless a second "raven" like unto Hedrick appeared—was a man whom I shall call A.Q., who owned the homestead next to mine. Thus far he had been something of a myth. His quarter section on which he had filed "sight unseen," had turned out to be absolutely no good except for rough pasture and not very good for that. He earned his sour-dough bread and flapjacks by cutting and hauling logs for the homesteaders from the distant timber, and spent a minority of his time on his claim. He kept some stock on the place and had a good well with a windmill and a trough. His tiny, one-roomed house of unhewn stone, so low and gray that it fairly melted into the general landscape, was only a mile from my cabin but the way was so rough that, between lame feet and fear of loose cattle, the distance was practically prohibitive...Up to this time I never had seen the man, but someone told me he was a "right decent little bachelor."...

He was slow of speech but at last the argument began.

"Well—I ain't here always, you know. I've took up two claims—this here one and a desert claim away out yonder. When I ain't haulin' I'm liable to be at the other place. Couldn't Heathlowe's kids help you out? There's enough of them."...

"Heathlowe intimated that women alone like myself had no business on the plains, but I'm here and here I mean to stick and prove up—I have a RIGHT to. I may need a bit of help but—others may need my help some time. If they do, I'll give it if I can—up to the handle. If I had a well and horses and you needed water...and of course I expect to pay anything within reason."

"We—ll...." He was now chewing his braided straws. I felt encouraged. "Matter of fact when I'm right busy you couldn't pay me what'd pay me. See what I mean? How would seventy-five cents a barrel be? Time is all the money I've got. I can't promise to be regular nor often, but I'll do the best I can once I start in—that's my way. You hang a rag of some kind over your hitching post when you need me and when I'm home to see it I'll come over with a barrel full."

I walked back to Cabin O'Wildwinds almost on air—the wind blew so fiercely. The water problem taken care of was one long step toward success. I even forgot to watch for horned brutes. At once on reaching the house I got from my trunk a length of turkey red cotton which I happened to have and with a building slat, rigged up a signal flag and when the water in the barrel was more than two-thirds gone, tied it to the hitching post so that it hung high and flapped for my neighbor to see. Sometimes he happened to be at home and within a few hours his good horses with the stoneboat would be at the door. Sometimes it hung several days. Once it was out for two whole weeks with consequent anxiety and much inconvenience....

I had filed on my quarter section under the description of hay-claim and could have satisfied the Government without further attempt at cultivation by proof that I had cropped the hay. But my ambition ran tall. I was filled and thrilled with the thought of soil redemption—the taming of the wilderness so that it should produce grain and support human life. So I meant, in addition to cropping the blue stem that covered my flat land, to see what could be done to cultivate the rough greasewood-and-cactus-covered rises, on one of which little Cabin O'Wildwinds was built.

While these first months of being fitted into the new life were moving by, my grass was growing splendidly for there had been an unusual snowfall and some good early rains. A civil engineer who had been on the plains for many years and understood soils and their cultivation down to the last syllable, told me—sketchily—as mere men so often give information to mere women—that my greasewood "r¹ were "a proposition" agriculturally considered.

"Of course," he drawled, "cultivation can do something for this gumbo but it will take time. If you have money to spare to hire labor it will not do any harm to experiment."

Experiment! I meant to have a vegetable garden, flowers, and, as a beginning, ten acres of oats. That was settled. I had bought seeds in the very earliest day of spring—I laugh now as I think of that ambitious, careful list which I mailed with a hard-to-spare check to a good florist in the state. And before the frost was out of the ground I had prevailed on A.Q., the only available man with horses and machinery, to promise to break an acre of ground for my garden near the house and ten acres for the oats. He shook his blond head and smiled. "Well, it's your funeral!" I thought he was a pessimist. I knew a little something about gardening and I mean to know more.

I had been reading everything I could find about the breaking up and cultivation of new ground and had my campaign all mapped out! Oats, that first year, ten acres of them; then winter wheat on that ten acres and an additional ten in oats; then alfalfa to follow the wheat, wheat to follow the oats, and ten more acres for oats—wheat—alfalfa. So before my homesteading term—which was five years when I filed, but was changed to three later on—was over, I would have a permanent stand of thirty acres of alfalfa and if I had two crops a year, that would be a big help. The father of a distant neighbor was an alfalfa enthusiast and I had learned even to make alfalfa tea—a brew that was supposed to be full of nourishment and vitality-essence; the word vitamin was not on the map then.

Very big I felt with all my acquired wisdom.

But I had reckoned without experience and the first snag I struck was A.Q.'s mortal slowness in getting around to break the ten acres—one week he was too busy, another week the ground was too wet, another week he simply was not to be found, and at last it was admittedly too late to do anything that year. But he did get the one acre for garden broken up and perhaps I shall not be too greatly laughed at if I narrate that when he was all ready to turn the first furrow, I begged to have my hands on one of the plow handles and help the shining share cut the first sod on my own land. I can still see A.Q.'s superior, tolerant smile. Oh, but I was proud! All the latent love in me of Nature, of soil, of growing things, surged to the surface. And I was a true patriot and pioneer—helping to develop the beloved country of my adoption.

I had studied Government bulletins about plowing. Ever since I can remember, the sight of a smoothly plowed field ready for the living seed has inspired a wonderful, almost a holy joy in me. So I waited eagerly to see my acre plowed. Ah me! I suppose A.Q. did his best but the rows of overturned sod that should have been even, level, the responsive soil, rippling along like waves, were anything *but!* Every few feet, the plowshare, guided by A.Q.'s inadequate strength would leap clear of the ground refusing to do battle with the tough sod and snags of greasewood. Then again the bright steel would bite deeply and cast up a mound out of all proportion to the rest of the furrows. 'Twas a rough job....

I was slow to convince. I did not propose to be beaten. I had bought a complete outfit of good garden tools, so with new spade, new hoe, new rake, new spud, new trowel, new stakes for string and new string for the new stakes, I set out to have a garden and grow food for the coming winter.

The Great Mother seemed to smile on me: The Rocky Mountains, loomed above the horizon in marvelous peaks and shoulders of shining, snow-crowned beauty; the birds—meadow larks, curlews, tiny song birds whose names I did not know—filled the air with joy; the tonic air was as wine; the enterprise on which I had embarked was thrilling—sacred even....

I struck my shining hoe into the soil. I forbear to write the complete story of my defeat. Enough to say that after three days of futile struggle I staked out a scrap of ground about the size of a kitchen table and by dint of sweat of brow and ache of back, thrashed it into an appearance of smoothness and planted a few hardy seeds—lettuce, radishes, onions. Beside my little porch I buried hopefully some morning-glory and scarlet bean seeds in memory of a vine-covered summerhouse that had been the joy of my early childhood.

Somewhere in my reading a word had caught my imagination and I now comforted myself with it. *Fallow.* When ground that had been ploughed lay fallow, I understood, the fingers of the light and the rain did a work all their own upon stubborn soil until it was rendered friable—willing to support green life. Perhaps it was just as well that A.Q. had not bothered to harrow the acre—it should just lie fallowing for a twelvemonth. Lie fallowing. The words tasted good in my mouth and consoled me as I made out a list of canned stuff to take the place of the lovely things I had meant to garner from the land that autumn for the coming winter.

Day by day and week by week I watched my kitchen-table plot. Not a thing sprouted. There was almost no rain. The sun was scorching hot. The gumbo was unkind. One morning-glory seed sent up a pale leaf which died. I swallowed and then smiled, surveying my grass land. No failure there!...

Of the hundreds of questions asked me by people curious to know the experiences of an elderly city woman "holding down" a homestead all sole alone on the Great Plains, two have been put more frequently than others and always accompanied with a tone of consternation or a note of actual horror: "Did you not get fearfully lonely?" "And weren't you AFRAID?"

[T]o both questions, a big, emphatic yes. But there is more to tell than this mere admission. *How* I lived through the loneliness and *how* I finally conquered fear, are a vital part of these simple annals which contain nothing of mystery, little of romance, no heroics, but a great deal of genuine human struggle....

[T]here came a day when I drained the cup of solitude to its dregs. It was during my first winter in Cabin O'Wildwinds. Following a snowfall that had turned the great expanse of the plains to a blinding unrelieved white, there were ten days of such intense cold that only those ventured out who were forced to go. Faces froze in the dry still air before their owners knew what was happening to them. From my windows all I could see was blazing empty stillness with the silent mountains on the horizon and at night the silent wheel of the pitiless stars. Not a cloud in the sky, not a shadow on the ground, not a sound in the world save the creak and snap of the wee house's timbers. In all that time I was alone with one thing to do—keep warm and alive and as busy as my inventiveness could keep me. I sewed, wrote, read, cleaned a perfectly clean little house, tidied perfectly tidy shelves, broke up a packing case and made myself an extra table, answered all my letters at quite un-necessary length and stamped them ready for mailing only heaven knew when, visited the chickens in their horrid little shed expecting to find them frozen every time I did so, experimented in cooking new dishes out of the same canned goods, and then did everything over again—spending much time peering out of my window until vision went black from the glare.

And the second Sunday—Sundays always seemed more lonely—was the tenth day. I awoke at dawn possessed by a nervous energy that could have accomplished almost anything but there just was nothing to do. Childishly, at noon, the sun still unclouded, the trails still empty, the cold still unbroken, the wind still asleep, I decided to have a party. What I was really doing was trying to keep my nerve, tensed almost to the breaking point. So I got out my best tablecloth and napkin, set the new table I had made with my prettiest possessions, cooked an elaborate creamed vegetable soup which took a long time to make, having to be run through a colander, put on my one party dress, even stuck a velvet rose in my hair, and bidding Lassie and Betsy Bobbett, my perfectly serene and comfortable dog and cat, sit on two chairs near the table, proceeded to dish up. I filled a valuable blue plate with the savory hot soup and on the way from kitchen to table, stumbled, the soup burned my hand, and—with a scream which I never knew was in me, hurled the full plate across the room and running to my bed, burst into convulsive crying. The little scald on my hand was nothing. The explosion was in my mind.

In the midst of the storm I realized perfectly something had to be done—I had to see someone or go somewhere, no matter what the danger of freezing on the way. I would see if possibly A.Q. was at home and either go to him or get him to come to me. Yes, smoke was coming out of the stovepipe, the smoke of a freshly built fire. I took my big dishpan and a huge iron spoon, and standing on my back porch made such a clatter as that peaceful world had never before heard. In a few minutes the little man was out beside his house to see what it was all about, waved an arm to me and I knew he would come over. Presently he did and as I opened the door and his three dogs pushed into the warmth of the house, I grabbed his sleeve and almost crying again, cried, "A.Q.! If you don't come in here and talk to me I shall go crazy! I haven't seen a soul—"

He gave me a keen comprehensive glance and saying, as if to reassure me, "That's—perfectly—all—right!" came in, divested himself of several mufflers and coats and sat down beside the stove, asking no questions until I of myself had confessed to the tale of my nervousness and the broken soup plate. "If you had not been home," I said, but he did not let me complete the sentence, but lifting an admonitory hand assured me once again, "That's—perfectly—all—right! Good gosh! I don't blame you none. If I didn't have my horses and work that takes me into town every so often, I'd be the same. I get goofy sometimes up in the timber—or I would if I didn't have to get the logs out and keep goin'. I don't rightly see how you stand it here—it's no place for a woman alone. Now some of these here girls who stake out claims, they just naturally draw folks—the young fellers see to that. But with an older woman, it's different...Right smart cold, isn't it?" and therewith we began to talk on any and every topic. It never occurred to me to ask my enforced caller if he had had his dinner. We discussed homesteading, homesteaders, politics, religion, crops—the great crop I was going to have the coming autumn. The four dogs and the cat stretched and snored by the fire. The wood fairly melted in the stove. The shadow of the house on the snow steadily shifted. It drew on toward dusk. Then I made coffee and set out a lunch—a mere snack. I rather loathed food just then. As I poured my guest a third cup of coffee, somehow he brought out that this was his first meal that day. He had come in late the night before almost frozen stiff. Had put two stone jugs of boiling water in his bunk and getting "good and warm" had not ventured forth until not long before he heard my rataplan calling him. He had cared for his horses but had not had time to care for himself. "And you've had nothing to eat since some time yesterday?" I cried, ashamed of my selfishness. "Can you stand it a little longer?"

So then I got out the best I had and cooked a real meal and had my reward in seeing the man eat and in my own renewed appetite. The meal over, we renewed our fireside conversation—books, farming, crops for new homesteads—alfalfa, oats, rye, flax, corn, wheat, logging, homesteading in all its aspects, politics, religion. The dogs were let out and let in. The brilliant light of the full moon on the floor made the lamplight look sickly. I began to feel tired. A.Q. began to yawn. The animals were dead in sleep. Then—"I wonder what time does it say by that there clock o' yourn? Is it right?" suggested my guest, flushing to the roots of his hair. My Big Ben was on the shelf above my head—I had not glanced at it since cooking the late dinner. I took it down, listened— it was running steadily—held it out to A.Q. He roared with laughter and uttered a smothered "Good Gosh!" It was Monday morning and more. We had talked twelve hours straight and it is safely to be conjectured that in all his sober, conscientious, well-moderated life, little New England A.Q., bachelor, never before had been guilty of visiting the clock around alone with a woman! The humor of the situation overcame us both, and our laughter was good for my nerves. I accompanied my guest outside to see what the thermometer had to say. Forty-six below in the moonlight and still dropping. I speeded the parting guest, who stood to give me a backward glance and say humorously, "I'm thinking it's a might good thing we've got no neighbors. They *might* talk!" and our mutual laughter again rang out in the frozen world.

When I awoke toward noon of the next day, as refreshed as a child from happy sleep, the entire face of the plains was changed. Shadows drifted across the snow, wind and mercury were rising, there were teams and riders on the trails, and before the afternoon was gone, friends at the door. But I told no one of the episode just narrated—it would do no good and would only add to my neighbors' anxiety about me and they had enough of their own.

Very little effect has solitude had upon me since. I learned in those years on the plains how to do without the physical presence of people....

There was one vast unknown I greatly wished to explore but it took some time before I could command myself sufficiently to go forward. After the sun was gone down I found it more than difficult to stay out-of-doors in the darkness. On moonlit nights I sat on my little porch—my back close against the wall of the house—and drank in the wonder of the scene—the distant mountains veiled in snow, stars whose brilliance were not overcome by the moonlight, and the stretching of the level plains, away and away and away to the horizon. But in the dark of the moon, I could not sit out for long, and I simply could not get any distance from the house, even with my flashlight. There "was something about it," as we say for want of a more intelligent phrase, that "got" me. I was familiar with every foot of my quarter section and the adjoining acres were the same as mine. I knew the roads and trails. I knew who lived in the widely-scattered shacks that winked their evening eyes at me; there was no wild life to fear—coyotes are cowards and they were the chiefest of the untamed things that still survived the coming of man. I would watch the sun go down—and the magnificence of those sunsets are beyond any power of mine to describe, would watch gentle night slowly slip into the room of day and know beyond a peradventure that the face of the plains was unchanged save for the venturing forth of small and harmless beasties that would flee before my slightest move. But for all this I could not stay out-of-doors for more than a brief sojourn—and would cravenly seek the comfort and stay of lamplight and enclosing walls.

I knew very well the Great Mother had secrets she could reveal to me if I would watch with her in the night and I determined to know the night fully as well as I knew the day.

I had a solid platform built around my pump, which was in front of the house and perhaps one hundred feet away. I installed on this platform a comfortable chair and a sizeable wooden box. Then when weather—and wind—permitted, I would light my good lantern, take it to the platform, smother its light in the box and seat myself back to the house, face to the mountains. And there I tried to sit. It really was ridiculous. I was indeed a finished product of that artificial life and habit which robs man of the natural equipment with which he comes into the world—the occult sense by which he could feel at home anywhere and at any hour in the presence of Nature.

My self-imposed schooling was at first not easy and all my attention was taken up with the will to stay. But little by little I lengthened my sittings, forcing myself to think on themes more or less connected with my marvelous environment....

In time I formed the habit of being out alone under the sunless sky and little by little the leaves of the great book of nature began to turn before my wondering watch. The vast procession of the constellations with here and there the brilliant—and relatively slow—passage of a meteor on its unguessed way. The whisper of the wind as its wings brushed the earth or its great song as it swept far above on errands to the uttermost ends of the world. The call of some wild creature to its mate. Sleepy chirps of birds hiding in the grass, or nesting in the low greasewood and under the protection of the cactus thorns. Then that marvelous experience of listening to the silence, the inner self calm, new thoughts floating into consciousness from one's deeper depths, perhaps to be recalled by the weird cry of a coyote, distant or not so distant, with the keen realization that this little wild brother also had his right and place in the scheme of things.

'Twas a great experience and turned into my spiritual coffer wealth which worldly standards cannot measure, wealth that has remained with me.

It would soon be spring! I besieged A. Q. while yet the frost was in the ground to promise he would plough and harrow ten acres and seed them to oats. All he would say was, "We—ell—I'll do my best. You can't get anyone else?" He knew I could not. Men who came to the plains to farm in earnest were too busy with their own strenuous proposition to bother with a small job like mine....

Nature and A. Q. combined defeated me again so far as getting in the oats was concerned.... But he had "made out" on two brilliant moonlit nights to put the one acre near the house into pretty good shape and I staked out an eighth of it for my vegetable garden, deciding to let the balance lie fallow—the liquid syllables of that word still held a sort of fascination for me—and next year put it into potatoes. I had seen and eaten some marvelous potatoes grown on the new ground and felt that there would be an easy sale for all I could raise!

In the one-eighth acre I planned to plant peas, beans, cabbage, cauliflower, rutabagas, carrots—oh, just everything! Why not? I had most industriously worked the soil beside the porch of Cabin O'Wildwinds where I would plant the morning glory and scarlet bean, adding a few seeds of wild cucumber, a self-sowing annual that would take care of itself once well started. I pictured the vine-covered shelter I should have from the heat of the sun. Someone had told me that if I would succeed as a gardener I must keep my hoe bright. Bright it was! I worked till every muscle was sore and every joint creaked. I planted my seeds with sweat and tears and occasional drops of blood. Then I invoked the kindness of all the gods of things as they should be and waited.

Slowly there struggled into warped and stunning being, perhaps half a dozen onion spears, half as many lettuce plants, two or three radish tops which fleas promptly destroyed. By the porch side wild cucumber squeezed itself out of its hard gumbo cast and spent such vitality as remained to it in climbing some five feet up a string and then died. And that was all—no, not quite. Over the entire unplanted portion of the acre, following the lines of disk and drag, something green appeared, a lusty weed. When it was a few inches high I examined it and gasped. I was sure it was Russian thistle and there were millions of it. This was too much!

Well I knew what a pest the Russian thistle is for it has made as deadly a record for itself in the peaceful areas of agriculture as ever Tartar hordes left on Russian steppes....I had a hatred all my own for the Russian thistle. I had ridden behind the half-broken bronchoes of the plains when they stood straight up on their hind legs or danced a break-down when the big prickly spheres blew against them. I had watched them bound and roll before the wind on dreary days when the clouds hung low and they were the only moving thing on the landscape. I had seen fences flattened by their mass against which the wind flung its weight. I had crossed coulees filled with them....

And now, on this beloved land of mine, which I had dedicated to fruitfulness, here was the pest! Could I by any possibility hoe out the young plants before they matured? I estimated the work. Surely I could. "It's dogged as does it!" I simply would not let them conquer me. So that very hour I set to work, bent on doing so much every day till the last nasty weed was laid low. Heroic task! And not profitable in dollars. And I needed dollars.

One morning, I was resting a moment on my porch when a cowboy rode in and asked me for water to fill his water bag. I was so tired that I pointed out the barrel to him, begging him help himself and adding, "If you want fresh water, you can get it over there," indicating A. Q's. "Like some fresh, yourself, wouldn't you?" he asked genially and taking my two pails, walked away in the direction of A.Q.'s pump. He was a handsome, likable lad and as I watched him go I envied the good son he could be to a good mother. He came back with full pails and hunting up a cup, brought me the "fresh drink" I so seldom had and seated himself beside me on the porch, frankly curious to know how I was "a-makin' it all sole alone." As hungry for talk as I had been thirsty for water, I found myself telling him some of my troubles and among them this Russian thistle aggravation.

I escorted him to the scene of struggle, he pulled up a handful of the weeds and looked, then threw his head back in a hearty laugh and patted me on the shoulder. "Shucks, lady! You ain't wise! Them thar ain't Rooshin' thistles—I kinda thought they weren't—I've knew folks been fooled before. Them thar is nothin' a-tall but a rotten alk'li weed. It don't hurt none—ploughs out and dies."

He rode easily away and I watched him disappear in the dust of the road—one of the last of the cowboys....

One evening, not long after this, I was out walking and as I passed along A.Q.'s fence and in sight of the little stone hut, there floated, out to me on the still air a new sound. I stood stock-still and Lassie looked inquiringly into my face. Had I heard aright? Plainly it came a second time—that sweetest of music, the voice of a happy little child: Mamma! I stared around. Had the voice come from A. Q.'s hut! There was no other place for it to come from. What had my neighbor been up to? Wondering, I walked nearer. A woman came out of the hut and saw me. Simultaneously we called greetings and she came rushing down to the fence and tore at the wire gate.

"For Heaven's sake!" she cried. "A woman! Come in! Come in! Do you live over there?"

After surface questions and answers, the thin, tired-looking young woman, shouting back to her children to "go on now and get to sleep," began to tell me her story. She and her man and their two kiddies, a boy and girl, aged respectively six and four, had been living meagerly on a small rented farm. Homesteading and land of their own and a chance for the children to grow up with the country looked good to them.

So they sold all they had—and I gathered that was not very much—and had come to Nesterville with one trunk and a team of horses. They had known little or nothing about travel and had come "clear from Ioway," spending more money en route than they could well spare.

Ada Melville Shaw's dog, Lassie, was her companion on her 160-acre homestead in Yellowstone County. ILLUSTRATION BY IRVIN "SHORTY" SHOPE. REPRODUCED COURTESY OF THE SHOPE FAMILY.

They had lunched from the time of leaving the farm on food carried in an old suitcase and arrived in Nesterville almost sick, tired out, hungry, bewildered, with no idea of what to do next. And there in the lobby of the expensive, comfortless, ramshackle "hotel" they "met up" with A.Q. The two men got to talking and my bachelor neighbor understood their plight and came to the rescue....

And so I met Mrs. Simes and her babies.

"Gosh!" she exclaimed, as I turned to go back to my Cabin. "I'll sleep easier tonight knowing there's a woman within reach. Queer he," meaning A. Q.—"said nothing about you being here. He seems to be a shut-mouthed little cuss. But good hearted...

Say, but you've got your nerve to live out here all by yourself. Kind of old, ain't you, to be taking up land? Got a nerve, I'll say! But women are made that way, I guess, if there's something to be done—they do it. Leastways, that's the way I was brought up.

"This country beats all, doesn't it? Cactus and snakes and them coyotes—ain't seen one yet but I heard one all last night—couldn't have been nothing else. And wind! Honest to Gosh, when we was down to the depot if I hadn't have grabbed onto Babe by her clothes I don't know where she'd be now....

It was a week later. We had seen each other almost every day. The children were shy and did not respond to my advances but on this morning they came to the house quite early bringing a note from their mother. The handwriting was good and the spelling perfect. This is what I read:

Dear Neighbor: I hustled out yesterday and shot us a rabbit—a regular daddy one and fat—weighs a lot. So we're going to have lots of fresh meat for dinner and here's the little old girl knows how to cook rabbit. And I'm cooking it on my brand new kitchen range. You'll be surprised. Come on over at noon by your sun clock.

Mrs. Simes

My sun clock was the shadow cast by my hitching post.... I dressed up a little in honor of my hostess and promptly at high noon presented myself at the little stone hut....

Mrs. Simes greeted me with a smile. "Great day!" she called. "We've got a man for company too. Meet the school clerk! He's out scouting for young uns but mine are too little yet. I invited him to stay." The stranger was a quiet man with observant eyes and a good smile. "Ain't this old soul got the nerve," she said to him, "to live in this forsaken country by herself? And you'd ought to see her house! My, but it's fixed up fine and dandy. Turn around." she gently rotated me. "Make you acquainted with my brand new kitchen range—latest model. Now what you got to say? Don't you think I'm smart? Say! I just had to have something to eat besides flapjacks and canned beans so I took his gun and roamed around while the young uns were asleep and shot us a rabbit. And there it is—cooking!"

I stared—and thrilled. With the stones from A. Q.'s building that still lay about the door she had built a body for the fire, with cunningly contrived hole in the front for draft, chinking the cracks with gumbo. From the rubbish piles...she had gathered some discarded five-gallon kerosene cans, rusty but whole, and cutting them open and lapping one piece of the tin on another had covered the top of the stove—this same top having to be removed when fuel had to be added. Wandering far and wide over the plains, she told me, she had found several of these rubbish heaps, and salvaged therefrom, pieces of bailing wire, lengths of rusted and long-abandoned stovepipe, and—a real treasure trove—a huge baking pan that only needed to be scoured to do service. There was a small pile of A. Q.'s coal left from winter. There was a pipe hole in the wall, evidently A. Q. had thought to have a stove in that corner sometime. The pipe from the heating stove went up through the middle of the roof. The fire was burning merrily and on the tin top of the brand new kitchen range the dinner was cooking in three vessels: A. Q.'s overgrown, smoke-blackened coffee pot, a tin pail full of spuds and in the salvaged baking pan the "regular daddy one" was sizzling and browning to a turn. When I had surveyed the miracle, I collapsed wordlessly on the one chair: what had I ever accomplished, what could I ever do that would compare with a feat like this?

"Pretty good range, eh!" said the miracle worker, her eyes dancing at my wonderment. "At that it doesn't smoke any worse than the one I had to cook on back in Ioway. I hit off that front draft pretty good, didn't I? And say, look at my fur!" dangling the rabbit skin before my eyes. "My dad taught me how to get the skins without spoiling them. I'll tan this and have me a dandy fur cap for next winter. And lookit— what do you know about this?" pointing to the spread table. "Butter and jell and bread and cake right from home!"

I did not see how that could be but the happy pioneer explained. "Two of our neighbor boys was coming through here—they're going to locate too—and Ma packed a box for them to bring. They rode out here late last night after you were to bed or we'd have come over. She couldn't send much because they didn't have room—they just brought a big telescope for the two of them—they aim to locate side by side. But anything Ma sent would taste like heaven to me! Now, if you'll hold your raging horses, I'll mash the spuds and make the gravy and then we'll sit up. My, but this is going to be a party!"

It was a party. As real a one as I ever attended. Out of the trunk had come a sheet that covered the table contrived out of a barrel and some boards. There were five plates of five different styles and sizes—A.Q.'s small collection. Those who had knives had no forks and those who had spoons had no knives. "It's rabbit we're getting, not dishes," quoth the light-hearted hostess, "and as Pa used to say, fingers and teeth was made first." There were five receptacles for the clear, fragrant, strong, good coffee: a tin cup, a shaving mug, a cracked jelly glass, a pint mason jar, a small bowl....

Inside of two weeks the Simes family moved on. A. Q. told me "he" had a good job hauling and they had rented a shack on the edge of town. Then I heard they had moved on to a homestead many miles distant and were "getting along fine." And the courage, kindness, initiative, sheer grit of that wife and mother have been as lights to my path ever since.

•

At one time, hearing that a young lawyer in Nesterville was greatly in need of a stenographer who could take ordinary dictation, read her own notes and make a decent transcription of them on the typewriter, half in fun and half in earnest, I applied for the job....

I dared the young business man to take on, at least temporarily, a woman old enough to be his mother. He was a good sport and called my bluff. I applied for and was given permission to vacate the homestead for two or three months, found a place to board and renewed my youth, at the same time putting myself in position to observe closely the mushroom growth of a town where but a short time before cowboy and cattle had ranged the fenceless miles....

Surveying Nesterville one day from an elevation of rimrock I could think of nothing but a litter of child's bright building blocks spilled over the cactus-sage-and-greasewood sod with a crude attempt on the child's part to set the confusion straight. Depot, warehouse, two general stores, post office, seven saloons, meat market, drug store, lumber yard, grain and seed house, real estate "offices," with shacks of various shapes and sizes, some built on the owner's lots, some occupied "free gratis" pending the sale of the lot from under them. Out a short distance from the town were the two tiny competitive churches, and at the upper end of the long street two or three fairly well-built houses and a pretentious school building. Nesterville had all the necessities of life, even to a well....

When my weeks of work for the young lawyer were completed, I returned to Cabin O' Wildwinds reimbursed as to cash, rested, strengthened, resolved to "stick." I dreaded the winter to come but I was ready for it. In the wagon in which I rode out from town was a supply of comestibles that would see me well into the cold months.

I was not so tenderfooted as I had been. The environment had done a good work in me. Imperceptibly but surely under the stern training of the wilderness, my powers of observation grew keen—sight, hearing, smelling, feeling, or "sensing" as we say, all took on new sharpness. It no longer needed deep-cut ruts in the ground to tell me that hoofs or wheels had passed the cabin while I was away or in the night when I was asleep. The tilt of grass blades, a mere brushing of the surface of the soil, a faint disturbance of the dust of the porch, a fallen straw, a thread or horsehair caught in hitching post or porch post, shouted to me the fact of human presence and passing. In that vast ocean of silence where the wind had become a companion-at-large, my ears learned to catch and sift out sounds and scents and interpret them with accuracy. I could detect the slightest fugitive whiff of tobacco brought to me on the breeze, the smoker being far off, and Lassie and I would keep an eager eye on the trail to glimpse the human being although he might not be—very seldom was—headed Wildwinds way. In winter when the snow lay virgin white on the ground, it was most novel entertainment to read the tracks that told how the plains came to life at night—some of them very close to the cabin door explaining why Lassie so often woke me by her excitement to be out and after 'em.

But there were still the newcomers to the plains who had to work out an understanding of these things. Some were at first unfortunate from one cause or another, but having their families with them and having burned their bridges behind them, hung on till the tide turned in their favor. There was a large quota of failures—there could not but be, all things considered—some failing through ignorance and pig-headedness, others who, put them where you would, did not have the elements of success in them for stability was left out of their mental make-up....

One morning while eating breakfast my ears were greeted with an unmistakable sound, one I had not heard except in Nesterville—indeed, a sound I had not heard so very often in my life but often enough to have registered it clearly: the odd muffled sound of a plank dropped directly on other planks.

Planks? I stood up from the table, ears intent. Yes, planks, one after the other. I rushed out-of-doors, looked in every direction, and there to the southeast on the quarter section cornering mine was a lumber wagon and a man unloading the planks. That meant building, building meant builders, people—a new shack perhaps?...

Day by day boards clattered, saws sang, hammers beat out the blessed music of house building, home making, folks coming. And then one night, one dark, dark night following a day of misty rain when I had not been able to make out even with my glass just what was going on around the new house, a light suddenly pierced the gloom—the light of a kerosene lamp.

"How far that little candle throws its beams!" I whispered to myself, a rush of hot glad tears turning the lowly earth star into a burst of rays that glowed like a tiny sun. The newcomer's light had crossed the gulf of isolation for me—the only neighbor light to brighten the darkness since I had come to Cabin O'Wildwinds, save that first light I had seen beneath the rainbow arch and which, strangely, I never had seen again....

It was well there was no one to witness my feelings when I first saw that low-shining beam a mile away behind which an unknown sister woman spread their evening meal and hushed her little ones to rest. The light burned late—I yearned to go over to see if I could help in the settling. The next morning was Sunday. Indeed, Sundays were special days with me—not always red-letter days, it is true. But this was to be a gold-letter day. The sky was still stormy but nothing could have kept me away from the new house. I tried to wait a decent time after I saw the first smoke ascend from the chimney, then I was off.

The Optimist had been prompt and thorough with his fence building and as the road was at the far side of his quarter, no gate as yet connected his fence corner with mine. Their house was near the fence, however, and as I searched for a cactusless depression in the ground on which I might flatten myself out to roll under barbed wire, I heard a child's sweet voice pipe up, "Papa! There's a lady out there—is she coming here?" Then, a little boy of about six came running out shouting eagerly, "My Mamma she says for you to come right on in—she's bathing the baby and can't come to the door!"

Beside her kitchen range I found her, sweet Lizzie, the Optimist's wife, her naked babe laughing on her lap, not a girl wife but a mature woman to whom love and motherhood had come in her maturer years. At once we embraced like long separated friends. The little boy clutched my skirts and bubbled over with glee. The babe kicked and chuckled. The Optimist stood about and beamed upon us, an unfinished cup of coffee in his hand, his hat on his head.

"Take off your things—help her, Papa. Do make yourself at home! Isn't it good to have a neighbor come right at once! You won't mind the mess, will you?—we only got in last night."

Mess? What I saw was a lovely confusion of home-in-the-making: lumber and tools, furniture crated and uncrated, trunks and boxes, a pail of fresh milk, firewood dumped on the new floor, little clothes drying on strings stretched across a corner, the remains of a picnic breakfast on half a table, the other half piled with just unpacked dishes. Not a mess!—the possibility of a home.

"Oh, Papa, take your hat off in the house!" gently chided the mother to her beaming man. "Our neighbor will think we are savages."

"I'll never find it again if I do. Anyway, it looks to me as if this lady would be glad to have even a savage to speak to!"

I sat down beside the stove, the children were given some toys, and the man of the house went off to the barn. Lizzie's tongue and mine kept steady pace with the old Seth Thomas clock perched on top of a barrel until there could be a shelf built for it. And in what seemed to be no time at all it was noon.

"Why, of course, you'll stay to dinner! We can't let you go so soon! Don't know what there is to eat but there'll be something—this place seems like heaven to me after that awful shack down by the tracks."…

Hours later, tongue, and the clock still were keeping pace,…as the clouds had broken away and the level rays of the setting sun came through the unshaded windows I looked about for my hat.

"You're not *going*? But why? Oh, you must stay for supper! I'll stir up some pancakes. Can you drink milk—like it? We have a real good cow. And I have three eggs left from some I bought from a woman we passed on the road—she let me have part of hers she had just got in town."

It was something more than pancakes and milk that was shared with me that evening—angels' food and wine of fellowship, with a bowl of morning's milk and scraps for Lassie. Then we sociably "did" the dishes, strained the milk and set it away for morning cream, the children were put into their night clothes and allowed to tumble about a bit before being tucked up on a pallet in a corner with a quilt hung on chair backs to keep the light from their faces.

Once more I essayed to go—the moon was shining and the way was direct, I had but to follow the fence line from their house to mine.

"Oh, but couldn't you stay all night?" urged Lizzie and I could see she meant it. "Please do!—if you can stand us."

"I expect her bed is more comfortable than we can make her," said the Optimist, tenderly regarding the wife's wistful face.

"Oh, but—" her lips trembled, "I haven't seen a neighbor woman since I left Mother…" That settled it. I'd have slept on a tick stuffed with greasewood after that.…

The mail!—letters from friends, magazines and dailies with news of the "outside" world that seemed so far away and sometimes almost like a dream—how much we counted upon the mail!…I was long miles from the Nesterville postoffice and my trips to the town could be but few and far between. Despite the kindness of neighbors and friends, I sometimes was weeks without mail and when the fat bundle came I was lost to everything else until the last word of the last letter had been read and reread, the papers scanned, and the magazines at least paged over to see what they offered.

At the time of which I am now writing, a young couple, Jed and Jennie Thompkins, nearly three miles west of me, picked up my mail whenever they or "he" went to town and kept it at their house until connections could be made more or less easily.…

"There," said Jennie, selecting one letter from the fat budget in my hand, "that's the one—open that first."

I wondered what there was about it that looked so important to her for I had an extensive correspondence and many of my letters were in "business" envelopes. However, I obeyed, and opening this letter ran my eyes over the typewritten lines, Jennie watching my face. At first, in my hast to read, I did not take in clearly what it was all about and read it a second time.

"What's the matter?" asked my neighbor. "Nothing wrong is there? You got news? I knew it was news!"

"News?" I cried. "I should say it is news—more than news! Why, Jennie! What do you think? I've got—or I can get—a job! A good job on a magazine! Did you ever?" and with trembling voice and an awed heart, I read the letter aloud. It was from the editor of a monthly magazine to which I had sometimes contributed, in a distant city—a member of the staff had been taken ill, they needed help, they had been "keeping tab" on my homestead experiment, they thought my knowledge of editorial work plus my added knowledge of country life would just fit me for the place. If I was free to leave, would I consider the matter?

"But you've not proved up yet," said Jennie. "If you'd do that, you'd have to commute. Four hundred dollars is an awful lot of money to put on top of what you've already spent in fences and the house and all. And you wouldn't want to lose the place now you've stuck it out this long. What'd you have to do? Write stories for the paper? I couldn't do nothing like that! I wanted to be a teacher but I had to stay home and work. I couldn't have married Jed if Pa hadn't married again after Ma died…Think you'll go? You've got a good lot of grass land and this is a right cute little house—you might be able to sell your relinquishment but there's no telling. Would you want to live in the city again? I wouldn't!" She talked along in her gentle monotone while I tried to get the import of the letter clear in my mind. Its message had brought to my inner hearing the always beloved song of the printing press, I could even smell the atmosphere of the composing room—gasoline, printer's ink, the sweaty bodies of the men at the stones,…better that I should ever know the world of agriculture I knew the world of the printing presses.…

In my eight-by-eight kitchen I had a cook stove given to me by a homesteader woman who had thrown up the game.…

Came a three-day blow with the wind running a fifty-mile-an-hour race. In the middle of the third night I heard a twang and snap of wires, a bang and bound and knew that my kitchen chimney was rolling merrily away to the rim of the world. No more cooking for me for a bit! Oh, well, I should manage somehow. I had learned how to put a long-handled skillet of bacon through the door of the heater and hold it over the flame or coals, and how to boil coffee by setting it down inside the stove over a low fire. It was not cold and women with children to provide for sometimes had to do with less convenience than this. I had just fried my breakfast bacon when Lassie gave her company-coming bark. A hasty glance showed me something like a procession coming from the direction of the Optomist's. I got my field glass and what I saw touched me to the quick—the Optimist and Lizzie at either end of a ladder, Lizzie carrying the baby on her free arm and the Optimist loaded down with a burden I could not make out. The little boy was trudging along side with a bright tin pail in one hand and a basket in the other. I went out to meet them. This was a Sunday, too! The betther the day, the betther the deed, said Judy O'Grady.

"We've come to fix up that pipe of yours—we missed it this morning—you know we always keep on eye on your smoke—and knew what had happened. Feed is scarce just now and we don't like to break the horses' day of rest so we just toted the ladder. Now don't say a word—it's lots of fun. A picnic."

Fun and a picnic to tote a heavy ladder a mile over the cactus trail—through two fences—with a baby—with lengths of stovepipe which they "luckily happened to have on hand"—with a roll of wire and tools!

A commonplace incident in an ordinary day—yes, if you like to think of it that way. It was more than that to me.....

Toward evening the wind rose and the storm was wild indeed, the rain coming in gusts, the thunder and lightning seeming to come from all sides at once. I lighted a fire and enjoyed the cosiness of the Cabin. I had brought back some new books with me. There was fuel in the house and food on the shelves and water coming down out of the sky to water the wild grass and the civilized oats....

I looked out the window at the oat field—gasped with dismay: a "bunch" of more-than-half-grown steers was coming down the middle of the oat field—eight or ten big brutes—their horrible hoofs sinking deep into the rain-soaked gumbo. How they had broken in I did not know. That they must be gotten out and that as speedily as possible I did know—they would churn the seeded acres to destruction.

I was a bit city soft. I rebelled. But there was nothing to do but get busy so I bundled up in my storm outfit, took a good club and faced my job.

First, without frightening the slowly moving, watchful, nervous bunch, I had to get to the gate nearly a quarter of a mile away and open it. Then I had to walk back, get quietly behind the brutes and head them for the gate, praying while I heaved one foot after the other out of the clinging gumbo that they would not take it into their several heads to break away in the opposite direction. How I did it I hardly know for they watched me as steadily as I watched them but somehow I kept them moving, quietly edging toward them so as to get them next to the fence at the other end of which was the open gate....

The lightning blazed and the thunder roared, the wind nearly took me off my feet, the clinging, slippery mud was maddening, the rain beat on my face and ran down my neck. Once, the leader of the bunch with lowered head booed in my direction as much as to say, "Who are you anyhow?" and wheeling started to run in the way he should not go where upon I turned my back and walked away from the herd as fast as I could go, hoping they would think they were rid of me and keep on moving gate-ward—which is precisely what they did.

Once for a minute the entire bunch got out of hand and then I ran at them, brandishing my big stick and yelling a cowboy Hi-yi-yi! until they were again bunched by the fence, headed for the gate. Once I caught my feet in a root and fell face down in the mud, one hand striking into a cactus clump as I fell and gathering in a beautiful crop of thorns. A greasewood thorn tore my cheek from ear to chin. I lost my hat. But I kept those children of Satan steadily moving away from the oats until they came to the gate. For some reason they did not like that gate and bunched there, bawling the matter over among themselves while I waited, almost exhausted, to see what they would do. With a sudden snort, as if to say, "Oh, what's the use—let's rid of that critter that's following us!" heads down, tails flying, they plunged through the opening and away into the darkness of the open road.

I got the gate up and then, breathless, leaned my head on a gate post while the rain came down harder than ever. There was still the long walk back to the house which was wholly invisible as I had not lighted a lamp before I left. But I made the trip successfully, guided by ceaseless lightning, got rid of wet clothes, made some tea and called it a day....

First news of the breaking out of war overseas had reached me that summer of 1914 oddly enough. Mary Heathlowe had sent her youngest son, a twelve-year-old, over on horseback with a treat for me—nothing less than a cherry pie made from the last can of fruit she had canned on the home farm before coming to the new homestead. Ted and I were good friends and when the boy came he liked to linger to look over my books and study the maps I kept on the walls—he was "good in geography," his mother told me and more than commonly interested in events of the day.

"Aren't you sorry the President's wife died?" he asked me casually. "We like Wilson at our house."

"Ted!" I exclaimed. "Tell me about it—I haven't heard—"

"You haven't? Oh, then maybe you don't know about the war either?"

"War? No." I turned to the map on the wall where, aided by the Chicago dailies which I received in smaller or greater batches according to how long my mail was held up at a neighbor's, I had kept geographical track of the unrest in central Europe. "Over here—in Serbia?"

"Yes! Over there—everywhere—Germany—Belgium—looks like the whole of Europe was going in—France, all of them....

That very afternoon, urged on by the boy's vague report of what was happening, I walked to Jennie Thompkins' for the accumulated mail....

That night, having read till the print swam before my eyes, for the first time I felt clearly that my residence on the Great Plains could not be a permanent thing. I had been led to Cabin O'Wildwinds by an invisible hand for an inscrutable purpose—to learn lessons I needed to learn—to gain strengths I needed to gain—to "find myself" in a bigger and better way. Now the sway of events was tending to lead me away from the homestead. Several times Lizzie had reiterated her fear that the second winter away from the plains would finally cement my ties to the city but I had reassured her. I had to see the twenty acres of winter wheat mature and I fully meant to complete the required term of residence, proving up to the entire satisfaction of Uncle Sam. I had gone too far, invested too much, struggled with too many problems, overcome too many difficulties, to let everything go now....

Spring again and eagerly as any homing bird, again I turned my face west. Never had the west looked so good to me as then. "Blessings brighten as they take their flight." I had been offered a permanent position with the firm which I had served during two winters and had given tentative promise that if the proving up were satisfactorily concluded I would consider their proposition. But my heart of hearts was with the soil. If the twenty acres of winter wheat did very well indeed, I felt I might be tempted to stay on and with the Optimist's cooperation—for he said he would use more land if he could get it—enlarge the grain acreage. I was between two stools—I was inherently farmer-minded and a nature lover and though, by life-long experience habituated to the city and all her ways, I knew I should always be more deeply happy on the land. Well—we should see.

As never before during that third spring and summer the beauty of the wide plains thrilled me. Having overcome my tenderfoot fears and dreads, with good neighbors within more or less easy reach, my heart was at leisure to revel in the wonders of the unspoiled earth and the always matchless sky. Every hour of every day and night there was something new, something strange, wonderful, amazing, to see—only those with earthbound vision could fail to be enthralled.

It was while the wheat was "jumping" out of the ground that I went through the really thrilling process, at the county seat, of proving up and in due time receiving my patent for my homestead. It was a proud hour for me!...

It was about a week after I had measured the height of the wheat, that Alhambra [a teacher friend] and I were...awakened in the middle of the night by a noise like machine gun firing, at first one sharp shot at a time, a few seconds between each, then a bombardment that was truly unbelievable. I got into bed with my friend but even with my lips against her ear could not make her hear for the roar of the hail on the roof and walls. We got up—lighted candles—I was afraid of the kerosene lamps. My companion was actually ill with fright and we were both shaking as in an ague. I ran to my emergency cabinet and we each took a heroic dose of old-fashioned Jamaica ginger and in a few minutes the fiery draught had brought our blood back to normal circulation. We gathered ourselves together as best we could, waiting and watching—we knew not for what. There was nothing to do—nowhere to go. Now and then a window pane went but the house stood and the roof kept intact. At last the hail ceased as suddenly as it had begun and the first minutes of dead silence were almost as terrifying as the attack had been. I went out on the porch and gathered a big pailful of huge stones, transparent spheres of compactest ice that had been hurled at us from the skies. I thought of Lizzie and her babes and went to the window with a lighted lamp—she was there ahead of me and neither of us moved the lights in our come-help-me-signal—as we might have had to do had the events of the night been more terrible than they really were.

"This is the end of the wheat—the end of every planted thing—heaven help the people!" So we mourned and prayed as we lay down again to wait as best we might for daylight. We were out at dawn and I saw through hot eyes only beaten, bare ground where there had been twenty acres of greenest beauty—fourteen inches high. While I was standing there, my friend in mute sympathy beside me, what should I see but the Optimist's wagon with all of the family, coming our way. What had happened to them to bring them out at that hour? Heartsick I waited. I was afraid to have speech with them. Of course there was the slenderest possibility that their fields had escaped—hail is freakish in its ways. But their pale faces told me the story before they put it into words: "Wiped out—clean. And our best young mare killed. We were so anxious about you two—here alone in this little house—we just had to come over—we'll take you back to breakfast with us."

I had not lost my nerve during any of the storms nor during this dreadful night. I had looked with dry eyes at my denuded wheat field but as these blessed folk came into the house with us, the Optimist and Lizzie and I mingled our tears, not alone for ourselves and each other, but for all who had felt the cruel force of that phenomenal storm, and they were not a few.

I did not say it aloud to these dear neighbors just then but that night and that storm—which was but the fifth of the seven that terrified us that summer—brought me to the final decision to close the Plains chapter. It had been a marvelous chapter to me and the thought of leaving Wildwinds hurt. But it had to be—I could see that now....

The next day I sent off a decisive letter to the city—I would accept the proffered position and leave Wildwinds to the care of the Optimist and his wife, giving him permission to do anything he liked with the land during the next year. Then came the packing up—good-bye words with neighbors and friends with whom I had shared the easy and the hard, the laughable and the tragic—then the last morning with the Optimist's wagon at the door—the last lingering look around at the mountains and the land, the sky, A. Q.'s little hut, the far distant shacks here and there—the key in the door—the sob in the throat—the looking back and back and back—the Cabin out of sight—the shriek of an engine—the train—"Good-bye! Good-bye! God bless you!"—the Adventure of Cabin O'Wildwinds was ended.

Chapter Twelve

A HOMESTEAD NEAR SMOKEY BUTTE: CATHARINE CALK MCCARTY

IN 1915, AT THE LAND OFFICE in Miles City, Montana, thirty-two-year-old Catharine Calk filed a squatter's right on unsurveyed land in Garfield County, close to her brother's homestead. Her brother immediately went to the Missouri River Breaks to get logs for her shack. When he returned, he went to Sumatra for supplies. While he was gone, she was alone—completely alone. It was 8 miles to the nearest post office in Smokey Butte, 20 miles to the nearest town of Jordan on the Big Dry, and 120 miles to the nearest railroad.

This lonely and desolate landscape was far removed from Mount Sterling, Kentucky, where she was born in 1883. As she described in her memoir *Blue Grass and Big Sky,* published in 1983, "Kentucky is an enchanting land with waving blue grass swaying in the early morning breeze, deep shadows cast by shady trees, green hills...."[1] As one of six children, she grew up in a busy household in an 1816 oak log home modeled after an English manor house. She was accustomed to a comfortable lifestyle. They had a cook, for example, "Black Sarah," who lived in a cottage in their yard.

Despite her deep affection for Kentucky, Calk became a committed Montanan for the rest of her long life. "Adventure beckoned," she

This portrait of Catharine Calk, taken on November 18, 1918, was published in Montana newspapers in August 1919, along with Irene Cummings' article from the Opheim Observer. Calk, who filed on her homestead in 1915, proved up on 320 acres in 1920. PHOTO BY JANSRUD. MONTANA HISTORICAL SOCIETY RESEARCH CENTER, PAC 95-34 6.

wrote.[2] She first came to Montana in 1914, but soon after her arrival was involved in a car accident. She did not walk for four months and was on crutches for another eight. An aunt and uncle in Bozeman nursed her back to health, and she went ahead with her plans to homestead. Her memoir details her homesteading years. Her shack was a log house on the side of a hill on the open range, with a dirt floor and dirt roof. But it "seemed a haven" in the summer of 1916 when "the hot winds, parching the land as well as the face, seemed never to end."[3] She encountered wild horses, a band of antelope, grey wolves, and coyotes. She was often entirely on her own, but there were neighbors, including a Mrs. Tuttle, who showed her how to gather mushrooms. Calk spent summers on her homestead to complete the required residence. During the winter she worked "in order to make ends meet." Her aunt Emma Culloden, a widow from Bozeman, stayed with her the second summer and filed on adjoining land. Calk proved up on her 320-acres homestead in 1920.

In the winter of 1916 to 1917, Calk worked as an enrolling clerk at the Montana legislature in Helena. She also acted as secretary to

Catharine Calk with her horse, Tramp, and her dog, Cam-me, at her homestead in Garfield County in 1916. MONTANA HISTORICAL SOCIETY RESEARCH CENTER, PAC 95-34 3.

the Democratic and Republican floor leaders. In her memoir, she wrote about how the senators teased and taunted her because she had to work for a living. "They always said, 'Catharine, why are you always working so hard?' One day Senator Sales came with the same question and I replied to him, 'Why, Senator, I have to work for a living.' He thought this was a joke and repeated it around the Senate and House. Then someone would call to me, 'Catharine, I hear you have to work for a living,' and then laugh. I was very sensitive about it and some of the girls were not very happy either."[4]

During and after World War I, Calk worked for the Red Cross as the executive secretary of the Dawson-Garfield-McCone chapter; she assisted often disabled returning servicemen secure the benefits they were entitled to. She assisted the widows and parents of servicemen who died overseas, as well. Many of the discharged veterans had become transients, and she had to track them down throughout the vast territory of Dawson County.

She also worked as clerk of the State Livestock Sanitary Board, where she met Albert J. McCarty. A homesteader from Ireland and a veteran, he was employed in her office as the county engineer. They married in 1921. Their first child, a daughter, was born a year later, but lived only a few days. In her grief and despair she "plunged into the [m]any affairs of civilian welfare as well as those of veterans."

In 1922, she decided to run for representative to the Montana legislature and was chosen in the November election on the Democratic ticket. As she wrote in her memoir, "That was before the time of woman's lib, and the 'powers that be' in this little political world of Dawson County considered it amusing. I have never considered at any time that I have been turned down because I am a woman. President Harding had taken the country by storm two years before and Republicans were in the saddle in Montana as well as in the Nation. It would seem that a woman who was a Democrat was little threat."[5] She paid little attention to the campaign, being busy with her Red Cross cases, but was elected nonetheless. Calk McCarty was the first woman and only

Democratic legislator to be elected from her county. She was one of four women elected that year, three of them Democrats.[6]

Calk McCarty served two terms in the legislature. She introduced bills concerning minors and disabled persons and funding for schools, particularly county and district schools. A conservative Senate killed all her bills except for one that provided vocational training for persons with disabilities. She gave birth to a daughter, Jerree, in May 1924, but ran for reelection nonetheless. Her aunt offered to move to Helena to help care for her daughter. She was the only woman elected to the nineteenth legislative session. She later wrote, "No one mentioned a lawmaker going to the Legislature with an infant. When I went in the House all the men wanted to know about the baby and would I bring her to the Capitol. As far as I know, I am the only mother who was ever elected to the Montana Legislature with an infant."[7]

In 1928, Calk McCarty campaigned for presidential candidate Alfred E. Smith: "I took Jerree in our Model T Ford and went over the county putting Democratic literature in mailboxes. How my husband stood it, I do not know. Sometimes it would be late when I came home and Jerree would be asleep in the car with her head in my lap."[8] Calk McCarty and her husband continued ranching on her homestead in Garfield County, and in the late 1920s she filed on an additional stock-raising entry—she needed pasture to run some cattle. In 1932, she had to ask for an extension of time for final proof "on account of drought conditions, as my brother Jas. C. Calk, and myself had to move all our stock from this ranch in Garfield County, Montana, over 150 miles, east of Glendive, Montana, and winter them; that in addition, affiant brought her brother's family consisting of wife and four children, and supported said family as they had no funds on account of drought, and that it is now necessary to continue to help them."[9]

Only a few of the details of Calk McCarty's busy and distinguished career of family, community, and public service can be given here. She was an employment officer with the Dawson County Selective Service Board in World War II. She operated a volunteer school for foreign citi-

Cowboys in front of Catharine Calk's homestead shack, circa 1916. MONTANA HIS-
TORICAL SOCIETY RESEARCH CENTER, PAC 95-34 4.

zens, and was a state Democratic committeewoman. She was instru-
mental in organizing the Democratic Women's Club in eastern Montana, and she managed Mike Mansfield's eastern Montana campaign.
She was Montana Businesswoman of the Year in 1956. In her memoir,
she devoted a chapter to her interest in Native Americans, noting that
the Assiniboine, Lakota, and Crow tribes were located close to Glendive
and that through her Red Cross work she got to know many of them.
Many were veterans. She wrote, "These Indians often confided their
family troubles in me and I was always ashamed of their poverty. We
had actually taken their land from what was once a proud people."[10]
Her memoirs end in the 1930s, yet she continued on in Glendive for
another four decades or so. She moved to Phoenix when she was approximately ninety years old, and died there at age 107.[11]

McCarty's excerpt has been condensed from two sources. The "Story
of a Montana Girl Homsteader and the Fine Farm She Developed," by
Irene M. Cumming first appeared in the April 22, 1919, *Opheim Observer*
and ran in other Montana newspapers. Also included here is Chapter
Five about Christmas in 1916 from McCarty's memoir, *Blue Grass and Big
Sky,* published in 1983 by the Stockmore House in Phoenix, Arizona.

STORY OF A MONTANA GIRL HOMESTEADER
AND THE FINE FARM SHE HAS DEVELOPED
Irene M. Cumming

Opheim Observer, *April 22, 1919*

Away back in colonial days, a Montana girl's great-great-grandfather accompanied the famous Daniel Boone into a country that at that time was truly "No Man's Land," but today is known as the state of Kentucky. It was the middle ground between the northern and southern Indian tribes where they met for battle and sort of free-for-all hunting preserve.

The young woman who is here pictured is Miss Catharine Calk. Her great-great-grandfather was William Calk, who left his Virginia home one day in 1775 and, braving the dangers of the mountains, Indians and elements, journeyed with Daniel Boone into the Blue Grass region. They built the first log cabin in the state. With its sod roof and dirt floor, the cabin seemed a mansion to these men who had been shelterless for many months.

The story of the pioneer life of William Calk so impressed his great-great-granddaughter that she vowed that when she grew up she, too, would travel to a sparsely settled country, build with her own hands a duplicate log cabin and help settle a new country as her famous ancestor had done. Her family laughed at Catharine's childish dreams and she was reared in the beautiful home in Mount Sterling, Kentucky, that had been the home of four generations of "Calks," built by William Calk in 1778.

Catharine was taught all the arts of home-making and it was hoped that the wild ideas of pioneer life would be forgotten by the time she had finished school; but one day after she had graduated, Catharine announced that she was going "out west" in quest of a bit of land of her own and as a side-issue planned to teach school.

CAME TO MONTANA

She reached Montana seven years ago; but her reception was not as she had planned it. Shortly after her arrival, she was hurt in an automobile accident and for a year was practically invalid. During this time and while still on crutches, she taught herself shorthand and typing and was able after her partial recovery to take a position in a business office in Bozeman. Undaunted, however, by ill health, she still persisted in her plan to establish a home of her own and later filed on land in Garfield county near Smokey Butte. Here she built the cabin of her dreams—one hundred and twenty five miles from a railway. With her own hands she made the sod roof and smoothed the dirt floor. The house is a duplicate of grandfather Calk's.

Miss Calk lived on the land every summer and went to Helena in the winter where she was employed at the state capitol. In this way she financed herself. At the conclusion of her fifth year in the state, she "proved up" on her land and secured her final papers. Today she owns 320 acres of improved land valued at $6,000. Miss Calk last year was clerk of the Live Stock Sanitary Board at the state capitol.

ACTIVE IN RED CROSS WORK

She was a fervent relief worker in the state throughout the war and it was a bitter disappointment that she could not serve the Red Cross overseas. However, the opportunity came to serve, when the Red Cross activities of the Dawson county chapter could no longer be handled solely by volunteers. The executive committee of the chapter looked about for some one who would be competent to supervise the detail work at the country Red Cross headquarters in Glendive. Miss Calk was chosen and is now the executive secretary of the chapter.

Twelve hundred men, the majority of whom are homesteaders, ranchers, and cowboys, entered the service at the beginning of the war from this sparsely settled territory that covers so vast an area. Miss Calk has kept in touch with most of the families of the men in her district during the war. Many live 100 to 150 miles from a railroad and in numerous instances it has taken two months for mail to reach them from Glendive; but this energetic young woman considers herself a Montana product, so she is familiar with the conditions that exist in these rural communities, the difficulties encountered and how to meet them.

Through the services of the home service section of the Red Cross, extended by Miss Calk, scores of families whose men were overseas have secured their government allotments regularly. Now the men are returning home and as they learn of the splendid services rendered their families during their absence, they naturally turn to Miss Calk when it is necessary to have their affairs straightened out. Last month, the home service section of the Dawson-Garfield-McCone county chapter made out applications for arrears in pay, bonuses, travel pay, legal papers of many descriptions and requests for the conversion of government insurance for nearly 300 men. It also rendered service to many families living in the district and gave information to scores of returned men who visited the office.

Miss Calk is known as the most popular girl among the cowboys in eastern Montana.

A HARROWING EXPERIENCE

Last winter, while hunting rabbits, she became lost in the impenetrable, or nearly so, forest of Canyon creek. Fighting her way through the forest, she encountered driftwood, and logs thrown out at floodtide by the creek. They had lodged in the timber and made barricades ten to fifteen feet high. There was no way to get around them, so she climbed trees and went "over the top" only to run into a series of heaps of driftwood. It was nearly dark when she found a stream with ice-fringed banks. She decided to wade. In mid-stream she floundered into a hole nearly shoulder deep from which she extricated herself after a plucky fight. From time to time she fired her rifle and called for help; but aside from the hoot of owls or the howl of a distant coyote, there was no answer. When she had about given up hope, she discovered from a tree she had climbed, the dim outline of a clearing and not far away the flash of a light from a ranch house. Arriving at the house she was given a change of clothing and was apparently none the worse for her exposure.

Do you not think that Miss Calk's childhood dreams have come true? She has her log cabin with its sod roof and floor. She is serving humanity and has encountered many of the dangers met by her great-great-grandfather; so the thrills of the pioneer day tales have become a reality.

BLUE GRASS AND BIG SKY
Chapter Five
Catharine Calk McCarty

Homestead days in eastern Montana were at times days of loneliness, sometimes of adversity, but always of adventure.

I well remember December, 1916. My homestead, 20 miles west of Jordan, was 120 miles from the railroad. The Montana Legislature was meeting in January, and I was looking forward to a job in that body, as homesteaders always needed money.

A cold winter had been predicted by Indians and old-timers; a heavy coat of fur covered the cattle and horses. Early that fall jackrabbits had turned snow white. Nature had prepared them for the winter ahead.

We had no car; all my travel was by horseback and it would be diffi-cult to get to the railroad that way. It was late in December and no way had come for me to travel, so when a distant neighbor came in a farm wagon on his way to Jordan, I pleaded with him to take me along.

For days the weather had been near zero or below; so in a heavy coat and wrapped in blankets I made the 20 miles to town with him without incident. The snow had not drifted enough for the road to be impassable. When we pulled into Jordan, I had made the first 20 miles to civilization; I felt encouraged.

There, Dr. Baker, the only physician in that country, offered to take me to Miles City, 100 miles south, in his Model T Ford. We started out December 22. A blizzard was brewing out of the northwest and snow was coming down in gusts of wind. Everyone shook his head. We would never make it, they said.

And we didn't. About four miles out of Jordan, the snow drifts were deep. Dr. Baker realized the Ford would go no farther. We dug out and with difficulty made it back to Jordan.

Was I crestfallen! I was stranded in Jordan, unable to get back to my homestead where my brother was, and without enough money to stay indefinitely in Jordan.

When I went into the hotel, a man called to me, "Mr. Butz, a cattleman who trailed his cattle south of Miles City for winter feeding, has come for his family. He can't get out by car, and he is at the stable putting a sheep wagon on runners. I hear he is taking passengers to Miles City for $6. Why don't you try him?"

I ran all the way to the stable where Butz was busy at work.

"Oh, Mr. Butz, take me with you," I cried.

"I'm sorry," he said, "but I have all the passengers the wagon will hold."

"Please get me in, some way," I pleaded.

He looked me over, and then said, "You don't weigh much. Maybe I can sandwich you in between the men. But don't take much baggage!"

My spirits soared! I would get to the railroad after all.

In sub-zero temperature, with wind-driven snow cutting our faces, we left Jordan December 24. In addition to Mr. and Mrs. Butz and their two little girls, there were a Miles City lumberman and his mother, a homesteader, a "grass" widow, a Scottish sheepman named Alex Cameron, and myself.

When we started from the hotel, Cameron wore a long sheepskin coat and carried a beautiful fur coat. He immediately insisted that I wear the fur coat over my other clothing. It later proved a lifesaver.

The sheep wagon box, covered with canvas, had boards on the sides where the passengers sat; in the back were chairs where Mrs. Butz and the girls were. A little camp stove to warm the wagon had a supply of coal and wood around it. Four young horses pulled the improvised sleigh. The wind increased, piling up snow drifts which made travel difficult. When dark came, it was bitter cold, but we made the little post office, Cohagen, about 20 miles south of Jordan. Here were two stores, some frame houses and a rooming house or inn. Butz found everything full, occupied by homesteaders who had come in from distances around, all hoping to get to Miles City for Christmas. They were all stranded, unable to get back home, or go on.

There literally was no room for us at the inn. The kind storekeeper let us stay in his store for the night. How or what we ate I do not remember. It was a sad Christmas Eve; a man was dying in the back room; a girl was sobbing by the pot-bellied stove. It was to have been her wedding night. Others sat around sad and forlorn.

The wind howled outside, shaking the building every time a door opened, the cold air made us shiver and hug the stove closer. We were thankful to be inside. That night I slept, wrapped in the fur coat, on the store counter.

Christmas day came early, and with it wind, snow, and the eternal cold. The men talked of 40 below zero. After a good breakfast, Butz had talked the storekeeper out of a piece of meat, two cans of tomatoes, some macaroni to make soup as we traveled and some wood and coal. When the soup was ready for the tomatoes, Mrs. Butz asked me to finish it up, as I was nearest the stove. Unfortunately, I added the macaroni too early; it went to the bottom of the iron kettle and burned. But our Christmas dinner of burned soup was hot and we ate it with relish, and there were no comments from the other passengers.

The blizzard grew worse; it was dark in midday, and often one of the men went ahead with a lantern. The lantern's rays could hardly be seen in the flying snow. The poor horses floundered in deep drifts, where the wagon tilted, and often we expected it to upset. When this happened, I had to choose between being thrown on the hot stove or catapulted under the horses' hind legs.

Christmas day came to an end at the "Halfway House," a stop for freighters on the 100-mile trip between Miles City and Jordan. Seen ahead in the dark, it was a small three-room unfinished frame house. The little room we entered had the usual pot-bellied stove, a welcome sight for weary travelers.

The people got us something to eat—not a Christmas dinner, but it was hot. The men, they said would have to sit in chairs, but they had beds for the women and children. We were ushered into an unfinished room, with no stove, filled with frozen clothes festooned across the room on ropes. There were two mattresses on the floor. The lumberman's mother and I crawled in, piling our coats on top. There was no thought of removing clothes.

The cold came through everything. We started to chill; we shook. Sleep was impossible. I remembered Dr. Baker's parting gift, a half pint of Kentucky Bourbon. "For emergencies," he said. I reached for my bag, took out the flask and offered my companion a drink.

She took a "swig," then I took one. It warmed us, so we dozed off, only to awaken shivering again. We took another, dozed off, and another. Again the cold came through.

The flask was empty. Morning would never come. About 4 o'clock we got up and joined the men around the stove, turning one side, then the other to be thawed out. Finally, after some breakfast, we were off again before daylight.

The bitter cold continued; the wind with fine snow hurled itself around the improvised sleigh with increased fury. At the "Halfway House" they had had no fuel to spare; we prayed that the little we had would hold out to our next stop, the "Stone Shack," about 20 miles from our destination.

This day proved the most difficult and coldest of our journey. The poor horses were hard hit and traveled with difficulty. Many times they were belly deep in drifts and had to be dug out by the men.

Night came suddenly that December 26th, and with it all our fuel had gone. In minutes the wagon became an icebox. The cold air cut our lungs like fire. Outside there was no sign of habitation, living thing, fence or tree; just a vast expanse of shifting snow and desolation. We were alone in a cold world.

One of the girls became ill, adding to our uneasiness. I took her in my lap and wrapped the fur coat around her, as it was large enough for us both. Mrs. Butz held the other girl, wrapped in a blanket. We were all shivering, and our jaws were chattering so we could hardly talk. Butz, who had been walking ahead of the horses for some time, came to the wagon and climbed in. In a frustrated voice, he sadly said, "Folks, we're lost. We are off the road. I don't know what to do except turn the horses loose. Maybe they will take us someplace."

For a time no one spoke; finally Mrs. Butz said sadly, "You know what that means. If we do not get someplace, all of us will not be here when morning comes."

I hugged the little girl closer and said a silent prayer. The widow sobbed. Everyone was silent in the wagon. Soon, however, Cameron and the lumberman began to talk of unimportant things and the tension lessened. The faithful horses went on and on. About midnight, they stopped suddenly.

Butz jumped out. He came back, shouting joyfully, "We're up against a shed. I do believe it is the "Stone Shack." He looked around and found a low-built house and asked Mrs. Butz to come with him to see if anyone could be raised. We could hear them pounding on the door; finally a light came on, a door opened, and they went in.

We waited to hear from them. They did not return, and as we were getting colder by the minute, if that were possible, I asked Cameron if he would carry the child in. I went ahead, stumbling up some steps, and opened the door.

A strange sight we found. Mrs. Butz sat in a chair, tears streaming down her face. Her husband stood behind her bewildered. At a door leading to another room stood a fat man; dominating the scene was a little man, with bulging eyes and snow white hair seemingly standing on end. He was waving his arms and shouting "Crazy people! Crazy people! Who wants to have crazy people in their homes?"

When he saw the child in Cameron's arms, he jumped up and down, waved his arms with renewed energy. "And children, too. Where's the sheriff in this country? These people should all be arrested. Nobody but crazy people would be out on a night like this. Crazy, all crazy!"

There was a cot in the room and I went to it, Cameron following, and I said, "You can lay her down here."

With that, the little man ran over, saying "You can't put anyone there. That's a workingman's bed. Not for crazy people."

Although I was the youngest adult of the group, that really aroused my Kentucky temper. I raved back at him in no uncertain terms, ending with, "You don't belong to this country; no one who lives here would act like you are doing." Turning to the fat man, I asked, "Who is this man, anyway?"

Meekly he answered, "He's my brother who came out from Indiana to spend Christmas with me."

With that Butz went out for the others in the wagon and our shivering party took possession. When Butz came in after caring for the horses, he said, "It's 54 below zero, folks, by the thermometer out there." We believed him.

We gathered around the stove. Could we ever get thawed out, we wondered? Finally Mrs. Butz asked the fat man, who proved to be a roundup cook for a large cattle outfit, if he could get us something to eat.

Very reluctantly he went into a kitchen and soon we were ushered into a bare room, with table, chairs, and a cupboard in the corner. He brought out some watery coffee, dry bread and a pork roast, solid fat except a thin showing of lean. It was not even browned. I have never seen fat pork since without feeling my stomach turn.

Finally I asked him if he didn't have something else to eat. He went to the cupboard and brought forth a dark mass on a platter; it had a thick white covering glistening in the lamplight.

I exclaimed, "Oh, a Christmas cake."

Disgustedly he looked at me and muttered, "Head cheese."

It struck me so funny that I began laughing. The men joined me and we almost had hysteria. Mrs. Butz kept asking us to stop. "They'll throw us out," she exclaimed.

We slept in a bed that night, in a room with a stove, and the men kept the fire roaring all night. In the morning, the cook softened his heart and gave us a good breakfast—sourdough pancakes, butter, syrup, bacon and good coffee. It was 43 below zero when we pulled out of the Stone Shack; the little man from Indiana still thinking we were crazy and a case for the sheriff.

As we traveled that morning, the wind went down; the snow

stopped. The horses had an easier time. In the afternoon the sun came out. About 4 o'clock we crossed the bridge over the Yellowstone River into Miles City, with its welcome homes belching smoke straight to the heavens. What an inspiring sight!

At last we could get our clothes off, get a bath and a good meal. At the Olive Hotel where I registered, the clerk, would not believe it possible that people could live in a covered, improvised sleigh through the worst blizzard he had ever seen.

I had a date for dinner with Cameron and the lumberman and his wife. I took a bath, thought I had a half an hour to dress, so fell into bed just for a nap. The next thing I knew, there was a terrific pounding at the door. I could hardly realize where I was; it was like coming back from a far away country.

My friends had been back time and time again for me, the clerk saying that I was not in my room when he rang. Finally they demanded an investigation. It was nearly midnight. I joined them in a few minutes and we ate the best belated Christmas dinner I can remember.

It was a hilarious occasion. We had reached civilization safely; trains were going through; I would get to Helena in time; life was full of hope.

Chapter Thirteen

LIFE IN THE BADLANDS:
PEARL DANNIEL

THE LAST WORD BELONGS TO Pearl Danniel—of the women featured in this book, she was the last to homestead.[1] Although she filed
on her own homestead on Black Spring Coulee in the late 1920s, this
was not her first experience with homesteading. She and her first husband, Clarence Unglesbee—both from Illinois—and their two daughters homesteaded in the "Big Dry" of eastern Montana beginning in
1918. They chose the badlands, a harsh and unforgiving environment,
and the family, which included Pearl's disabled brother, suffered severe
hardships. The marriage broke up, and Clarence left for Wisconsin.
They had just reconciled when he died of a heart attack in the late
1920s. Pearl transferred ownership of the homestead to her daughters
and filed on her own homestead in the same vicinity. She did not remain single for long. In 1929, she married Perry Scott Danniel, one
of a "new breed" of homesteaders who lived off the wild horses of the
badlands.

In the early 1930s, Pearl discovered that she could write, and it
became her passion. Her first article, called "Hunting Wild Horses for
Food in the Bad Lands of Montana," was sent as a letter to a friend who
submitted it to the *St. Louis Post-Dispatch*. It graphically described the

Pearl Danniel stands at the door of the homestead cabin she returned to after her husband Clarence Unglesbee died in Wisconsin in 1927. Among the handwritten notations Pearl made on the back of this photograph was this observation: "Our little home where the Crickets used to make me feel that it was always summer. They sang in the walls all winter." MONTANA HISTORICAL SOCIETY RESEARCH CENTER, PAC 95-7 1.

harsh life of the Depression in Montana." She wrote: "This is a hard, hard land, any time, desert-like in this particular locality, most years. Though lavish are nature's gifts when it rains, as it does some years, just like it does everything, by extremes. It is almost always too hot or too cold, too wet or too dry, and life is like that here also, gray, lonely, chilling...It is now four years this summer since we raised any crops. Only a few people live here."

Pearl Danniel's land was flooded by the Fort Peck Dam. She was supposed to be paid for her land at market value, which was very little following years of drought and depression, but she initially refused to sign a statement saying she had received fair market value. She signed "under protest" in 1939 and was left with only the badlands portion of her land. Fort Peck Dam flooded the bottomland, the only farmable land in the Rock Creek area. Pearl's husband left, and she tried a variety of ways to earn money including cooking for construction crews and home care for an invalid.

During the 1950s and 1960s, she had a regular column in the *Glasgow Courier* and the *Circle Banner* called the "Rock Creek–Bonin News." She wrote a great deal, completing one novel and 300 pages of a history of the world in rhyme, much of which was never published. She continued to live year-round on her homestead until her last years, when she moved to Miles City to live with her daughter Nell McCartney. She died in 1975 at age ninety. Her cabin was vandalized just before her death and her papers were strewn all over the floor. Montana Historical Society Research Center archivist Ellie Arguimbau did a tremendous job of fitting the pieces together, publishing a fascinating article on which this introduction is based.

MISSOURI WOMAN'S FIGHT FOR
EXISTENCE ON THE MONTANA PLAIN
Pearl Danniel

St. Louis Post-Dispatch, *March 27, 1932*

Bonin, Montana. This is a land of phantoms. A land of broken dreams.
A hard, hard, land. Tumbledown, windowless houses, ruins of old stone
walls, farm machinery rusting away, weed-grown plow land, once-
loved gardens with rhubarb stalks dry and dead, a rosebush now and
then, iris, death-defying, in lonely clumps... A specter walks here, so
fearful, so grewsome, that mayhap this shall never again be other than
a land of phantoms. It is the specter of starvation. Save for the wild
horses that roam the range we would be in his clutches now.

This year even the wild horses may perish, so short is the grass.
Out among the bleak buttes of the badlands, men ride. They sight a
bunch of wild horses, leave their own mounts tied to sage brush or with
dropped reins if they will stand, creep to the crest of a hill, get near
enough to pick out a "slick." The gun roars. Flying hoofs. The herd
scrambling away in panic. But one has fallen. A slash across the throat
and the ground is dyed red.

That night the coyotes will walk all round, circling nearer, at last to
feast on the waste left by human failures.

Just when the World War drew near they came here, a flood of emigrants. Pilgrims, the cowboys called them. Home builders, freighting their
household goods, their poultry, pigs and cows, settling here, 40 miles
from the railroad, to build homes, churches, schools, roads, communities,
civilization. My husband and I among them. Missouri farmers, getting
nowhere after years of toil, making a new start, filled with high hopes....

Nearby was a shack owned by a single man who had gone to war.
We lived in that while building our house. A neighbor loaned us a
stove, the kind known as a laundry stove, with an oven around the
pipe. Another neighbor gave us a table and Daddy [her husband]
made us chairs out of some old boards.

With my bedding and the dishes from the old home we were fairly well equipped. We slept in a "wall" bed on borrowed springs. The bed hung from the wall under a wide shelf in daytime and was let down at night. Bert's [her brother's] bed had to be made under the table, the cabin was so small.

We were squatters, for the land where we had settled had never been surveyed. Those who came before us had attempted a sort of rough survey, then "plowed in"—put a furrow around what land they thought would be allowed them. A more careful survey showed that they had overstepped. That is why we had a T-shaped place. It was hard to fence and mostly a string of rocky hills. In the little coulees, like dimples between the smiling hills, was water, soft and free of alkali or soda, but the nearest water was three miles away....

We planted a garden on newly-plowed ground and marveled how it lived in the heat, but live it did and later in the summer, when the rains came, there were large, crisp heads of lettuce and big turnips and corn that had braved a dreaded summer and won.

Our flour gave out. Looking back now I feel I was a poor sport. I was hungry every day. I wanted bread, but no one had it. Then we had no sugar. We had meal, milk and butter. That is all until our garden came on. The children were far gamer than I. They guzzled milk and found no fault. Then one day Daddy killed a sagehen. That made a feast. But sagehens were scarce, and we only saw one rabbit that whole summer. Now a small cotton tail we call a rock rabbit is here. They are good to eat, their meat fine grained and white.

As an experiment, an acre of sugar beets was planted. They grew regardless of drouth. We thinned them and ate those we took out. Everyone living near got some. I think none of us had ever eaten them before. I believe they saved me from starvation.

We had good times as well as hardships. We had baseball teams. Cat Creek rivaled our Rock Creek team. There were dances and picnics and dinners. Each woman would bring a dish, crock or pan of food and we put in all on a long table and ate together. Around us, as we drove to these merrymakings, there were herds of horses, but in those days, hungry though we were for meat, we did not dream of taking those animals which were not ours for food.

That fall we had no bread, no sugar, no money. The walls of our sod house were laid, but there was no lumber to finish the work. Daddy got a job building a sod barn for a neighbor. With what he had earned I went to Butte and he went to North Dakota to work in the harvest fields. We left the children until I could earn money to send for them. I sent them some groceries, and in a month I was able to send for them. During that month they went to the school that a young teacher had started in an abandoned cabin.

After threshing was over in North Dakota, Daddy came back and finished our house. We returned to it in March, with bacon, seed and some money. That summer we farmed....

We had planted flax. It grew nine inches high and stopped. We tried to cut it by hand, down on our knees with hand scythe, butcher knife, even scissors. We cut a lot of it too. Daddy finally rigged up a buncher out of some old binder canvases and cut the rest with a mower. We planted navy beans. They refused to ripen.

Winter was coming and we were not much better off than the year before. There was no school. The community was now three years old, and everybody in it was poorer than when they came. Except us—we could not get poorer. We had our flax, but there was no machine anywhere to thresh it. We decided to try to winter where we were. If anyone could, we could. We would beat out our flax, we decided, and we did. We sat around on the dirt floor of our house, with a cloth apiece, a hammer, a stick and a bunch of flax beside us, and pounded, and finally we threshed that flax.

We had a small dictionary. We took up word study, wrote rhymes, played cards.

The range horses, as usual, were all around us, pawing the snow away to get the grass....

Then came a year when we had wonderful crops, but it would take several crops to pay the debts and the 10 per cent interest. Discouragement set in....

We were going backward. The spirit of the old West was getting us. Our club dissolved, there were quarrels among the members. Quarrels arose on every hand. Instead of helping one another as we had done, neighbors sat up nights thinking up ways to hurt and hinder....

The breaking up had come. People kept drifting away. The summers grew dryer. The little trees died. Blizzards swept the prairies. Weeds grew so rank they choked themselves. And herds and herds of horses grazed where once had been fields and gardens.

My husband and I would go away winters, to work, coming back to farm in the summer. One winter, when we were working in Wisconsin, he died. I came back and my brother and I made a last stand. I hoped to make money to clear the debts. I had faith in the place. I still have. But now, with the last year's drouth, the land is in the grip of starvation, save for the food that the wild horses give.

Sometimes I walk up to the little hill where my husband built that sod shanty and gaze about me at the wreckage of our dreams, wondering if I shall ever see anything here but phantom homes. Those of us who remain have lost the romantic vision, lost the dream that brought us here. I look less than a mile from my old house and see seven phantom homes. Dry and deserted, I see the fields where plows have gone patiently up and down, now weed-grown, the fences down. And I feel the hand of desolation.

I look a little farther and see one tiny house. So small appears that fenced field, but it is not small, except by comparison with the vastness of the untilled land about it. I look again, and in the immensity of the unbroken acres of range land, white against the hills, is a sheep wagon. And around the little tilled patch, among the scattered bunches of cattle, beyond the sheep wagon, are horses.

These horses are our only hope. We have no feed for them. They must fend for themselves, pawing away the snow to get what little grass there is, and they must be strong enough to pull sleds or wagons 18 miles to the nearest store. If our horses starve, and if the wild horses starve, we will starve...

Through my tears I see them still, the phantom homes. Dear, painted, shingled houses where now are only sod houses and tarpaper shacks...Stacks of grain...Trees tended by loving hands...Gardens loved and cared for...And fat, gentle, sheltered horses.

Endnotes

INTRODUCTION
Montana's Solo Women Homesteaders

1. Anna Scherlie Homestead file, Montana Historical Society Research Center, Montana State Historic Preservation Office, Helena, Montana.

2. Anna Scherlie told Nellie and Leon Cederberg about her work for the Hill family. But in her nomination form to the National Register of Historic Places, this story is described as an unverified "local legend"—although her Saint Paul bank account suggests a link to that city. James Hill died in 1916 at age 78, so if Anna Scherlie worked for the Hills, it must have been with his children and grandchildren. See Claire Strom, *Profiting From the Plains: The Great Northern Railway and Corporate Development of the American West* (Seattle and London: University of Washington Press, 2003).

3. Gary D. Libecap, "Learning About the Weather. Dryfarming Doctrine and the Homestead Failure in Eastern Montana, 1900–1925," *Montana: The Magazine of Western History*. 52, no. 1 (Spring 2002): 27.

4. United States National Archives and Records Administration, (NARA), General Entry Land File, Gwenllian Evans, Section 4, Township 4-N, Range 10-W. Serial number MTMTAA 056560.

5. Patrick F. Morris, *Anaconda, Montana: Copper Smelting Boom Town on the Western Frontier* (Swann Publishing, 1997), 16.

6. Walter Ed Taylor, "Landmark Stands Near Anaconda," *Judith Basin Star*, 8 March 1936.

7. NARA, General Entry Land File, Margaret Macumber, Section 24, Township 2-S, Range 5-E, Serial number MTMTAA 042878.

8. Andro Linklater, *Measuring America: How an Untamed Wilderness Shaped the United States and Fulfilled the Promise of Democracy* (New York: Walker Publishing Company Inc., 2002), 223.

9. I have borrowed the term "immaculate grid" from Linklater (ibid.). Chapter 12 of his book is entitled "The Immaculate Grid."

10. Douglas W. Allen, "Homesteading and Property Rights: Or, 'How the West Was Really Won,'" *Journal of Law and Economics,* vol. 34 (April 1991): 2.

11. Quoted in Dyan Zaslowsky and T. H. Watkins, *These American Lands: Parks, Wilderness and the Public Lands* (Washington, D.C. and Covelo, CA: Island Press, 1994), 110.

12. "Montana: Homesteads in Three Years," Great Northern Railway, 1913. , Montana Historical Society Research Center, 2.

13. Ibid., 29

14. James Muhn, "Women and the Homestead Act: Land Department Administration of a Legal Imbroglio, 1863–1934," *Western Legal History* 7, no. 2 (Summer/Fall 1994): 285. Many thanks to James Muhn, Land Law Historian for the U.S. Department of the Interior's Bureau of Land Management, for his assistance with my research and for sending me an offprint of his article.

15. Tonia M. Compton, "'They Have as Much Right There as Bachelors': Provisions for Female Landowners in Nineteenth Century Homestead Legislation." Paper presented to the Western History Association, Oklahoma City, October, 2007: 1–2.

16. Quoted in Ibid., 6–7.

17. Quoted in Muhn, 287.

18. Muhn, 291–2.

19. H. Elaine Lindgren, *Land in Her Own Name: Women as Homesteaders in North Dakota* (Norman and London: University of Oklahoma Press, 1991), 76.

20. *Montana 1912* (Helena: Independent Publishing Co., 1912), 295.

21. Muhn, 286.

22. Library and Archives Canada (LAC), Record Group 13 (RG 13), Department of Justice, vol. 2247, file int. 25: 74/ 1896, memorandum, 8 Nov. 1894.

23. *Montana 1909* (Helena: Independent Publishing Co., 1909), 48.

24. James Muhn indicates that Mormon women involved in plural marriages were able to file on homesteads until 1878, when the General Land Office ruled that they would no longer be permitted to do so (pp. 290–291). Katherine Benton-Cohen, however, found that Mormon women "finessed homesteading law to accommodate plural marriage or to help children born in Mormon colonies in Mexico to obtain land in the United States." Katherine Benton-Cohen,

"Common Purposes, Worlds Apart: Mexican-American, Mormon and Midwestern Women Homesteaders in Cochise County, Arizona," *Western Historical Quarterly* 36, no. 4 (Winter 2005): paragraph 5 of on-line version.

25. See for example Paula Bauman, "Single Women Homesteaders in Wyoming, 1880-1930," *Annals of Wyoming* 58 (Spring, 1986); Dee Garceau, *The Important Things of Life: Women, Work and Family in Sweetwater County, Wyoming, 1880–1929* (Lincoln: University of Oklahoma Press, 1997); Florence C. Gould and Patricia N. Pando, *Claiming Their Land: Women Homesteaders in Texas* (El Paso: Texas Western Press, 1990); Lindgren, *Land in Her Own Name: Women as Homesteaders in North Dakota;* Sheryl Patterson-Black, "Women Homesteaders on the Great Plains Frontier," *Frontiers* 1 (Spring, 1976).

26. Muhn, 283.

27. Sherry Smith, "Single Women Homesteaders: The Perplexing Case of Elinore Pruitt Stewart," *Western Historical Quarterly* 22 (May, 1991): 164.

28. Benton-Cohen, paragraph 16 of on-line version.

29. Sunday Anne Walker-Kuntz, "Land, Life and *Femme Sole:* Women Homesteaders in the Yellowstone River Valley, 1909-1934," (Master's thesis, Montana State University–Bozeman, January 2006), 46.

30. Lindgren, *Land in Her Own Name*, 224.

31. *Hinsdale Tribune*, 21 Dec. 1917.

32. Lindgren, 20.

33. Henry L. Armstrong, Geraldine Anderson, and Geraldine History Committee. *Spokes, Spurs and Cockleburs* (Fort Benton: River Press, 1976), 79–80.

34. Egly Country Club, *Trails, Trials and Tributes* (Fort Benton: 1974), 40.

35. Geraldine History Committee, *Spokes,* 205.

36. Liberty County Museum, *Our Heritage in Liberty* (Chester: Liberty County Times, 1976), 184.

37. Research done by Gretchen Albers and Amy McKinney using census data and BLM records of women homesteaders in Valley County. Statistics are based on information they were able to find; many of the women were absent from the census records.

38. *Footprints in the Valley: A History of Valley County, Montana* (Glasgow: Glasgow Courier and Printing, 1991), 421–2.

39. Ibid., 423.

40. Ibid., 552.

41. "Louise La Fournaise," clipping file, Montana Historical Society Research Center, Helena, Montana.

42. After the war LaFournaise continued her nursing career in California, working in the veterans' hospital in Palo Alto. In 1926 she married Raymond Lee Schneider of Missouri. She died in 1984 and was buried with full military honors at the Presidio in San Francisco. See the display in the Valley County Museum, Glasgow, Montana.

43. NARA, General Entry Land File, Bertie Brown, Section 3, Township 19-N, Range 21-E, Serial number 04062; BLM MTLTN 0004062. She signed her name "Bertie" but her obituary says "Birdie." *Fergus County Argus Weekly*, 18 May 1933.

44. Grass Range History Committee, *From the Foothills to the Plains: A History of Grass Range and Southeastern Fergus County* (Lewistown: News-Argus Printing, 1999), 287–8.

45. Highwood Women's Club, *Trails and Trials of the Highwood* (n.p., n.d.), 85–6.

46. Sun River Valley Historical Society, *A Pictorial History of the Sun River Valley* (Shelby: Promoter Publishing, 1989), 269.

47. Jack K. Castor, *Carter, Montana: Homestead Boomtown 1909–1930s* (San Rafael, CA: Tumbleweed Publications, 1991), 118.

48. Carter County Genealogical Society, *Shifting Scenes: A History of Carter County, Montana* (Billings, MT: Artcraft Printers, 1978), 687.

49. Ibid.

50. Ruby Langel, *Rudyard Images* (n.p. 1985), 905–7.

51. *Report of the Public Lands Commission* (Washington, D.C.: Government Printing Office, 1905) Senate Documents Vol. 4, Document No. 189, 58th Congress, 3rd Session.

52. Ibid., xvii.

53. Paula M. Nelson, *After the West Was Won: Homesteaders and Town Builders in Western South Dakota, 1900–1917* (Iowa City: University of Iowa Press, 1986), 42.

54. Ibid., 187, note 5.

55. Lindgren, *Land in Her Own Name*, 209–225.

56. Garceau, *The Important Things of Life*, 115.

57. Smith, 167.

58. Garceau, 113.

59. Ephretta J. Risley, *"The Golden Triangle": An Account of Homesteading in Montana By One Who Lived It* (Montana: The Meagher County News White Sulphur Springs, 1975), 5.

60. Roy History Committee, *Homestead Shacks Over Buffalo Tracks* (Bozeman, MT: Colorworld Printers, 1990), 92.

61. Walker-Kunz, "Land, Life and *Feme Sole*," 52.

62. Lindgren, 221.

63. Libecap, "Learning About the Weather," 27.

64. Libecap, 27.

65. Ibid., 30. See also Gary D. Libecap and Zeynep Kocabiyik Hansen, "'Rain Follows the Plow' and Dryfarming Doctrine: The Climate Information Problem and Homestead Failure in the Upper Great Plains, 1890–1925," *The Journal of Economic History* 62, no. 1 (March 2002): 86–120.

66. Joseph Kinsey Howard, *Montana: High, Wide and Handsome* (Nebraska: University of Nebraska Press, 1943), 196.

67. Garceau, *The Important Things of Life,* 123.

68. Seena B. Kohl, "Memories of Homesteading and the Process of Retrospection," *Oral History Review* 17, no. 2 (Fall 1989): 25.

69. Ibid., 26.

CHAPTER ONE
Lone Woman Homesteader: Mattie T. Cramer

1. Biographical details are from the finding aid to the Mattie T. Cramer Papers, Montana Historical Society Research Center, from a three-page biographical sketch of William Mathers in these papers (no author, no date), and from obituary notices for: (1) Mrs Eliza Mathers, the *Enterprise,* 14 Aug. 1919; (2) Mattie T. Cramer, *Phillips County News,* 2 July 1959; and (3) Mattie T. Cramer, *Great Falls Tribune* 1 July 1959. The dates of birth given for Mattie T. Cramer vary. The *Great Falls Tribune* claimed she was born in 1858 and died in 1959 at age 101, while the *Phillips County News* said that she was born in 1867 and died at 92. Although her gravestone in the Malta cemetery says 1858–1959, census research suggests that 1868 or 1869 is more accurate. In the 1900 census when she was living with her mother and her son Harold, she gave her age as 31. In 1912, when she applied for her patent, she gave her age as 40. In a 1921 document in her land file, she had taken even more years off, as she then claimed to be 42. See NARA, General Entry Land File, Mattie T. Cramer #1 Section 11, Township 30-N, Range 30-E. Serial Number MTGLS 0002473 and #2 Section 21, Township 30-N, Range 31-E.

Serial Number MTGLS 0041890.

2. Curiously, census research indicates that in 1920, a B. Frank Cramer was living in Jarvis, Illinois, at age 61. His wife, listed as with that household and not absent is Mattie, age 58, and they have a son. In 1930, this couple is living in Troy, Illinois, and have a son Clifton, age 46. This is an older Mattie, born in 1862. Could there have been two B. Frank Cramers married to two different Matties?

3. There are other mysteries about Mattie T. Cramer that emerge through census research. In the 1910 census, Harold C. Cramer, age 15, and born in New York, was listed as living with his mother and stepfather in Valley County, Montana. His mother is listed as Mattie Osgood, age 38 (which is Mattie's age according to the 1900 census) and his stepfather Raymond Osgood, born in 1869 in Pennsylvania. It was noted that this was her second marriage, and that her mother was born in England. There is little doubt that this is Mattie T. Cramer and her son Harold. Were Mattie and Osgood married? If so, what became of the marriage? And of Raymond Osgood? In a fragment of a typewritten letter in the Cramer papers (undated) written from her Malta homestead, there is a mention of Osgood. She wrote "Mr. Osgood is in British Columbia now, he sent some very pretty cards—views of the country—the other day. His last address was Elko, B.C." and "We keep the milk in the cellar since Mr. O made it so large it's as cool as a refrigerator, almost." Census research reveals that in the 1920 census, Raymond Osgood is living in Clarke County, Washington. Mattie Cramer moved to Washington in 1919. Thanks to Amy McKinney for this research in the census records.

4. *Enterprise,* 16 Sept. 1908.

5. Bureau of Land Management website, Western Land Patents, Eliza Mathers, South ½ North West and North East South West Section 11, Township 30N, Range 30E. Serial No. MTGLS0000506.

6. "James Jerome Hill, Empire Builder," by Mattie T. Cramer, Cramer Papers, Montana Historical Society Research Center.

7. Mattie T. Cramer Papers, MC255, Montana Historical Society Research Center, Box 1, Folder 1.

8. Cramer Papers, Box 1, Folders 2–3.

9. Cramer Papers, Box 1, Folder 9.

10. Cramer Papers, Box 1, Folder 2.

CHAPTER TWO

A Shack Near Big Sandy:
Adelia Elizabeth Hawkins Sturm Glover

1. Adelia Elizabeth Hawkins Sturm Glover Papers, Overholser Historical Research Center, Fort Benton, Montana.

2. NARA. General Entry Land File, Adelia E. Sturm (Hawkins), Section 5 (4) Township 25-N, Range 15-E, Serial number MTHVR 0018633.

3. Frank Hyde, "Area Woman Homesteaded in the West," *Post-Journal,* Jamestown, New York, 8 July 1878 and 15 July 1878. Glover Papers, Overholser Historical Research Center.

CHAPTER THREE

"In My Own Home At Last":
Metta M. Loomis

1. Metta M. Loomis, "From a School Room to a Montana Ranch," *Overland Monthly* (January 1916): 59–64.

2. Thanks to Ken Robison, Overholser Historical Research Center, Fort Benton, for sharing his census record research with me on Metta M. Loomis. E-mail 23 May 2006.

3. Dee Garceau, *The Important Things of Life: Women, Work and Family in Sweetwater County, Wyoming,* 1880–1929 (Lincoln: University of Nebraska Press, 1997), 123.

CHAPTER FOUR

The Sumatra Adventure:
Grace Binks, Ina Dana, Margaret Majors

1. Kent Midgett, *Traces on the Landscape,* ed. Douglas Midgett (Parkersburg, Iowa: Mid-Prairie Books, 1998), ix.

2. Census records research, Amy McKinney. NARA, General Entry Land

File, Grace Binks (Price), Section 12, Township 15-N, Range 34-E. Serial number MTMC 0011918.

3. NARA, General Land Entry File, Ina Dana, Section 12, Township 15-N, Range 34-E. Serial number MTMC 0011917.

4. Midgett, 8.

CHAPTER FIVE
Lone Tree, Montana:
Nan ("Nannie") Pritchard Francis

1. "My Experience Homesteading," by Mrs. N. P. Francis, Overholser Historical Research Center, Fort Benton, Montana.

2. NARA, General Land Entry File, Nannie P. Francis, Section 7, Township 21-N, Range 14-E. Serial Number MTLTN 0009654. Francis declares herself to be a "deserted wife" in her 7 April 1910 Homestead Entry. This document is witnessed by her relative George F. West and by Fred E. Brunskill.

3. Thanks to Ken Robison, Overholser Historical Research Center, for his census records research on Nan Pritchard Francis.

CHAPTER SIX
Crossing the Border for Land:
Laura Etta Smalley Bangs

1. Betsy Cohen, "Women's History Month: Out of Canada: Etta Smalley Homesteaded a New Life..." *Missoulian,* 23 July 2007. missoulian.com News Online. http://www.missoulian.com/articles/2007/03/16/new/local/news04.txt

2. *Edmonton Bulletin,* 21 May 1910.

3. *Manitoba Free Press,* 24 May 1910.

4. Ibid., 18 June 1910.

5. Georgina Binnie-Clark, *Wheat and Woman* (1914 rpt. Toronto: University of Toronto Press, 2007). Intros. Sarah Carter (2007), Susan Jackel (1979).

CHAPTER SEVEN
Evelyn Cameron Photographs of
Janet ("Jennie") Williams and Other
Montana Women Homesteaders

1. Donna M. Lucey, *Photographing Montana 1894–1928: The Life and Work of Evelyn Cameron* (New York: Alfred A. Knopf, 1991), ix.

2. Ibid., xii.

3. Ibid., x.

4. NARA, General Land Entry File, Jennie M. Williams, Section 6, Block 12-N, Range 54-E, Serial number MTMC0002706.

5. Lucey, 174.

6. Evelyn Cameron Papers, Montana Historical Society Research Center, MC226, Box 5, Folder 17, Scrapbook, pg. 11.

CHAPTER EIGHT
A Homestead Near the Little Crooked:
Mia ("May") Anderson Vontver

1. Biographical information is taken from the finding aid to her file in the Montana Historical Society Research Center, and from the May Anderson Vontver reminiscence in that file, the "Memoirs of May Vontver," SC 958.

2. It has appeared most recently in Caroline Patterson, ed., *Montana Women Writers: A Geography of the Heart* (Helena: Farcountry Press, 2006): 129–136.

CHAPTER NINE
2 Letters, 5 feet of Snow:
The Mildred Belle Hunt Diary

1. NARA, General Land Entry File, Mildred Belle Hunt, Section 21, Township 22 –N, Range 8-E, Serial number TGF 0010947. Letter from Register, Department of the Interior Land Office, Great Falls to Mildred Belle Hunt, 18 March 1910. All

of the correspondence quoted here is from this file.

2. Mildred Belle Hunt papers, Obituary, 18 March 1953, Overholser Historical Research Center Archives, Fort Benton, Montana.

CHAPTER TEN
Dead, Plucky, or Proved Up:
Women Homesteaders in the Montana Press

1. *Glasgow Democrat* 8 Sept. 1916, p. 5.

2. NARA, General Land Entry File, Nora Nereson, Section 5, Township 32-N, Range 32-E, Serial Number MTGLS0050707. Affidavit of George Schneider, 25 Oct. 1920, Greve, Montana.

3. NARA, General Land Entry File, Nellie T. Holt (Smith), Section 4, Township 34-N, Range 25-E. Serial Number MTHVR 0045663. Affidavit of Nellie T. Holt, 4 March 1921, Havre, Montana.

4. NARA, General Land Entry File, Maud Miller, Section 34, Township 22-N, Range 7-E, Serial Number MTGF 0025570. All correspondence quoted here is from this file.

CHAPTER ELEVEN
"A Sure-Enough Pioneer":
Ada Maud Melville Shaw

1. Many thanks to *Drumlummon Views* for publishing Ada Melville Shaw's memoir in its entirety at drumlummon.org. Thanks also to Rick Newby of *Drumlummon Views* for sending me the final installments before publication. This biographical information is taken from the introduction to installment two of "Cabin O'Wildwinds: The Story of a Montana Ranch," *Drumlummon Views* (Fall 2006–Winter 2007).

2. NARA, General Land Entry File, Ada Maud Melville Shaw, Section 32, Township 4-N, Range 24E. Serial Number MTBIL 0006368.

3. Janet Galligani Casey, "'This is YOUR Magazine': Domesticity, Agrarianism and *The Farmer's Wife*," *American Periodicals: A Journal of History, Criticism and Bibli-*

ography, vol. 12, no. 2 (2004): 179–211.

4. [Editor's note, footnote original to the text] It was possible to buy the quarter section from the government by the payment of this fixed sum of money, this payment releasing the homesteader from all future obligations of residence or improvement.

Chapter Twelve
A Homestead Near Smokey Butte:
Catharine Calk McCarty

1. Catharine Calk McCarty, *Blue Grass and Big Sky* (Phoenix: Stockmore House Ltd., 1983), 7. See also Joan Bishop, "To Turn the Dark Cloud Inside Out: Catharine Calk McCarty and the American Red Cross Home Service in Montana, 1917–1925." *Drumlummon Views.* (Fall 2006–Winter 2007): 109–124.

2. McCarty, 13.

3. McCarty,, 18.

4. Ibid., 28.

5. Ibid., 54.

6. The other women elected that year were Florence Facey of Malta (Republican), Jessie Roscoe, a lawyer from Butte (Democrat), and Mrs. K. Hamilton of Dodson (Democrat).

7. Ibid., 63.

8. Ibid., 73.

9. NARA, General Land Entry File, Catharine Calk McCarty, Section 21, Township 18-N, Range 35-E. Serial number MTBIL 0028085.

10. McCarty, 113.

11. *Great Falls Tribune,* 4 November 1991.

CHAPTER THIRTEEN
Life in the Badlands:
Pearl Danniel

1. Ellie Arguimbau, "Pearl Danniel: Homesteader in Big Dry Country," *Mon-

tana: The Magazine of Western History 46, no. 3 (Autumn 1996): 62–70. The Pearl Danniel papers are in the Montana Historical Society Research Center, MC 237. Her article from the *St. Louis Post-Dispatch* of 27 March 1932, excerpted here, is in folder 32, box 3, Danniel Papers.

References

Mattie T. Cramer
> Mattie T. Cramer Papers, 1888–1958, MC 255, Montana Historical Society Research Center, Helena, Montana.

Adelia Elizabeth Hawkins Sturm Glover
> Adelia Hawkins Sturm Glover Papers, Overholser Historical Research Center, Fort Benton, Montana.

Metta M. Loomis
> "From a School Room to a Montana Ranch," *Overland Monthly* (January 1916): 59–64.

The Sumatra Homesteaders
> Grace Binks Price album, PAC 92-62, Montana Historical Society Research Center.

Nan ("Nannie") Pritchard Francis
> Francis Papers. Overholser Historical Research Center.

Laura Etta Smalley Bangs
> Etta Smalley Bangs Reminiscence, SC 116, Montana Historical Society Research Center.

Evelyn Cameron Papers and Photographs

Montana Historical Society Archives, PAC 90-87, Montana Historical Society Research Center.

Mia ("May") Anderson Vontver

"Memoirs of May Vontver", 1905–1939, SC 958, Montana Historical Research Center.

Mildred Belle Hunt

Overholser Historical Research Center. Transcribed by Ken Robison.

Women Homesteaders in the Montana Press

"Young Lady Killed," *Hinsdale Tribune,* 14 July 1916, p. 1; "Tragic Death of Irene Van Kleek," *Lewistown Daily News,* 30 December 1910, p. 1; "Nellie Holt and Her Stolen House," *Opheim Observer,* 17 June 1921, p. 2; "Girls Freezing, Pen Notes," *Glasgow Democrat,* 11 February 1916; "No Montana Teachers Were Frozen to Death," *Great Falls Tribune,* 8 February 1916, p. 3; "Montana Homesteaders Who Are Women," *Ronan Pioneer,* 15 December 1916, p. 4.

Ada Maud Melville Shaw

"Cabin O'Wildwinds: The Story of a Montana Ranch," *The Farmer's Wife,* 1931–1932; *Drumlummon Views* (Fall 2006–April 2008).

Catharine Calk McCarty

"Story of a Montana Girl Homesteader and the Fine Farm She Has Developed," *Opheim Observer,* 22 August 1919, p. 7; *Blue Grass and Big Sky* (Phoenix: Stockmore House, Ltd, 1983), Chapter 5.

Pearl Danniel

Pearl Sparks Unglesbee Danniel Papers, 1885–1975, MC 237, Montana Historical Research Center.

Index

Page numbers in italics indicate images.